THE NECESSARY
REVOLUTION

THE NECESSARY REVOLUTION

How Individuals and Organizations
Are Working Together to Create
a Sustainable World

PETER SENGE, BRYAN SMITH, NINA KRUSCHWITZ,
JOE LAUR, SARA SCHLEY

DOUBLEDAY

New York London Toronto Sydney Auckland

DEDICATED TO THE INSPIRED INNOVATORS EVERYWHERE
WHO ARE SHOWING ALL OF US THE WAY TOWARD
A DIFFERENT FUTURE.

DD

DOUBLEDAY

PUBLISHED BY DOUBLEDAY

Published in the United States by Doubleday, an imprint of The Doubleday Publishing Group,
a division of Random House, Inc., New York.
www.doubleday.com

DOUBLEDAY is a registered trademark and the DD colophon is a trademark of Random House, Inc.

All trademarks are the property of their respective companies.

This book and its jacket were printed on paper that contains 100 percent postconsumer-recycled
fibers and is certified processed chlorine free. The interior was printed using soy-based inks, and the
jacket was printed using vegetable-based inks. For more information about the environmental
savings from the use of this paper, please visit http://www.ecologiquedenature.com/en/, and for
environmental savings information regarding the jacket stock, please visit
http://www.neenahpaper.com/NEENAHGREEN/.

Book design by Chris Welch

Library of Congress Cataloging-in-Publication Data
The necessary revolution : how individuals and organizations are working together to create
a sustainable world / Peter Senge . . . [et al.].—1st ed.
p. cm.
1. Sustainable development. 2. Industries—Environmental aspects.
3. Social responsibility of business. I. Senge, Peter M.
HC79.E5N436 2008
338.9'27—dc22
2008013878

ISBN: 978-0-385-51901-4

PRINTED IN THE UNITED STATES OF AMERICA

5 7 9 10 8 6

contents

part III
GETTING STARTED

part IV
SEEING SYSTEMS

part V
COLLABORATING ACROSS BOUNDARIES

part VI
FROM PROBLEM SOLVING TO CREATING

part VII
THE FUTURE

part I

ENDINGS,
NEW BEGINNINGS

[1]

A Future Awaiting Our Choices

A nyone visiting Australia today cannot help but notice massive billboards in all the major cities encouraging people to conserve water. A natural response would be to think these are the result of recent drought conditions, and indeed they are—in a way. But though the signs are new, the drought they were erected in response to has gone on for years and shows no sign of improvement. Across the nation, water reservoirs are at roughly one-quarter of capacity and have been declining for a decade—thanks to a combination of subnormal rainfall and rising temperatures widely attributed by leading scientific panels to climate change.[1] Starting in 2007, water became the focus of national debates; one popular suggestion even called for the complete elimination of the nation's large citrus crop. This sounds drastic, but when there is simply not enough water to go around, hard choices need to be made, even if that means sacrificing an important crop in an industry that accounts for roughly 3 percent of GDP. The country's national election in fall 2007 was the first in the world in which climate change was the number one issue (and the candidate deemed most dedicated to addressing it won), a possible harbinger for other countries in the coming years, including the United States.

But in addition to conserving resources such as water, innovative Australians everywhere are also seizing the opportunity to rethink and re-create their lives and the infrastructures that govern them. They are working together in communities across the country to come up with renewable energy solutions, and beginning to consider sweeping changes in energy and water industries. Business, long dominated by mining and minerals industries, has become a vocal advocate for investment in innovative alternative energy technologies, such as wind and solar.

Half a world away, Sweden has parted ways with other industrial economies to completely sever their dependence on imported oil—and the vulnerability that goes along with it. Under former prime minister Göran Persson, a commission was established in 2006 that laid out a fifteen-year plan to cut fossil fuel use to zero by 2020. This momentous shift was, in fact, the outcome of decades of work by remarkable networks of public and private sector leaders committed to making northern Sweden the world's first "bioregion," in which all energy needs are met from sustainably produced biofuels.

Similar changes are occurring in businesses the world over. In response to the turmoil of world oil markets and oil-producing regions, DuPont, one of the largest and oldest companies in America, has set itself on a course to shift its product line from petroleum-based to bio-based feedstocks. Like many companies around the world, DuPont has worked for years to reduce waste, including carbon dioxide (CO_2) emissions. But it now sees that the real innovation opportunities lie in the creation of new products that break the company's dependency on conventional oil and gas entirely. Similarly, Nike has reduced its "carbon footprint" by more than 75 percent. But, again, by looking for the truly innovative opportunities for the future, the company has declared its intent to achieve zero waste, zero toxicity, and 100 percent recyclability across its entire product line by 2020. "Our company and our customers care about health; our products and ways of producing them should embody this," says Darcy Winslow, former head of the women's footwear division. "But to do this we are having to completely rethink how we design, produce, and distribute those products and how we recover them at the end of their lifetime."

———

There are many types of revolutions. History talks mostly of political revolutions, dramatic events that all too often represent little real change over the long term: The cast of players in power shifts and new political philosophies come into vogue, but when it comes to the daily realities of most people, little changes. But occasionally something different happens, a collective awakening to new possibilities that changes *everything* over time—how people see the world, what they value, how society defines progress and organizes itself, and how institutions operate. The Renaissance was such a shift, as was the Industrial Revolution. So, too, is what is starting to happen around the world today.

Perhaps surprisingly, the most visible signs of this new revolution are a mounting series of environmental and social crises.

While Australia's water situation may seem extreme, it is hardly unique. Both the southeast and southwest regions of the United States are facing a similar need for rationing and possible permanent cutbacks. In developed countries around the world, previously taken-for-granted aspects of daily life—food, water, energy, predictable weather—seem less and less reliable.

Each of the last several summers has brought record heat waves to much of Europe, as well as other strange occurrences such as extreme flooding, crops that come to season a month early, and the appearance of mosquito-borne diseases previously known only to the Southern Hemisphere—events that scientists have linked to global warming and increased atmospheric CO_2.[2]

In the United States, there have been repeated scares about contaminated food imported from Asia and *E. coli* outbreaks from crops grown in our own backyard, recent warnings to parents about the rapid spread of poison ivy caused by higher CO_2 levels in the atmosphere (which both speed the plant's growth and increase its toxicity), and a historic shift in the politics of energy. Even former protectors of the oil-fueled economic status quo now recognize that America's energy consumption (we consume 25 percent of the world's fossil fuels with only 5 percent of the population) cannot continue.[3] Our rampant consumption and protect-the-source foreign policies no longer offer a reliable path for the future. As President Bush admitted, "America is addicted to oil."

While environmental crises get most of the headlines today, the simple fact that the wealth of the 200 richest people in the world exceeds the combined annual income of the world's 2.5 billion poorest people should give anyone pause, as should the knowledge that almost half of the world's population lives on less than $2 per day while the average American earns $130 per day.[4] The belief that economic growth alone will solve the problems of poverty is simply not borne out by the facts. And the drive to satisfy legitimate ambitions for material progress is forcing developing countries such as China and India toward unprecedented rates of fossil fuel consumption—a poignant reminder that our social and environmental crises are joined at the hip.

But the real problem is not these crises per se but the likelihood that our responses will be completely inadequate.

If we see each problem—be it water shortages, climate change, or poverty—as separate, and approach each separately, the solutions we come up with will be short-term, often opportunistic, "quick fixes" that do nothing to address deeper imbalances. Take the recent frenzy in the U.S. over ramping up production of corn-based ethanol as an alternative to imported oil. The number of ethanol plants is expanding rapidly (there will be almost 200 by the end of 2008) and vast amounts of corn are being grown to supply them.[5] Not only is this driving up food prices around the world, but ethanol from corn arguably takes us in the wrong direction in terms of reducing greenhouse gases. Greenhouse gas emissions from using corn ethanol in cars do not differ substantially from emissions from using gasoline in cars. The net effect of using corn-based ethanol may even increase greenhouse gases due to land-use changes, as farmers worldwide clear forests and grasslands to grow corn in response to higher prices and demand.[6] More sustainable alternatives such as cellulose-based biofuels from forestry and crop wastes are being developed, but the search for a quick fix, as opposed to creating a truly environmentally sound energy system, has put the attention on corn ethanol.

Fortunately, more and more people are beginning to sense that the mounting sustainability crises are interconnected—symptoms of a larger global system that is out of balance. As soon as people understand this, their view of the problems shifts. They start to see the extraordinary opportunities for innovation that can occur when we abandon fearful, reactive mentalities. They start to realize the deep problems we face today are not a result of bad luck or a greedy few. They are the result of a way of thinking whose time has passed.

All ages end—from the Iron Age to the Bronze Age, from the age of the Renaissance to the Reformation, from the rise and reign of empires such as Rome's to more modern empires such as Britain's. No era—no matter how influential or how far-reaching—lasts forever. The Industrial Age, which has shaped our lifestyles and our worldview for generations, is no different.

To many, the term *industrial* itself seems rather quaint, since most of us in the developed nations appear to live in a world dominated by bits and bytes, not smokestacks and coal mines. Seventy percent of the American economy, for example, is driven by the spending of consumers, people who for the most part work in service or white-collar industries.[7] Relatively few Americans work in factories today, fewer still in mines or on farms.

But immediate circumstances can be misleading. In fact, the last quarter century has seen the most dramatic increase in industrial activity the world has ever known. The number of automobiles in use in the world has grown from about 50 million in 1950 to about 800 million in 2008. The annual growth rate in the global production of automobiles (over 6 percent) is now at least four times the growth of human population in percentage terms.[8] Since 1980, annual steel production worldwide has almost doubled. While U.S. industrial production grew by only half a percent in 2007, China posted a 13 percent increase in industrial production in 2007, Vietnam 17 percent, and India 10 percent.[9] More coal is mined than ever before. As customers and consumers, we are tied to industrial production for our computers and PDAs, cars and trucks, and flat-panel televisions. And we are dependent on the energy required to make them work, over 70 percent of which comes from burning fossil fuels, as it has for the past 150 years. Yes, products and industrial processes are far more information-intensive than ever before, but such shifts in the mix of dominant technologies, such as the move from gaslights to electrification or from mainframe computers to the Internet and personal computing, have been a recurring feature of the Industrial Age, not a signal of its demise.

But something important has happened in this last stage of the industrial era that sets it apart from the past: Globalization has brought a level of interdependence between nations and regions that has never existed before, along with truly global problems that also have no precedent. This includes environmental crises such as increasing levels of waste and toxicity (which often spill over from one country to another) and growing stresses on a host of finite natural resources, but also the widening gaps between the wealthy and the poor and alarming political reactions to these imbalances in the form of global terrorism. Just as the Iron Age didn't end because we ran out of iron, the Industrial Age isn't ending because of the decline in opportunities for further industrial expansion. It is ending because individuals, companies, and governments are coming to the realization that its side effects are unsustainable.

Ages do not end abruptly. Everyone does not just wake up one day and say, "This isn't working. We must change." Quite the contrary. When faced with challenges of this magnitude, the vast majority of people and institutions try harder to maintain the status quo. As neuroscientists say, the brain "downshifts" under stress—in other words, we revert to our most habitual (and more primitive) modes of behavior. Societies are no different.

Fortunately, societies are not monolithic. At the same time that many companies resist change to outdated methods and technologies, governments refuse to implement needed regulations, and individuals resist change to their established lifestyles, others wonder instead about what *could* be. What would an economy look like that operated entirely on "our energy income rather than our energy capital," as the pioneer systems thinker and inventor Buckminster Fuller used to say? Or that embraced the natural systems principle, as articulated by William McDonough and Michael Braungart, that "all waste equals food for another system"? Or one in which Marshall McLuhan's image of the "global village" was not merely a clever metaphor—but a principle for a world of interdependence, where the unilateral pursuit of "national security" is like chasing a shadow; none of us is secure if all of us are not secure?

Endings are also beginnings. The Industrial Age has brought extraordinary improvements in public education, human rights, and material well-being, but it has also destroyed ecosystems, swallowed up traditional cultures that had thrived for centuries, and created a way of life that cannot continue for much longer. With regard to each of these interconnected problems, the same fundamental choice exists: Do we protect the ways of the past or join in creating a different future?

People and organizations around the world are already planting the seeds for new ways of living and working together. Yes, they are a minority. No, they are not part of the mainstream, either within their industries or usually within their own organizations. But, unlike previous periods of profound change, it is unlikely these seeds will take centuries to mature and spread, because in today's interconnected world, the problems *are* global, and the changes will be as well. Pressures for change are building rapidly, and solutions and opportunities—and news of what works and how to build on it—are spreading equally rapidly.

CREATING THE FUTURE

Amid all the uncertainties, three guiding ideas stand out as essential for creating a more sustainable future:

1. **There is no viable path forward that does not take into account the needs of future generations.** The term *sustainability* is widely used to express the need to live in the present in ways that do not jeopardize the future. When a process is sustainable, it can be carried out over and over again without negative environmental effects or impossibly high costs to anyone involved. The belief that we can attend only to our own needs and goals is tantamount to discounting the value of the children, families, communities, and businesses who will inhabit that future. Businesses can no longer expect to compete in the future without taking into account the larger problems that stand between now and then.

2. **Institutions matter.** Today's world is shaped not by individuals alone, but by the networks of businesses and governmental and nongovernmental institutions that influence the products we make, the food we eat, the energy we use, and our responses to problems that arise from these systems. No one person could destroy a species or warm the planet

no matter how hard he or she tried. But that is exactly what we are doing collectively, as our individual actions are mediated through the web of institutions that interconnect the world. It is folly to think that the changes needed in the coming years will not involve fundamental shifts in the way institutions function, individually and collectively. Ironically, despite increasing interdependence, most institutions are more consumed than ever by short-term thinking, frenzy, and opportunism. The gap between the need to think and act interdependently and our abilities to do so sits at the heart of all the most difficult problems we face today. Still, as you will see from the stories below, the leadership needed to close that gap is now emerging from business and non-business organizations alike, and often in partnership.

3. **All real change is grounded in new ways of thinking and perceiving.** As Einstein said: "We can't solve problems by using the same kind of thinking we used when we created them." While institutions matter, how they operate arises from how we operate, how people think and interact.

In short, to shape a sustainable future, we all need to work together differently than we have in the past. And that is what we will be describing in the pages ahead.

In *The Necessary Revolution*, we will talk about the challenges we face in three interconnected areas—energy and transportation, food and water, material waste and toxicity (what we make and discard)—and the consequent imbalances that result when too many resources are concentrated in too few hands.

We will look at how these problems have arisen, and how they are all symptoms of a way of living that we have come to take for granted, which has produced great progress but also growing side effects. Seeing the deeper pattern that connects many different problems is crucial if we are to move beyond piecemeal reactions and create lasting change.

But we are most interested in exploring the extraordinary opportunities these problems represent and how business and social entrepreneurs are stepping forward to create flourishing new businesses, networks, and organizations of all kinds based on these opportunities.

No one has *the* answer to the question of how 6 (soon to be 8 or 9) billion people can live together sustainably. But an ultimate solution is exactly what is *not* needed. No one had a plan for the Industrial Revolution. No ministry was put in charge. No single business led the way. Instead, countless acts of initiative and daring created a critical mass of unstoppable changes. The Industrial Age was not planned but innovated. The next age will be no different.

The difference between many random initiatives that add up to little and a revolution that can transform society itself boils down to a shift in thinking. The Industrial Age has often been called the "machine age" because the rise of machines and the way they operated transformed the way people thought and worked. It wasn't long before people were expected to work like machines and the assembly line became the icon of efficiency and standardization for all organizations. Gradually, machine thinking shaped much more than manufacturing: Economic progress became synonymous with increases in efficiency and productivity; cultural advance became equated with dazzling new technologies; and nature, including the other creatures with whom we share the earth, was reduced to "natural resources," inputs to the economic machine.

A sustainable world, too, will only be possible by thinking differently. With nature and not machines as their inspiration, today's innovators are showing how to create a different future by learning how to see the larger systems of which they are a part and to foster collaboration across every imaginable boundary. These core capabilities—seeing systems, collaborating across boundaries, and creating versus problem solving—form the underpinnings, and ultimately the tools and methods, for this shift in thinking.

For over a quarter of a century our work, first at the Massachusetts Institute of Technology and then through the Society for Organizational Learning (SoL) global network, has involved helping organizations of all sorts to "learn how to learn"—which naturally leads to the question, "Learning for what?" For many years, precedent provided the answer: learning so that companies could be more innovative and profitable, so that schools could help students learn, so that governmental organizations could better serve their constituencies. For the past decade, however, we have begun to also see a larger answer: shaping a sustainable, flourishing world for life beyond the Industrial Age. This represents perhaps the greatest learning challenge humans have ever faced, and it will require extraordinary leadership from institutions of all sorts.

This is not pie-in-the-sky rhetoric or intellectual idealism, but in fact is reflected in ways organizations and individuals are already working together. The organizations and people you will meet in the pages that follow are starting to enact new ways of managing, leading, and ultimately creating value, not just for today's real needs but for tomorrow's, and their practices are spreading to hundreds of businesses and non-business organizations of all sizes around the world. There is no silver-bullet formula for putting these ideas into practice widely, but there are principles, practices, and ways of getting started.

A FINAL WORD

One thing we have learned from working on organizational and systemic change is that the leaders are hard to identify in advance. Sometimes they are CEOs or presidents, but often they do not occupy positions of obvious power in a corporate hierarchy. They are not the flag wavers, campaigning vocally for change, but rather passionate individuals working to transform their organizations from the bottom up. They are most often open-minded pragmatists, people who care deeply about the future but who are suspicious of quick fixes, emotional nostrums, and superficial answers to complex problems. They have a hard-earned sense of how their organizations work, tempered by humility concerning what any one person can do alone. They often do not think of themselves as leaders, but time proves them wrong.

This is the sort of person for whom we have written this book. You may find it hard to get a handle on the immensity of the challenges we face today. But you likely understand those aspects that are more immediate— air quality or waste where you work, local water shortages or contamination problems where you live, the anxiety people in your community feel about the future. You see the larger imbalances and sense that major changes are needed. You may have found it hard to see how all the problems fit together and to know exactly what you—and the organization you work in—can do to help. But you know these problems are important to you, and you genuinely want to contribute to addressing them.

If that is true for you, welcome. You are the person for whom we have written *The Necessary Revolution,* and our highest hope is that it will help you in your work.

[2]

How We Got into This Predicament

THE WAGES OF SUCCESS

How did we get to the point where we are running out of the resources (such as oil) that support our way of life, and others (such as clean air and fresh drinking water) that support life itself? And how did entire industries, such as fishing and agriculture, find themselves in trouble as well, as chronic overfishing and the drive for ever-higher crop yields led to widespread depletion of fish stocks and a historic loss of topsoil?

How on earth did we get here?

The short answer is because of our success, success beyond anyone's wildest dreams.

In the first stage of the Industrial Revolution (1750 to 1820), the rise of large-scale manufacturing caused labor productivity in England to rise a hundredfold. But the Revolution did not simply change the way we worked; it transformed the way we lived, the way we thought about ourselves, and the way we viewed the world. Nothing like it had ever occurred before.

It didn't take long for innovations such as the assembly line to spread to other countries in northern Europe and to the hinterlands of the United States, whose exploding population and vast store of natural resources enabled the former colony to become the next industrial power. Industry was booming and so, too, were the material standards of living. As the United States' population increased from about 10 million to 63 million between 1820 and 1890, the country's industrial production grew thirty-fold. The resulting fivefold growth in output per person was even greater than the productivity gains on the other side of the Atlantic.

The impacts the Industrial Revolution had on quality of life were undeniable. As industrial expansion continued into the twentieth century, life expectancy in the industrial world roughly doubled, literacy jumped from 20 percent to over 90 percent, and benefits hitherto unimaginable sprang up in the form of products (from private cars to iPods), services (from air travel to eBay), and astounding advances in medicine, communication, education, and entertainment. With this kind of success, it is little wonder that the side effects of the Industrial Age success story went largely ignored.

But the downsides of this great prosperity were steadily accumulating from the very beginning. Some were hard not to notice. In the 1800s, England's level of fossil fuel combustion grew dramatically, and so too did levels of water and air pollution. In the late 1800s, London's infamous "fog," particulate emissions from burning coal, caused a virtual epidemic of respiratory diseases once confined to coal-mining communities. By 1952, air quality in London was so bad that the "great smog" (four days of toxic air trapped over the city) killed more than 4,000 people and galvanized the government to create air pollution regulations.[1]

Other side effects went unseen. Invisible CO_2 emissions in the United Kingdom rose from virtually zero to over a million tons per year by the end of the nineteenth century. During America's twentieth-century economic miracle, the amount of fossil fuels burned grew so much that by the end of the century CO_2 emissions totaled almost 2 billion tons annually, or about 7 tons per person.

Despite growing awareness of the importance of a healthy environment and successes in pollution reduction, even a cursory summary shows that things have mostly gone from bad to worse worldwide. Let's look at the problems by category.

Industrial Waste

- The U.S. economy consumes over 100 billion tons of raw materials per year; more than 90 percent of this, by weight, ends up as waste from extraction and production processes. That works out to about 1 ton of waste per person *per day*.[2]
- Solid and liquid industrial wastes (such as plastics and petrochemical wastes) disperse through groundwater, and airborne pollutants (such as acids) can travel hundreds or thousands of miles before they end up in rainfall, soil, and water. These pollutants affect health both directly (they've played a role in the significant increase in asthma since 1960) and indirectly (by decreasing food and water quality).[3]
- The "Asian Brown Cloud," a dense blanket of airborne, mostly industrial particulates, has been blamed for 500,000 deaths from respiratory illness per year in India alone.[4]
- Seventy percent of the developing world's untreated industrial waste is dumped into rivers, lakes, oceans, or soil.[5]

Consumer and Commercial Waste and Toxicity

- Approximately 8 billion tons per year of carbon in the form of carbon dioxide are emitted globally through the burning of fossil fuels for transportation, heat, and electricity worldwide. This is approximately 5 billion tons more than the biosphere can absorb.[6]
- Around the world, more than 90 percent of computers, TVs, video and audio recorders, PDAs, and other consumer and commercial electronics end up in landfills. About 20 to 30 million cars are taken off the road every year around the world; in the United States, about three-quarters by weight are recovered as scrap metal, but in the developing world, most old cars end up as waste in landfills.[7]
- Packaging waste has grown 400 percent in the past twenty years, mostly cardboard and diverse plastic containers and wrappings. While a few types of plastic containers are recycled at higher rates (such as water and soft drink bottles in developed countries), the vast majority of plastics worldwide—more than 90 percent—end up as solid waste. In the United States, for example, 93 percent of plastics end up in landfills.[8]

- Toxins embedded in everyday products also pose significant health risks even before they are discarded to landfills. For example, immunologists have shown that a great many diseases (such as many cancers) have become far more prevalent today due to toxins in our bodies that come not only from food ingredients but also from chemicals in products, dyes used in cloth, and plastic compounds in children's toys, computer screens, and household appliances.[9]

Non-regenerative (Non-renewable) Resources

- In a study commissioned by the U.S. government, the U.S. petroleum industry recently reported that world oil and gas supplies will be unable to keep up with rising global demand over the next twenty-five years, which could lead to continually rising prices (oil rose from $25 per barrel to $100 per barrel between 2000 and the end of 2007), shortages, and social instability in both producer and consumer economies.[10]
- The United States consumes about 20 million barrels of oil a day (about 25 percent of global consumption); China consumes about 6 million; Japan, 5 million. About 80 percent of the oil consumed in the United States is imported.[11]
- Other mineral resources in significant decline include zinc, copper, and iridium, all critical for technological innovations we've come to depend on, such as computers and cell phones.
- Coal is relatively abundant (known stocks are expected to last 50 to 100 years at current extraction rates) but problematic: It is the single biggest source of air pollution in the United States (and includes substantial amounts of highly toxic elements such as mercury), and CO_2 emitted per unit of energy (BTU) is roughly double that of natural gas. Coal generates 54 percent of the United States' electricity, 80 percent of Australia's, and 80 percent of China's growing electricity use.[12]

Regenerative (Renewable) Resources

- **Freshwater quality.** More than one-fifth of the world's people do not have reliable access to clean drinking water, and many are chronically dehydrated. Many natural water supplies—rivers, lakes, groundwater—have become increasingly degraded. Roughly two-thirds of the water we use goes to agriculture, and runoff from pesticides and fertilizers is the single biggest polluter.[13]

- **Topsoil.** Overproduction has caused severe or extreme soil degradation of over 1 billion hectares (or over two and a half billion acres) in the past fifty years—more than the size of India and China combined.[14]

- **Fisheries.** Over 70 percent of the world's fisheries are chronically overfished. Many species are so depleted that if drastic actions are not taken soon, their populations will likely be unable to recover. This will affect more than just consumers; the fishing industry itself will suffer, and as coastal economies are ruined, the unemployed will migrate, becoming part of the growing millions of unwelcome migrants worldwide.[15]

- **Forests.** More than a third of the world's forests have disappeared in the past fifty years. Their loss, especially in the tropics, affects the lives of many communities and species and reduces the rate at which CO_2, the main greenhouse gas driving climate change, is absorbed from the atmosphere.[16]

Our diminishing resources and growing waste underlie a host of related economic stresses and reflect environmental and social imbalances that all but ensure that, without significant change, these problems will worsen.

The first imbalance concerns nature's capacities to continue regenerating resources and providing the "eco-services" upon which human life depends—clean water, breathable air, fertile soil, pollination, and a stable climate. In economic terms, most of these services either have no substitute or are prohibitively expensive to generate by alternative means.[17] Today, according to the UN's Millennium Ecosystem Assessment report, one-third of the major ecosystems that provide these essential services worldwide—from forests to grasslands and wetlands—are in "significant decline," and another one-third are "in danger." Since 1900, more than half of the world's wetlands have been lost. Today, 50 percent of the world's five hundred major rivers are heavily polluted or drying up in their lower reaches. The acidification of oceans (primarily due to the absorption of CO_2 from fossil fuels) has, in the past twenty years, caused the loss of 20 percent of the world's coral reefs, while 20 percent more have been seriously degraded. Many of these reefs protect coastal areas from flooding and serve as critical breeding areas for marine life.[18]

As the Millennium Ecosystem Assessment report also discusses, declining ecosystems and increasing pollution tend to correlate with the erosion of our sense of spiritual and non-material well-being, in developing and developed countries alike. Growing social stresses are all too often taken as the norm today. In the developed world, we are plagued by anxiety, overwork, stress, mistrust, fear, and anger. America isn't the only advanced country "bowling alone," to borrow Robert Putnam's famous phrase for the breakdown of social community; similar signs of social stresses have been increasing in other nations, such as the tensions in Europe over growing African and Islamic immigrations.

In developing countries, environmental and social stresses often have a harder economic edge. According to the World Bank, from 1980 to 2000 the bottom quartile of the world's people found that their share of global income fell from 2.5 percent to 1.2 percent.[19] Today, about 50 million people globally migrate each year to cities, usually driven by the collapse of traditional economies and environmental degradation of land and fisheries (as noted previously). This migration rate is far greater than can be absorbed by urban economies, and as a consequence approximately 500 million chronically underemployed people currently live in squatter camps or slums.[20]

Inevitably, these underlying imbalances—deteriorating ecosystems and fraying social harmony—reinforce one another. The poor invariably bear a disproportionate share of the consequences of industrial waste and compromised ecosystems. This is one reason the extremes in inequity persist and are largely getting worse worldwide. Second, people living under growing stress, whether physical, psychological, or economic, have great difficulty acting as stewards for the future.

An inventory such as this can go on forever, becoming more exhausting as it becomes more exhaustive. The point, however, is not to be comprehensive but rather to be systemic: to see the deeper patterns behind all these problems, which at first glance might seem unrelated.

What these examples demonstrate is that the industrial system that has brought us so many benefits is now generating countless dangerous side effects that are swamping its ability to continue advancing standards of living. One of two outcomes is possible: Either we keep on with business as usual, leaving the accumulating side effects to continue growing until they overwhelm us, or we step back far enough to rethink where we are headed. Notice we said the first thing that needs to be done is to take a step back.

Not surprisingly, when we—individuals, companies, non-profits, governments—first acknowledge problems such as the ones we're discussing, our instinct is to do the opposite, to apply exactly the same kind of thinking that created these challenges in the first place. We focus on the symptoms in front of us—the river is dirty, we emit too much CO_2—and ignore the underlying forces contributing to them. We devise ways—usually through some combination of stopgap regulations or find-the-villain blame games—to try to fix the symptoms.

Focusing on eliminating the symptoms is always tempting. Taking two aspirin to relieve the pain of a headache can be an effective solution that works quite quickly. But if a person gets severe headaches every few days, there are probably deeper, longer-term sources of the problem, such as stress or overwork, that all the aspirin in the world will not help. In fact, the aspirin can even make matters worse by masking the pain, and along with it the signals that there are deeper sources of the problem. Over time, this neglect leads to a worsening of symptoms and the need for still more intense symptomatic fixes, such as more powerful drugs that simply continue the pattern of ignoring the underlying cause of the pain.

In most organizational situations, this pattern, known as "shifting the burden," often includes shifting the locus of responsibility for dealing with difficult problems to various "others" or "experts." Business executives have been doing this for years, hiring consultants to sort out their chronic management problems, safety specialists to reduce the number of accidents, and, today, environmental specialists, such as pollution experts, to scrub emissions from smokestacks.

The net effect of decades of shifting the burden to experts is that many people today regard issues involving water, waste and toxicity, energy, and

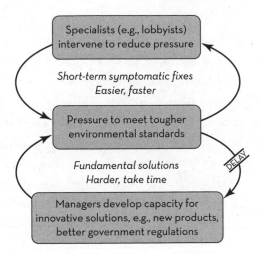

FIGURE 2.1 Shifting the Burden to "Expert" Specialists

community health as "someone else's problems." While businesspeople often have strong views about the ineffectiveness of government regulation, many also simultaneously advocate that it is up to government to tackle such problems. And many, rather than working proactively with government to come up with more innovative fundamental solutions (lower loop in Figure 2.1 above), have shifted the burden to lobbyists who fight to preserve the status quo (the upper loop).

Tips on Reading Causal Loop Diagrams

Throughout the book, you will find causal loop diagrams such as Figure 2.1, which portray interactions that give rise to patterns of change (or non-change) and forces over time. For example, in the shifting-the-burden pattern, the problem symptom "Pressure to meet tough environmental standards" can be addressed in two ways: a short-term symptomatic fix, such as using lobbyists, or a more fundamental solution, such as new environmentally friendly products or working proactively with government for better regulations. Think of these two loops as competing: If the symptomatic fix wins out, pressure to meet tougher standards diminishes and there is less need for funda-mental solutions. But this leads to new forces. If fundamental solu-tions are neglected, the problem symptom will eventually return: Since nothing is being done to actually address the underlying envi-ronmental problems, pressures will build up again. If the company still opts for the symptomatic solution when these pressures again need to be addressed (which is likely, given that the fundamental solu-tion is no easier and they now are used to working with the lobbyists), it will lead to still more lobbying. In this way, forces build over time to shift the burden to depending more and more on lobbyists.

And, of course, government leaders likewise have their own set of "ex-perts" for addressing symptoms in the form of environmental depart-ments and agencies to whom they shift responsibility. These groups are often isolated from the core functions of government such as economic and foreign policy, taxation, and national security, and as a result their actions have marginal impact.

But the time for shifting responsibility to others, or covering up deep problems with simplistic solutions that only make problems "go away" for a short time, is running out.

In the earlier phases of the Industrial Age, the wealthy simply moved away from factories and their waste by-products. Later, we found ways to dump wastes farther away from population centers (New York City ex-ports over 10,000 tons of solid waste per day).[21]

But in today's interconnected world, "away" is going away. As popula-tion and industrialization have continued to grow geometrically, waste generated in one region affects others. The earth, after all, is a finite sys-tem. Particulate emissions from Beijing affect air quality in Los Angeles, and those from Los Angeles affect asthma rates in New York. Our com-mon atmosphere, oceans, and groundwater systems have always con-nected us, but the scale of industrial activity has now reached a point where the consequences of local actions are no longer simply local. The space in which short-term, Band-Aid solutions to fundamental challenges will work is contracting as fast as the space for more landfills and toxic waste dumps. The time for rethinking and redesigning is at hand.

SEEING THE WHOLE PICTURE

For most of us, the endless litany of environmental and societal crises is overwhelming, both emotionally and cognitively. It is no wonder that so many simply "turn off" when confronted with another story of climate-change-related severe weather, water shortages, or toxic waste. The first problem to deal with is simply "How do I take all of this in without frying my circuits?"

"Systems thinking" has long been a cornerstone in our work on organizational learning, but the term often seems more daunting (it can easily sound like an intellectual task reserved for Ph.D.'s) than helpful. In fact, systems thinking is not about fighting complexity with more complexity. It simply means stepping back and seeing patterns that are, when seen clearly, intuitive and easy to grasp.

Several years ago, working with the Rocky Mountain Institute, an energy and resource research and consultancy group, we developed a simple "systems picture" to help people make sense of the situation in which we find ourselves today.[22] The gist of the picture centers on six basic ideas.

If you had to explain our predicament to a ten-year-old, this would be a good way to start:

1. The industrial system—what we make, buy, and use (from cars and TVs to buildings and power plants)—sits within the larger systems of nature.
2. This larger natural world includes living, regenerative resources, such as forests, croplands, and fisheries, and other resources that, from a human time perspective, do not regenerate, such as oil and minerals.
3. The regenerative resources can sustain human activities indefinitely, so long as we do not "harvest" them more rapidly than they replenish themselves.
4. The non-regenerative resources can only be depleted or "extracted." (That is why mining, oil production, and other similar industries

are called "extractive industries.") And not surprisingly, since they cannot be replenished, sooner or later—as is happening right now— many start to run out.

Because modern societies are set up to focus on the benefits and output of industry, we tend to either not see or pay less attention to the fifth and sixth features:

5. In the process of extracting and harvesting resources in order to produce and use goods, the industrial system also generates waste— waste from extracting and harvesting resources, and from how we produce, use, and eventually discard goods. This waste damages the ability of nature to replenish resources.
6. The industrial system also sits within a larger social system of communities, families, schools, and culture. Just as overproduction and waste damage natural systems, they also cause anxiety, inequity, and stresses in our societies.

These six ideas are captured in Figures 2.2a and b on page 25, starting with the initial phase of the Industrial Age, driven primarily by expansion of production and employment, and continuing into the last half century, driven increasingly by growing consumption. This includes consumption of both tangible consumer goods (such as cellular phones and iPods) and services (such as air travel and music downloads), both of which are produced by companies based on their capital equipment and facilities.

But seeing the whole picture is difficult (see figures on page 26). Until very recently, most politicians, businesspeople, and media have focused on only the "system within a system"—the industrial economy and how to keep it expanding. Concern for the health of the larger social and ecological systems within which the industrial system sits has been confined largely to the "back page," even though public concern for these larger systems has been growing for more than a generation. Only in the last couple of years have we seen more front-page articles about the economy, business, and technology that mention the declining health of the ecosystems that enable the global economic system to function.

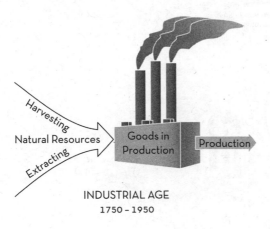

INDUSTRIAL AGE
1750 – 1950

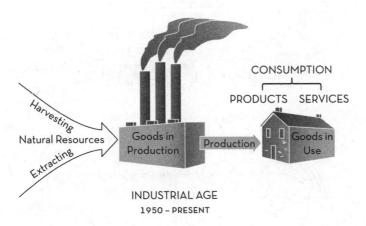

INDUSTRIAL AGE
1950 – PRESENT

FIGURES 2.2 a, b

That relatively few paid much attention to these larger problems is perfectly understandable. Ignoring unintended side effects is hardly limited to this environment. Indeed, it is one of the most common underlying patterns that we have experienced when helping companies understand systems thinking. For example, managers are often rewarded generously for cutting costs and improving short-term profits, but the side effects of their maneuvers, such as demoralized workers or angry customers, often end up costing the company more in the long run.

Put differently, we have gotten into our predicament today because of a way of thinking that focuses on parts and neglects the whole. We have

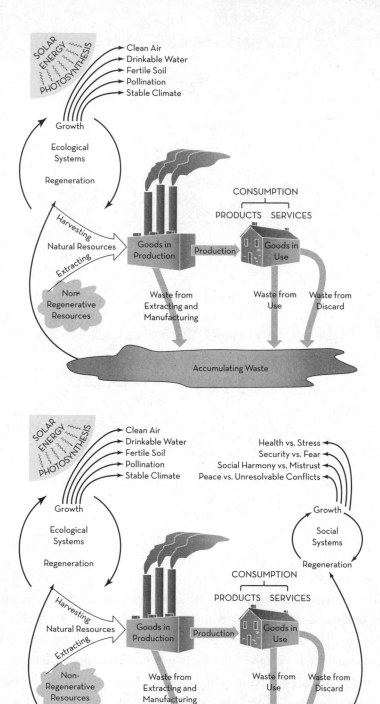

FIGURES 2.2 c, d

become masterful at focusing on immediate goals—such as short-term profits—and neglecting the larger systems of which quarterly profits are but one small part. But this is changing because the larger reality can no longer be ignored.

THE CASE FOR URGENCY: THE 80-20 CHALLENGE

Although the problems of the Industrial Age have been evident for decades, there is now one important difference, an increasingly inescapable mandate urging us to wake up and start operating differently: global climate change.

Though but one of many side effects of global industrial growth, climate change has two unique aspects: The current and prospective costs are enormous for both rich and poor, and it provides simple, numerical indicators of just how far out of balance we are—and how rapid and strong the adjustments must be if we are to avert disaster.

Although science rarely provides absolute certainty, a consensus has emerged among scientists, and among a small but growing cadre of influential leaders, that the changes needed to avert extreme and possibly uncontrollable climate change will be greater and must happen far more quickly than we imagined even a few years ago. In this sense, climate change is a particular sort of gift, a time clock telling us how fast the Industrial Age is ending.

As for the costs of climate change, they already are considerable, and will be far greater if we do not address the issue quickly and systematically. In 2007, Oxfam International, one of the world's largest and most respected civil society organizations (often called non-governmental organizations or NGOs), published the first study on climate change "compensation" costs for the poor—what it would take to compensate for the suffering from disease, failed crops, and dislocation arising from climate change. This report placed the costs at $50 billion globally and noted that they will rise precipitously in the coming years. In preparing the report, Oxfam's larger goal is to establish a method to make these escalating costs visible. The costs to the insurance industry already can be seen: Insurance premiums are rising dramatically—up to 40 percent in Florida, 20 percent in coastal Massachusetts, and 400 percent for some offshore oil rigs—reflecting the risks of climate instability. These rates make self-insurance (dropping coverage and taking your chances) more economical for many businesses and homeowners in high-risk areas such as southern Florida. The influential Stern Report, commissioned by the UK government in 2006 and led by a former World Bank chief economist, concluded that if dramatic changes are not made soon, the costs to the world of climate change in the next decade could equal or exceed the costs of World War II.[23]

Unlike so many other global social and environmental problems, in one sense climate change is simple—because its primary dimensions are measurable. Scientists now have extensive evidence of how rapidly CO_2 and other greenhouse gases are accumulating in the atmosphere, and how that compares with historical levels.

CO_2 concentrations in the atmosphere have been rising throughout the industrial era, with the current level more than 30 percent higher than in 1850.[24] This level is continuing to increase rapidly because the amount of CO_2 emitted from combusting fossil fuels in our power plants, buildings, cars, trucks, airplanes, and factories each year—about 8 billion tons of carbon equivalent per year worldwide—is more than double what can be removed from the atmosphere and absorbed by natural biomass (trees, plants, and plankton) and dissolved in oceans.[25]

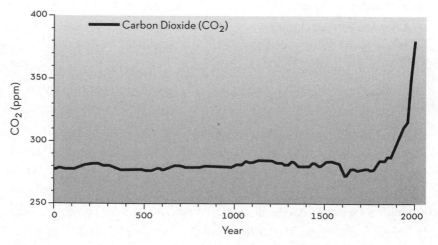

FIGURE 2.3

The CO$_2$ Bathtub

The difference between inflows and outflows of CO$_2$ in the atmosphere works just like a bathtub: The CO$_2$ level rises as long as more flows in than flows out. This simple fact has confused many people, including many in important leadership positions, who believe that curtailing emissions growth alone would solve the climate change problem.[26]

So long as the inflow of CO$_2$ emissions exceeds the outflow of CO$_2$ removed from the atmosphere, at some point the bathtub will "overflow." This means that unless we reduce emissions to equal CO$_2$ removed from the atmosphere—in other words, a 60 percent to 80 percent reduction of worldwide emissions—we will likely enter an era of irreversible climate change.

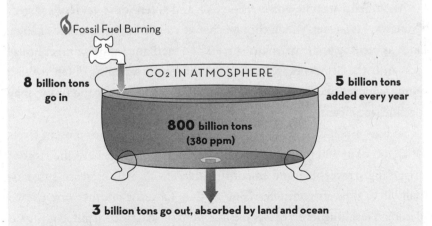

FIGURE 2.4 The atmosphere as a bathtub, with annual inputs and outputs of CO$_2$. The level in the tub is rising by about 5 billion tons per year (2.1 billion tons of carbon equivalent = 1 part per million (ppm) CO$_2$).

(An interactive simulation of the CO$_2$ bathtub is available at http://www.sustainer.org/tools_resources.)

No one can say with certainty how much CO_2 in the atmosphere is too much, but a few basic facts are starting to coalesce into a strong consensus.

First, current levels of CO_2 are almost one-third higher than at any other time in the past 650,000 years.[27] This includes much of human history, a period of time in which, despite periodic ice ages, the overall climate was conducive to human life.

Second, concentrations of CO_2 in oceans and biomass are far above historic levels, causing problems such as ocean acidification and raising questions about how much more these natural CO_2 sinks can absorb. If they start to absorb less, more CO_2 will concentrate faster in the atmosphere, driving global warming faster.

Third, there is a long time lag before the full effects of CO_2 are felt on temperature and climate; scientific estimates put this at thirty to fifty years. This means that the full effects of *current* atmospheric CO_2 levels will not be felt until 2050 or even later.

And finally, at some point, rising CO_2 and greenhouse gas levels trigger "runaway" effects in which climate change causes further climate change, such as melting arctic permafrost releasing methane (another greenhouse gas) into the atmosphere, leading to still more warming.[28] Once these "tipping point" feedbacks take off, our ability to influence the future may decline significantly.

So how much CO_2 is too much? Some scientists feel that present levels of CO_2 (about 380 ppm) are already too high. Others believe the risks of triggering irreversible and uncontrollable effects will increase substantially if CO_2 levels continue rising as they have for another one to two decades (reaching levels exceeding 425 ppm or so). By contrast, continued business-as-usual growth in CO_2 emissions would lead to midcentury CO_2 levels about twice as high (approximately 550 ppm) as the historic maximum for the last 650,000 years, and far more dangerous—levels that few with any sense of stewardship for future generations, let alone present ones, should tolerate.[29]

In some sense, the "How high is too high?" debate is academic because simply stabilizing CO_2 levels will require extraordinary and dramatic reductions in emissions worldwide—a crucial point to which the people of the world have just begun to awaken. A little more than a decade ago, a number of nations came together to shape the Kyoto Protocol, the first intergovernmental agreement to confront climate change (which the United States never signed). The accord focused on curbing emissions growth. But as we now know, stopping the rise of CO_2 levels in the atmosphere, the primary source of climate change, will actually require significant emissions *reductions*. Accomplishing this will require a sea change in the kinds of energy we use, cars we drive, buildings we live and work in, cities we design, and ways both people and goods move around the world, as well as other changes no one can even imagine.

Advances in climate science will continue to be crucial for understanding the specifics of how rising average temperatures are likely to affect rainfall and drought patterns, storm activity and intensity, the spread of disease, and significant increases in sea levels. But science can take us only so far. Sooner or later, it becomes a matter of making choices, not simply waiting for more predictions.[30]

Already, people and institutions around the world are starting to formulate bold "stretch goals"—aspirational targets that can galvanize the imagination, creativity, and courage truly called for.[31] Though the details of these goals differ, their central message is the same: To stabilize CO_2 in the atmosphere at levels that minimize the threat of catastrophic consequences will require a 60 percent to 80 percent reduction in emissions within the next two decades![32] We call this the 80-20 Challenge, the bell tolling the end of the Industrial Age.

While focusing on CO_2 levels helps us to understand the urgency we face, it is equally important to remind ourselves that climate change is not an isolated problem. Rather, it is part and parcel of all the other problems that are signaling the end of the Industrial Age: accumulating waste byproducts that derive from the take-make-waste industrial system; diminishing resources (some of which are driving CO_2 levels further upward: about 6 billion tons of CO_2 per year are released from deforestation— including the burning and decaying of wood—alone); deteriorating ecosystems; the intensification of social stresses (such as the United States' foreign policies, driven by dependency on Middle East oil). Climate change is but one thread in a larger cloth; we cannot simply remove the thread, but must reweave the cloth.

Because the side effects of globalization are interrelated, meeting the 80-20 Challenge of reducing emissions 80 percent in twenty years will require changes in all the major global industrial systems: food and water, energy and transportation, and the global production and distribution of goods. Little in our modern way of living will be unaffected.

In other words, the change will not happen without a radical shift in the thinking that has made the industrial era so successful—and so disastrous.

[3]

Life Beyond the Bubble

We are at the beginning of a long journey. Still, there is a simple overarching metaphor that has helped us appreciate the revolution we are starting to experience.

To understand this metaphor, you must first appreciate that we are not the first highly successful society to find itself in trouble. History is full of examples of people who've succeeded so thoroughly in expanding their way of living that they found themselves in circumstances for which they were tragically unprepared.

Historian and Pulitzer Prize winner Jared Diamond has chronicled (most recently in his book *Collapse*) how many once-dominant civilizations grew significantly and then expired, often quite suddenly. Few societies of the time, for instance, achieved such sophistication in mathematics, astronomy, and social structure as the Maya of Central America. Yet despite its accomplishments, the Mayan civilization—five hundred years before the Spaniards' arrival in their lands—all but disappeared within a generation, apparently the victim of an environmental collapse brought about by the unsustainable slash-and-burn agriculture the Maya had practiced for generations.

The larger the Mayan population grew, the more their agricultural activity deforested the areas where they lived. Deforestation, in turn, caused soil erosion, which eventually ruined the storage reservoirs that held their drinking water and destroyed their ability to grow crops. Without food and water, the Mayan city-states died and the people moved back to the jungles and forests.

Given the history of the Maya as well as the other examples Diamond shares of sophisticated societies that succeeded in destroying their own resource base, is our situation hopeless?[1] Hardly. In a recent article, Lester Brown, one of the elders of environmental analysis and founder of the Worldwatch Institute, recounts an example of a people who were successfully able to change.

Six centuries ago, Icelanders realized that overgrazing on their grass-covered highlands was leading to extensive loss of the inherently thin soils of the region. Rather than lose the grasslands and face economic decline, farmers joined together to determine how many sheep the highlands could sustain and then allocated quotas among themselves, thus preserving their grasslands.

Just as the Icelanders understood the consequences of overgrazing and reduced their sheep numbers to a level that could be sustained, we now understand the consequences of burning fossil fuels and the resulting CO_2 buildup in the atmosphere. Yet, unlike the Icelanders, who were able to restrict their livestock numbers, we have not yet been able to significantly restrict our CO_2 emissions.

Our success in doing so will depend on more than awareness of the side effects of global industrialization we discussed earlier. The real threats of collapse have more to do with denial than with unawareness, and it is here that we can build upon a metaphor frequently used by historians: the bubble.

We are all familiar with financial bubbles, the metaphor invented by economic historians to make sense of a recurring puzzle: How is it that financial overexpansion and collapse occur time and again, drawing otherwise bright and clever people into ruin?

The answer is that during a period of expansion, in effect, two parallel realities develop, one inside the bubble and one outside. Both feel equally real to those who live within them. But the more the bubble grows, the more people are drawn into its powerful reinforcing beliefs and perceptions. Eventually, those inside the bubble become so absorbed by their reality that they literally can no longer understand the point of view of those outside.

Recall the exchanges between those inside and outside the dot-com bubble of the late 1990s. Those inside the bubble were living in a "new economy" with new rules, and its success spoke for itself. What mattered was technology, hits to your website, "stickiness" (how long people stayed on your website once they arrived), and frequently a cool, anti-corporate image. Profit—that old-economy word—would come in time, the new-economy zealots argued. And many investors agreed—so much so that profitable old-economy businesses often saw their market value decline in comparison to their dot-com counterparts, despite the fact that the dot-coms had little or no profits.

But there was a larger reality outside the bubble where profits actually did matter. Eventually this larger reality asserted itself and the bubble burst, wiping out a great many paper millionaires and a few billionaires in the process.

As Diamond shows, societal bubbles can last decades or even centuries. In the meantime, the longer the bubble grows, the more people and resources get drawn into it, the more people may benefit from it, and the more its beliefs become deeply entrenched.

After generations, it becomes hard to even imagine an alternative, a way of living outside the bubble. But at some point the tensions and inconsistencies between life inside the bubble and the larger reality outside of it must be resolved. The bubble cannot continue expanding indefinitely.

We believe the Industrial Age constitutes an extended bubble of just this sort. Its expansion has continued for several centuries, so it is easy to assume that it will continue forever. But there is a world outside the bubble, what biologist E. O. Wilson calls "the real real world," and, as we are beginning to witness, signs that the Industrial Age Bubble has run its course are already out in plain sight.[2]

THE "REAL" REAL WORLD

As the saying goes, "Gravity isn't just a good idea; it's the law." The Industrial Age Bubble violates several aspects of the larger "gravity" of the natural world. Those of us who have been living inside this Bubble must now recognize this in order to see our path forward.

Consider, for example, how within the Industrial Age Bubble we go about meeting the fundamental human needs for energy, food and water, and products and services that ensure our physical security and well-being.

For some 2 billion years, life has flourished on earth based on one source of energy: solar radiation, the same energy that powers a forest, a prairie, a marine ecosystem, or a caterpillar.

By contrast, 90 percent or more of our energy within the Industrial Age Bubble comes from burning fossil fuels.

Similarly, in nature, most food is local (although in some cases seeds may be carried a great distance). Our food is rarely local, traveling instead

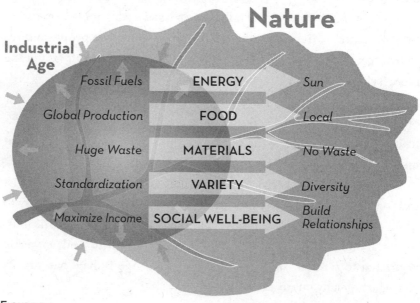

FIGURE 3.1

thousands of miles, and is often genetically modified or otherwise pre-
served so that it can survive the trip.

In nature there is no waste: every by-product of one natural system is a
nutrient for another. Within the Industrial Age Bubble, society generates
enormous amounts of waste.

The contradictions of the Industrial Age Bubble also extend to the way
society is organized and sets its priorities. For example, the Industrial Age
quest for efficiency and standardization has gradually unleashed relentless forces for homogenization, destroying cultural diversity just as it has
destroyed biological diversity. Today, people around the world watch
the same television shows, buy the same products, and, increasingly, embrace the same consumer ideals of the "good life." In stark contrast to this
drive to homogenize, everywhere we see nature's love affair with diversity
and uniqueness: No two trees, leaves, dragonflies, polar bears, or people
are the same.

For millennia, healthy societies that have endured have fostered a sense
of belonging and security, confidence that basic material needs will be
met, and the opportunity for each person to grow and express his or her
own unique gifts and aspirations. By contrast, within the Bubble, social
well-being is often reduced to material growth, specifically GDP growth.
Though we are regularly reminded of how important this is, few of us
actually *feel* more secure or happier when GDP rises. Indeed, research has
shown that after basic needs are met, there is little correlation between
increased material comfort and people's sense of well-being.[3]

These contradictions between how nature, including human nature,
works and how modern society works cannot continue indefinitely. The
question is not if the Industrial Age Bubble will end. The question is when
and how—keeping in mind Jared Diamond's point that collapse can occur
much more rapidly than those inside a bubble expect.

For a long time, those who have pointed to problems with the Industrial Age have mostly been relegated to the backbench of social critiques,
their arguments the stuff of academic debates, not practical policy and
organizational strategy. But the urgency of climate change is altering that.
The 80-20 Challenge demands immediate shifts in energy use and our
modern way of living.

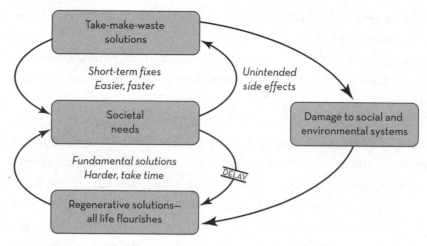

FIGURE 3.2

Which brings us to the question of how, the answer to which is relatively simple—although far from easy. Up until now, we have been shifting the burden to nature to handle the side effects of our fragmented, short-term take-make-waste solutions (see Figure 3.2).[4]

Either we continue on this path, perhaps making the occasional incremental adjustment (the equivalent of choosing between paper and plastic bags), or we invest seriously and immediately in building a regenerative economy and society that mimics nature as fully as possible.

THE CHOICE BEHIND OUR CHOICES

A core principle of a regenerative society is that life creates conditions for life.

When it comes to deciding how we deal with key issues such as energy, water, and other resources, we can either adopt that principle or resign ourselves to the fact that our time here will be short. Why? Because the more we opt for the old Industrial Age model, the more we compromise the conditions that support and generate life. And the more severe our sustainability problems become, the more difficult it becomes to invest in alternatives, because the increasingly stressed ecosystems will demand immediate, reactive efforts that limit our ability to truly innovate the future.

Obviously, the Industrial Age Bubble is a metaphor, but it is a useful way of looking at the current situation and can help guide our choices going forward. The Bubble is sustained by the choices we make every day—what we buy, what we make and how we make it, how we interact with one another. Choices that reinforce the extractive "take-make-waste" economy are based on a set of assumptions, beliefs, and ways of seeing the world that we have developed over time and that have by now become deeply embedded in modern society. For example:

- Energy is infinite and cheap.
- There will always be enough room to dispose of all our waste.
- Humans can't possibly alter the global environment. For instance, weather patterns will remain relatively stable no matter how we act.
- Humans are the primary species on earth; others are less important, and many are irrelevant.
- Basic resources such as water and topsoil are unlimited. If limits or problems are encountered, markets and new technologies will re-allocate financial resources so we can continue with our current ways of living and working.
- Productivity and standardization are keys to economic progress.
- Economic growth and rising GDP are the best way to "lift all boats" and reduce social inequities.

By contrast, life beyond the Bubble will be based on choices reflecting very different beliefs, assumptions, and guiding principles, such as:

- **Surf the flux.**[5] Live within our energy income by relying on forms of energy that come from renewable sources such as solar, wind, tidal, and bio-based inputs.
- **Zero to landfill.** *Everything,* from cars and iPods to office buildings and machine tools, is 100 percent recyclable, remanufacturable, or compostable.
- **We are borrowing the future from our children; we have to pay it back.** Our first responsibility is to leave a healthy global biosphere for our children, their children, their children's children, and so on.

- **We are only one of nature's wonders.** We are just one of the species that matter, and we all depend on each other in ways we cannot even imagine.
- **Value the earth's services; they come free of charge to those who treasure them.** Healthy ecosystems are precious and must be treated as such.
- **Embrace variety; build community.** Harmony amid diversity is a feature of healthy ecosystems and societies.
- **In the global village, there is only one boat, and a hole sinks us all.** Our mutual security and well-being depend on respect and concern for all. If any of us is insecure, then we all are.

Lastly, a regenerative society is a flourishing society. The revolution is not about giving up; it's about rediscovering what we most value. It is about making quality in living central in our communities, businesses, schools, and societies. It is about reconnecting with ourselves, one another, and our fellow non-human inhabitants on earth.

Over twenty years ago, the tiny country of Bhutan embarked on a project of devising a new set of indicators for national progress. What became known as the gross national happiness, or GNH, index included forest cover, child nutrition, education levels, and health of the elderly. Interestingly, in the years since it began using the GNH index, Bhutan has consistently been rated at the top of the performance index maintained by the World Bank for all countries that receive financing from its International Development Assistance arm, an index that takes into account both governance and social and economic indicators.

Life beyond the Bubble will require suspending "either/or" thinking. Assuming that we must choose either a better standard of living or healthy ecosystems and cannot have both is a by-product of the Industrial Age. This is not to assume that a regenerative society will not involve changes that will be difficult, such as adjusting to higher energy prices, having fewer material acquisitions, or taking greater responsibility for our impact on the world. But to assume that this is automatically a step backward in terms of overall quality of living is to assume that our answers from the past are automatically the answers for the future.

THE WAY IN IS ALSO THE WAY OUT

Just as our way of thinking got us into the situation we are in today, so, too, will our thinking—differently—help us find our way out. We can't attack the problems piecemeal. Solving isolated social and environmental problems will not get us very far; at best it will provide short-term relief. Neither will preserving the status quo while imagining naively that new technologies alone will somehow save the day.

We need to ask, "What would a way of thinking, a way of living, and ultimately an economic system look like that worked based on the principles of the larger natural world? And how do we create such a way of living in our organizations and societies, one step at a time?"

[4]

New Thinking, New Choices

As the Industrial Age worldview has expanded to draw in more and more of the world's people and resources, it has also created a level of interdependence that has never before existed. The average pound of food travels some 2,000 miles before being purchased by an American consumer. Many everyday products—from Nike sneakers made in China to Sony televisions made in Wales—travel as far or farther.

This is important for two reasons, one obvious, one subtle.

What is obvious is that our global economy is based on interdependence. Wealthy countries such as the United States and the European nations are dependent on people all over the world when it comes to producing the things we rely on in our everyday lives, and they in turn depend on us not only to buy their products but also to produce things they need.

But what many of us are unaware of are the invisible costs that come with this. The products we choose to buy affect people in distant places, not only through direct economic ties but through their side effects, such as CO_2 emissions and the depletion of natural resources. Our current methods of shipping and distributing food and other products over great distances consume massive amounts of increasingly valuable fuel and create another source of greenhouse gases. One glass of orange juice, for example, contains the equivalent of two glasses of oil, if you include transportation costs. Global distribution systems generate almost 10 percent of today's annual CO_2 emissions.[1]

As people gradually become aware of this interdependence, the immediate effects are disorienting and often frightening. This level of interdependence has never existed before, and it is catapulting us, as former World Bank vice president Mieko Nishimizu put it, into a world of "inescapable mutuality" and "a future that is truly *alien* to us."

We wrote this book in order to share the stories of people and organizations embracing this interdependence as they search for solutions for a sustainable world (as opposed to allowing themselves to be immobilized by fear or worry), and the inspiration and insights these stories carry. In our experience, once people recognize and accept this interdependence, they are able to begin looking for longer-term and bigger-picture solutions. Whether focused specifically on the 80-20 Challenge of climate change or on other symptoms of the Industrial Age's imbalances, they demonstrate the same sense of urgency—and the sense of possibility this urgency opens up.

In the stories you'll read in these pages, the same basic patterns repeat themselves time and again:

1. Thoughtful people see arising problems earlier than the rest of us.
2. They begin to understand how severe those problems are.
3. The combination of deep concern and sense of possibility for a better future causes them to think differently about the problems and how they are interconnected.
4. Different ways of thinking lead to different ways of acting. By focusing on long-term strategies, groups and organizations begin to take into account the larger systems in which they operate, instead of simply fixing isolated problems.

And there are thousands, probably millions, of such people searching for innovative ways to create a more sustainable world. To us, their work is the best evidence that a future very different from the Industrial Age is trying to emerge, and their actions are the best source of insight into how to help bring it into being.

Particularly, they demonstrate a mastery of three areas that have been core to our work in organizational learning over the years.

First, individually and collectively, they are continually learning how to *see the larger systems*—organizations, complex supply chains, industries, cities, or regions—of which they are a part. This gives them insight and perspective that shapes their strategies. They then work to design products, infrastructures, organizational and public policies, and business models that promote the health of these systems, rather than pursuing quick-fix solutions that often end up making the overall situation worse.

Second, they understand that it is crucial to *collaborate across boundaries* that previously divided them from others within and outside their organizations. Changing how unsustainable systems work cannot be separated from changing how *we* work. This starts with building relationships of trust and genuine mutuality among people who previously had little of either.

Finally, as people work together they also come to focus on what truly matters to them, and their thinking evolves from a reactive problem-solving mode to *creating futures they truly desire*. With this comes a level of commitment, imagination, patience, and perseverance far beyond what happens when we are just reacting to problems.

These three capabilities—seeing systems, collaborating across boundaries, and creating desired futures—must continually develop in institutions as well as individuals, for, as we pointed out in Chapter 1, institutions, and the networks they create, shape how our present world operates and hold the greatest promise for systemic change.

Lastly, these capabilities must develop together. Without a creative orientation, there is no genuine commitment to longer-term visions, goals, and desired outcomes, and it is easy to ignore the challenging work of seeing larger systems and transforming relationships. Without skills in collaborating, people do not learn how to develop the collective systems intelligence to tackle complex problems. Without the capacity to see systems and their place in them, people and organizations will naturally

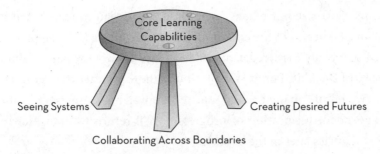

FIGURE 4.1 Learning Capabilities for Systemic Change

focus on optimizing their piece of the puzzle rather than building shared understanding and a larger vision. In short, all three legs of the stool are needed for creating regenerative organizations, industries, and economies; take away any one, and the stool collapses.

1. Seeing Systems

In a world of growing interdependence, it's more important than ever to learn how to expand the boundaries of normal management attention and concern in order to see the larger systems in which businesses operate. Failing to do so leads to policies and strategies whose side effects eventually sabotage the intended effects, as with the problems of growing waste and toxicity. Similarly, many regenerative resources, such as water, topsoil, and fish stocks, are declining because businesses and communities followed strategies of maximizing short-term production without stepping back to look at the larger system and see whether they're consuming resources more rapidly than they are being replenished.

Many companies are beginning to understand the limits they face. Because aluminum manufacturing is a highly water-intensive process, Alcoa gradually began to see growing water shortages affecting its business in the mid-1990s. As Alcoa looked into the future, it realized that this would only get worse. In 1997, the company set a bold goal of zero net water discharges, and proceeded to rethink and redesign basic aspects of how its plants worked. Coca-Cola faced even more daunting water challenges. After several years of focusing on improved water efficiency within its plants, Coke's senior management gradually began to realize that it was the overall health of the entire watershed in which a bottling plant operated that really mattered. Coke entered into a five-year partnership with the World Wildlife Fund (WWF) to build the technical expertise to achieve a new aim of "giving back to nature" the water it extracts and to set up independent verification of progress. (We'll return to both Alcoa's and Coke's stories later in the book.)

Expanding management boundaries and anticipating limits that might shape the future means challenging established ways of thinking and unquestioned mental models. Organizations that fail to develop these abilities tend to react to growing problems with shorter-term fixes more within their control. There is nothing wrong with this; indeed, Coke's work on water efficiency began with helping managers understand the importance of not wasting water and the costs of doing so. But often short-term solutions become part of a strategy of consistently avoiding deeper problems. For example, many companies react to water shortages by simply moving to different countries with laxer government regulations. Before long, companies are spending more and more money on lobbying and burnishing their image, while underlying problems grow.

At a certain point, expanding boundaries and facing deeper problems opens people's eyes to totally new opportunities—for Alcoa, it meant innovating radically different processes for making aluminum without using water; for Coke, it meant becoming a positive force in global water management. But organizations that fail to look beyond traditional management boundaries will never achieve these kinds of opportunities.

Systems thinking is widely espoused today, but many organizations lack the capacity because they lack the commitment to build the skills and the tools to help them do so. Buckminster Fuller used to say that if you want to teach people a new way of thinking, don't bother to teach them. Instead, give them a tool, the use of which will lead to new ways of thinking.

We will explore many different systems-thinking tools below, but the journey starts with seeing patterns, even if it's something as simple as noticing the unintended side effects of a proposed "solution." For example, companies cut customer service staff to improve profitability, but the unintended consequences of frustrated customers switching to competitors can cause profitability to fall even further. The pattern of unintended side effects is often part of a larger shifting-the-burden pattern of focusing on quick fixes instead of pursuing deeper, more fundamental solutions.

When dealing with complex issues such as sustainability, it helps to have a "pattern language," a way to visualize and talk about the deeper patterns. For example, companies can easily get into a shifting-the-burden pattern when facing an issue such as water scarcity. Relocating plants to an area with more water or less stringent water regulations might be fine unless you look ahead to determine that water will be becoming scarcer in general. If you do, you begin to consider a more fundamental solution: "Let's work with the local community to better manage the watershed." Being able to see this pattern—and especially how choosing the quick-fix symptomatic solution and avoiding the more fundamental solution may mean that the problems will come back, leading to yet more symptomatic fixes—can be a useful discipline to help management think more deeply about its choices.

There is nothing magic about seeing larger systems in order to encourage strategic choices; the magic comes from people actually doing it, and truly learning how to think together in the process.

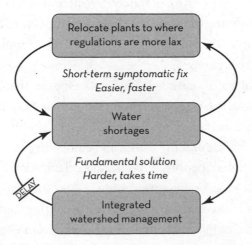

FIGURE 4.2 Water Shortages: A Shifting-the-Burden Pattern

2. Collaborating Across Boundaries

In a world shaped by organizations and networks of organizations, individual systems thinkers are, ultimately, of little significance. History has seen many wise people. This age is no different. The systems intelligence needed to deal with the challenges we face as the Industrial Age comes to an end is collective and must be built through working together at many levels, within and beyond organizations, in teams and networks that span industries, communities, and global supply chains.

In recognition of this, a rapidly growing number of collaborative initiatives have formed over the past decades, especially within the business community, and more recently between business and non-governmental organizations. For example, the World Business Council for Sustainable Development claims that its corporate members represent over one-third of the world's GDP. Ceres is a national network of investors, environmental organizations, and public interest groups that provide support for companies who understand and wish to address sustainability issues, and Business for Social Responsibility (BSR) provides such services to over 250 member companies and other enterprises. The Marine Stewardship Council (MSC) was founded by the World Wildlife Fund and Unilever to enable certification for sustainable fishing. Other collaborators focused on particular goals include the Green Power Market Development Group, created to promote the growth of renewable energy sources by guaranteeing large lead customers for green electricity, and the United States Climate Action Partnership, which promotes national policies for more aggressive greenhouse gas reductions.

But successful collaboration is easier to espouse than achieve, and many of these efforts have struggled to realize their founders' goals. For example, the MSC has fallen far short of Unilever's goals for certifying all major fish products around the world, and competing certification organizations have limited the spread of effective certification of forest products.[2] Many collaborative initiatives produce lots of talk and little action. As one executive and veteran of many collaborative initiatives put it, "These groups can be incredibly frustrating. We all seem either to agree on everything or have entrenched and irresolvable philosophical differences."

The problems come, in part, from underestimating the difficulties of learning among highly diverse groups. For example, in our experience in such settings, genuinely shared visions are rare. Far more often, one person's or one small group's vision is imposed, either subtly or otherwise, on others. Similarly, people know they need to learn together, whether in working teams or across complex supply chains, but they frequently avoid exploring difficult subjects because they want to avoid conflict. They know trust is important, but they often lack reliable strategies for building it. They may say they want to work collaboratively across boundaries, but ultimately provincialism prevails.

One reason for these shortfalls is that successful collaboration is often seen as a matter of good intentions rather than requisite skills. Our experience is exactly the opposite. Building the capacity to collaborate is hard work and needs to be seen as such. It takes time and a high level of commitment. Otherwise, well-established bad habits take over, such as avoiding conflict or launching into debates that merely reinforce previously held views.

These skills are all the more crucial given the challenging contexts in which these new collaborative initiatives are operating. The people involved often come from very different organizations and worldviews and have little history of working together. For example, leaders from businesses and NGOs often bring a history of combative relationships from the past. Plus, when people care deeply about the issues on the table, their emotional convictions can make them less than open-minded.

But, all these difficulties notwithstanding, real progress is being made in collaborations of all shapes and sizes. No one should be surprised at the difficulties that arise. There are few if any precedents for collaborative initiatives of the scale and complexity of those being attempted today. The very fact that many of these collaborative efforts exist and continue is a great sign of hope. Businesses *are* working together on carbon reductions, green energy, and more comprehensive sustainability strategies. Fish and forest products *are* getting certified. The imperative to collaborate across boundaries around such issues *has* been established. Now we just need to learn how to get better at it, quickly.

There is no turning back. As André van Heemstra, former Unilever management board member and co-founder of the Global Sustainable Food Lab (a global alliance of more than fifty organizations, including some of the world's largest food companies and NGOs, working together to bring sustainable agriculture into the mainstream), says, "Creating sustainable agricultural models will require bringing parties together that normally do not cooperate. As hard as this is, there really is no option because feeding 9 billion people sustainably means changes that cannot be achieved by any sector alone."

3. Creating: Beyond Reactive Problem Solving

Problem solving is about making what you don't want go away. Creating involves bringing something you care about into reality. This reflects a subtle yet profound distinction that, we believe, will make all the difference for the future.

Creating draws its energy from dreams or visions of what people truly want to see exist, in concert with accurate and insightful understanding of what is. Reactive problem solving draws its energy from crises, usually driven by an underlying emotion of fear—fear of the consequences if we fail to solve the problems.

This is not a black-or-white dualistic distinction. In the process of creating what we truly want, many problems will invariably arise, and effective problem-solving skills are vital to tackling them. The distinction lies in what is primary versus what is secondary. When problem solving is primary, we focus on figuring out what's wrong and avoiding outcomes we fear. When the creative orientation is primary, life becomes a journey of bringing into reality what you truly care about and addressing the many practical problems that arise along the way. Reality is no longer the enemy—indeed, understanding and reflecting on how different problems relate to one another, how they have come about, and how different forces contribute to the status quo are essential. But working with these forces is very different from reacting to what has gone wrong.

A sustainable future will entail collective creating of every imaginable sort. It will involve bringing into existence over time a new energy system,

new types of buildings and transport, and new ways to dramatically reduce waste and toxicity—based on new products, new processes for making things, new business models, and new ways of managing and leading.
It will require passion and patience, people working together toward aims
that have genuine meaning for them and opening themselves to ideas that
may seem foreign and even threatening. And it will require the courage to
act without all the answers, moving beyond the comfortable approach of
"figuring out the answer and then implementing it." The creative process
is inescapably a learning process, which means venturing forth into difficult and uncharted territory with openness and humility, continually discovering our shortfalls.

Tapping and developing the potentials of people and organizations to
create the future rather than react to the present rests on two foundations
that have always been at the core of our work on organizational learning:
visions for the future and an understanding of the present reality.

The power of genuine vision is understood in cultures around the world,
as reflected in the biblical admonition "Where there is no vision the people perish." But just as important is the ability to see the current state of
things as objectively as possible. This is often misunderstood by people
who appreciate the importance of vision but would rather not look at difficult or painful aspects of the current situation, as well as by those who
prefer to look only at the bad and not recognize what is positive about
their current situation that they can build on.

In particular, seeing the present systemically is crucial to creating the
future. Otherwise, people get so drawn into fragmented views of the "problem" that they often resort to superficial quick fixes. For example, people
everywhere today are reacting to different facets of the sustainability crisis,
but many of the efforts represent reactions to what are seen as separate and
distinct threats—climate change, high oil prices, growing waste and toxicity, unhealthy food, water shortages, social and political instability—as opposed to a deep reflection on the interconnections between these different
issues. In this sense, the ability to see systems and the creative process are
natural and essential complements to one another, as suggested by the
image of a three-legged stool at the beginning of this chapter.

Regardless of the words we use to describe it, many of us have felt the energy and passion of doing what we love—doing something because we want to, not because we have to. In each of the stories that follow, you will see different ways in which individuals, small groups, and larger networks of organizations gently yet persistently are cultivating this shift from reacting to creating. In each case, you can see how they move back and forth between encouraging visions of a positive future and telling the truth about present reality.

There is an old saw that says there exist only two fundamental sources of motivation in human affairs: desperation and aspiration. In the absence of the creative orientation, desperation prevails. But it need not.

The guiding ideas and principles for life beyond the Bubble are reflected in the vision, commitment, and actions of innovators hard at work bringing this new era into reality. Their stories and insights reveal that we all have one basic choice: to sit on the sidelines and wait for more like them to help in creating a different future, or to join them in the journey.

part II

THE FUTURE IS NOW

n Part I, we discussed the ending of the Industrial Age and the extraordinary opportunities this transformation in how we think, live, and work presents: to create a future truly in harmony with a flourishing world.

The first step, though, is knowing what kind of a world we want to create. For us, as authors, this is no idealized utopia but a living awareness based on amazing people and projects we have had the good fortune to know personally. For these people, a regenerative economy is no more or less than the answer to the simple questions "What is really needed?" and "What can I do?" Their stories can help us all remember that the changes needed for life beyond the Industrial Age Bubble will arise from countless actions of imagination and daring in countless settings: companies, NGOs, loosely organized networks, and working groups—communities where new thinking and new acting can take root.

In the following chapters, you will see how local businesspeople, city officials, students, and big auto companies have joined together to dramatically decrease an entire country's dependence on fossil fuels; how a group of architects, builders, and owners learned how to transcend the traditional turf warfare in an industry with the single largest energy footprint; and how a global corporation and a world-recognized NGO are working together to steward our most precious and scarce resource, water.

The stories that follow show how these transformations have been occurring under the most challenging of circumstances, led by people who lack the experience, the authority, and the resources typically thought necessary to usher in change of this magnitude. None of the people you are about to meet had all the answers when they started—and they still don't. But they knew that they could not stand on the sidelines and wait for change to happen.

They learned how to help themselves and others see the larger systems shaping their organizations and their world. They weren't afraid to take a hard look at the current state of their companies and industries and ask where they were headed. They tapped into their deepest desires in the hopes of creating a future that embodies those aspirations. And they gradually enlisted all manner of others along the way to help in realizing visions that all shared. Each came to realize that they had to do it themselves—and they couldn't do it alone.

As you will see, these innovators who are shaping life beyond the Bubble come from all kinds of backgrounds. Their specific approaches are as varied as their organizations, industries, and experiences.

There is no magic in their approaches, other than the "everyday magic" of tapping their own and others' imagination, intelligence, passion, and caring. Their lessons are for us all.

[5]

Never Doubt What One Person and a Small Group of Co-Conspirators Can Do

O f all modern industrial countries, Sweden is probably the furthest along in weaning itself from fossil fuels. Today, the country depends on oil for only 30 percent of its energy, down from 77 percent in 1970. (The United States, by contrast, depends on fossil fuels for 85 percent of its energy.)

Fifteen percent of all cars sold in Sweden in 2007 ran on ethanol, up from 2 percent in 2000. A car running on ethanol made from sugarcane or cellulose is estimated to emit about 85–90 percent less in greenhouse gases than a gasoline-powered car. As the production, distribution, and use of second- and third-generation ethanol increase (including ethanol produced from forestry wastes and other waste streams—not crops such as corn), there will be significant reductions in global emissions from fossil fuels. All the major Swedish motor vehicle manufacturers now offer ethanol-based cars or trucks; this includes Scania, the largest major truck manufacturer in Europe.

Behind these statistics and announcements is a timeless story of what historians call "basic innovation," fundamental changes in technology and organization that create new industries, transform existing ones, and, over time, reshape societies. Basic innovations—such as the emergence of electrification, the automobile, commercial air travel, digital computing, and most recently the Internet—involve not just a single new technology but a collection of new inventions, practices, distribution networks, businesses and business models, and shifts in personal and organizational thinking.

Learning to live outside the Industrial Age Bubble—and meeting the 80-20 Challenge, in particular—will require basic innovations of a scale and speed never seen before. That is one reason why the story we are about to tell is so important. But it's not the only reason; by learning exactly how Sweden was able to pioneer a future free of fossil fuels, we can also witness basic innovation from the inside.

After hearing of Sweden's achievements, you might have assumed that changes of this magnitude required a massive government effort involving tens of thousands of people, enormous financial subsidies, and years of extensively funded research. But in fact, for many years, there was none of this kind of support, government-sponsored or otherwise. Instead, countless local networks developed quietly, thanks to the efforts of small groups of committed and courageous individuals who set out to find others with similar aspirations.

Many basic innovations start out in exactly this seemingly disconnected manner. Because the myriad changes required for innovation can never be predicted in advance and can seem impossibly daunting, they are often catalyzed by small numbers of people who can both see larger patterns and focus on small steps that build momentum. This is how the automobile industry, commercial aviation, and personal computing were created. Though those involved have no way to know in advance what they may achieve, they are pulled forward, as George Bernard Shaw put it, by a "mighty purpose." In Sweden in the early 1990s, Per Carstedt was one such person.

FROM BRAZIL TO SWEDEN

Per Carstedt is the owner of a large Ford dealership in northern Sweden, a family business originally founded by his father. After several years of living in Brazil, during which he attended the Rio Conference, the first

global environmental summit, held in 1992, he found himself deeply immersed in what he called "big-picture questions."

"I started reading voraciously. I soon realized that we couldn't continue
on this path. It is simply not possible. The human race has been on this
planet for about 200,000 years. For the first 190,000 of those we were essentially hunter-gatherers. Over the next 10,000 years we became farmers.
Then, beginning about 150 years ago, there was an incredible explosion in
human population and activity, driven by access to cheap energy. In 1900,
there were about one and a half billion people on the planet. That grew
to two and a half billion by 1950, six billion by 2000, and stands at about
six and a half billion right now. It is almost impossible to understand the
consequences of the speed and magnitude of these changes."

Per Carstedt is living proof that you don't need a Ph.D. to think about
larger systems. The questions that he began to ask himself upon his return
to Sweden are ones that any of us can ask, if we simply learn to step back
periodically and think about the larger reality of which we are a part and
where the prevailing forces are heading. What often stops us from asking
such questions is the feeling that there is little we can do to change an
entire company, industry, or country. Unfortunately, such fatalism easily
becomes a self-fulfilling prophecy.

Carstedt found himself so caught up in the historic changes he saw
unfolding that he kept asking these big questions, even though he had no
immediate idea where this would lead him. The more he read and talked
to friends, the more connections he saw among different problems and
the more he saw the scope and scale of changes that were necessary. "But,
I asked myself, 'What can one person do?'"

An answer came when Carstedt was contacted by a foundation that
wanted help in getting ethanol cars into the Swedish market. "I had driven
ethanol cars in Brazil. For me it was no big deal, but people said they
wouldn't work in Sweden. It was too cold. They wouldn't start. There were
no filling stations. There was no market for them. No one had a clue about
them in Europe, including Ford."

After many inquiries, Carstedt eventually managed to find a person at
Ford in Detroit who was in charge of a small "flexi-fuel" vehicle program,
producing cars that could run on ethanol, gasoline, or any blend of the

two. "It turned out his wife had been an exchange student here; he loved Sweden. He saw me as a potential ally, and helped us buy three cars in 1995. Ford had no program for this and didn't even know we were doing it."

Carstedt thought that getting a few cars into Sweden would be "the end of it. People would see they work perfectly well, and that would create a demand that would lead Ford to import more. But I was wrong."

When it became clear that three cars were not enough to wake up the market, Carstedt negotiated with Ford to buy another 300 Ford Taurus flexi-fuel vehicles. The Taurus was larger than the kinds of cars most Swedish drivers wanted, but there was no alternative: They were the only flexi-fuel cars Ford had, and Carstedt needed a critical mass to realize his real objective, which was to build interest in the concept of European-built flexi-fuel cars.

All the car manufacturers he talked with were reluctant, however, citing market research that confirmed there was no market for such cars. Undaunted, he and a colleague from the Swedish Ethanol Development Foundation (later renamed the BioAlcohol Fuel Foundation) spent the next four years traveling from city to city until they formed a buyers' consortium of fifty municipalities, companies, and individuals committed to buying 3,000 cars.[1]

In Carstedt's mind, he was "simply doing the next logical thing," but he was also doing what comes naturally for an entrepreneur. Instead of debating with manufacturers whether there was a market or not, or organizing more market research or academic seminars, in essence he arranged a field test. Along the way he was also getting others engaged—primarily local government officials—to help build momentum for his idea. Before long, the BioAlcohol Fuel Foundation was working in concert with scores of individuals and organizations.

WHAT TO DO WITH CARS BUT NO FUEL?

But what good is importing cars that run on ethanol when there is no ethanol? "It was a real chicken-and-egg problem," says Carstedt. "We had no cars because we had no filling stations, and we had no filling stations because we had no cars." So, as he did when facing other problems, "We just got started."

By the time Carstedt and his colleagues imported the first fifty Fords, he had managed to persuade one filling station in his home region of Örnsköldsvik and another one in Stockholm to install pumps with ethanol. To expand to the number of stations needed to serve the hundreds and soon thousands of cars they were planning on importing, he and his colleagues from the BioAlcohol Fuel Foundation began a campaign of persuasion, approaching one retailer at a time, often coming up with the financing to install pumps themselves.

"By 2002 we had 40 stations in the entire country, and in June 2004 we inaugurated the 100th. I think I was at the official opening of the first 50," he laughs. Fortunately, after that his presence was no longer needed. The number of fueling stations doubled in 2005, doubled again in 2006, and reached 1,000 stations in August 2007, which represents 25 percent of the national network. "The first 100 stations took ten years to develop," Carstedt says. "Nowadays we add 100 stations every three months!"

Meanwhile, he and his colleagues were analyzing ethanol supply and learning about different options for sourcing, both short- and longer-term. In the mid-1990s, a modest amount of ethanol was being imported into Sweden, but it was enough for Carstedt to begin his work. As demand started to increase, however, the value of this business grew and the firm that imported ethanol was put up for sale. Carstedt organized a group of three energy companies to buy it, lest it get into "the wrong hands—people who simply wanted to exploit the opportunity of rising prices."

Several years later (but still before the biofuel boom that started in 2006), he sounded a prescient warning: "Opportunism is one of the greatest risks to this whole endeavor. People motivated only by short-term gain will exploit current fears about oil dependence and could do many stupid things that will lead to a backlash against biofuels in general. They will not think about the longer-term investments needed so that biofuels develop as one element of an alternative energy system."

With this aim in mind, the BioAlcohol Fuel Foundation set a course by 2000 to move beyond the "low-hanging fruit" of grain-based ethanol toward alternative sources—such as cellulosic ethanol made from forestry industry waste—that would not compete with food crops and would have significantly lower greenhouse gas emissions.

Continually thinking about all the different pieces of the puzzle and how they needed to come together over the long term was also vital, because the market did not expand quickly. For years, the flexi-fuel cars and filling stations were greeted with little interest beyond a small circle of enthusiasts. The reason was predominantly economic. In 1993, when Carstedt began actively getting involved in seeking out alternatives to oil, "the price of oil was $20 per barrel, and people just smiled when you talked about a need to free ourselves from oil.

"But existing market conditions had nothing to do with why we were doing this. Climate change was really the driving thing. But we couldn't get people to open fueling stations or bring cars to market because of a problem that didn't even exist for most people at that time. We struggled to get the kind of critical mass that would drive the market forces."

ENGAGING THE LARGE DRIVERS OF CHANGE

Reasoning that there were "two larger drivers of change," economic and political, he believed that getting the large car manufacturers on board was key. But whenever he talked with them, he heard the same responses: "There's no market for it, no infrastructure for it, lots of technical problems with no resources to solve them. Senior executives' careers depend on thinking in terms of less risky business opportunities with larger payoff in the short term than what we represented."

Undaunted, he gradually realized the problem was not that no one was interested, but that he'd yet to find the people who were. "You had to find the right individuals. You can't say, 'This is Ford, this is GM, and no one is interested.' Companies are made up of individuals, and if you are lucky enough to find those who are like-minded, you work with them and support them—that's how to get things moving."

Eventually, Carstedt found just such people at Saab. And to his surprise, they were not the technical experts he had mostly been meeting with.

In his countless visits to auto companies, he had met many engineers and researchers who understood a lot about biofuels, and even some who had been working to solve technical problems associated with them. But they tended to work with "unquestioned assumptions about prices and fuel availability, government policies, and sunk costs in the industry." Most didn't understand the dynamics of the market, as he saw them.

Those who did understand knew, as he did, that more and more people were reading about climate change and oil politics and wanted to make a difference. "Most people think people only do things for money," Carstedt says. "Then you ask them, 'Why do so many people recycle, even if it means hauling old magazines and soda bottles to the recycling center on Saturdays?' Obviously, making money is not the reason." Fortunately, the vice president of marketing at Saab Automobile understood the dynamics of what was starting to emerge in the marketplace. As people became more aware of environmental issues, he saw new market opportunities. "He convinced the technical guys."

Carstedt worked with the people at Saab even though he had better connections to the far larger Volvo (his older brother, Göran, had been president in the late 1980s and early 1990s). Volvo Cars was in the process of being purchased by Ford, his company, but this meant that they were not ready to pursue any other agenda at the time. On the other hand, the marketing people at Saab, a company that was struggling after having been acquired by GM, saw the promise of ethanol as a chance to differentiate themselves. They eventually found a way to redirect money from a marketing budget to fund a pilot program to produce a small number of ethanol cars to test in the Swedish market.

"You work with those who want to do this. You help them become winners, and they'll help you achieve your objectives. If you make Saab a winner, you don't have to worry about Volvo. They won't have an option—they'll have to follow."

MAKE IT SOMETHING PEOPLE CAN TOUCH

In many ways, however, Carstedt's biggest lesson still lay ahead and presented itself only once he'd stepped far enough away from the familiar. Up to this point, his focus, and his effectiveness, came from following a path that felt natural for him. His whole career was in automobiles. His international work experience had exposed him to different auto technologies. He knew the Swedish market. He knew the business. And, most of all, he knew lots of people in Sweden in the business. Getting biofuel cars into the country was just a logical step toward doing something about climate change, as he saw it.

But as it turned out, this too was just a first step. He knew it was not enough, since greenhouse gas emissions from transportation account for only about a quarter or less of all emissions. He kept thinking about "the whole sustainability challenge" and wanted to address it more completely.

Once again an opportunity presented itself. In 1997, he and a few colleagues decided to open a new branch of the family car dealership in another city in northern Sweden. Not long after that decision, he met an architect named Anders Nyquist; the two soon decided to work together to "build the most environmentally friendly car dealership in the world," says Carstedt. "I didn't know much about projects like this, but I knew the thinking behind them involved making buildings work like natural systems—recycling wastewater and such." Although he knew little about buildings, he knew that heat and electricity for the built environment contributed more greenhouse gas emissions than any other single economic sector, so the project appealed to him.

Not only did this new project represent a further step away from fossil fuels, but it led him to another kindred spirit in Nyquist. "You know, in all the talks and the like I was doing, I would find that there were many people who nodded but you knew they would do nothing, while with others, you know after two minutes they understand completely and you have a partner for life." He soon learned that unexpected innovations can arise from such partnerships. In this case, what began as the idea of building the "most environmentally friendly car dealership in the world" evolved into what he and Nyquist dubbed the Green Zone: a block of businesses, incorporating Carstedt's car dealership, a McDonald's restaurant, and a gas station (gasoline and biofuel, naturally), that would be as energy-efficient as possible.[2] They designed systems interconnecting the businesses—for example, excess heat from the restaurant kitchens was piped directly to heat the car dealership and the filling station. Overall energy use was cut over 80 percent from comparable developments.

The concept of fitting together different businesses in an integrated design where waste by-products in one become resources for another is known as "industrial ecology," and does indeed work like a forest. There were several showplaces of integrated complexes in Europe, most notably one in the city of Kalundborg in Denmark. But these were large manufacturing complexes. Carstedt and Nyquist's Green Zone was a cross section of smaller "everyday" businesses that could serve as a model to inspire others.

To Carstedt's surprise, his small pilot inspired many more than he had imagined. Soon it started to draw media attention from around the world. Between 2000 and 2006, the Green Zone attracted more than 500 official study visits.

"We had a Japanese TV crew there filming one day when it hit me. Here were these people who had come halfway around the world to see our little project, which in many ways I had thought was no big deal. After all, most of the technologies were readily available off the shelf, and I thought this was such a small step. But what I had missed was the importance of something that people could touch.

"A lot of my talks about biofuels, climate change, and the whole-systems approach were too theoretical for most people." When there was something concrete and tangible, "people 'see' the systems analogy."

Carstedt had discovered an important lesson in how visions take hold on a larger scale: While some people can imagine alternative futures with little help, most move from the concrete to the abstract—not the other way around. The Green Zone sparked people's imaginations because it was small and relatively simple, and involved businesses that people could understand and relate to. After seeing how the Green Zone worked, others "could start to take the next steps by themselves," explains Carstedt. "They didn't need me or others to tell them what had to happen."

Eventually, many did just that and began imagining an entire region that worked much like the demonstration site, scaling up the Green Zone into a BioFuel Region.[3] This too "would almost be like a physical thing people could touch," Cartstedt says. "They could visit and say, 'We've been there.' They could go home and say to one another, 'If they can do it, we can do it.' "

Gradually the vision of an entire industrial region free of fossil fuels started to take shape around three goals.

"First, we need to be a role model for the rest of the world for this process of change. By 2020," says Carstedt, "we should produce more renewable fuel than what we need to fuel our vehicles, and provide for our other energy needs."

The second goal is to guide the process to support industrial and regional development. "That's what the politicians began to pick up a couple of years ago. We need to build an industrial base for the next fifty years that is consistent with being independent of fossil fuels." All of a sudden, Carstedt's whole-systems ideas were about jobs and business development, and his economic and political "large drivers of change" were getting engaged.

The third goal is constantly developing new practices to share with other regions interested in becoming fossil-fuel-free, and pushing the envelope of innovation. "If we are seen by the world as a leader, we have to engage universities and other institutions in continual knowledge creation."

Today, the BioFuel Region vision in northern Sweden includes more than 200 people working actively in student projects, local businesses, building and urban design, feedstock development, and the continual advancement of ethanol production. For example, in mid-2004 a pilot plant was opened for producing cellulosic ethanol from wood chips, a plentiful waste by-product of Sweden's large forestry industry. The first demonstration plant will open in 2009, the second in 2012, and the third in 2014. "There will be lots of process improvements that we can share with others," says Carstedt. "The new production plant involves technologies that can be viable in many parts of the world."

As important, businesses, local governments, designers, and students are engaged in a deep and ongoing conversation to establish common goals and visions. "We're learning a lot, and very quickly," says Carstedt. "The key is to be thinking thirty to fifty years ahead and developing processes, designs, and sources of energy supply that are sustainable over that time horizon. To get the 80 to 90 percent reduction in emissions we need in the world, we need systems change. This means people working together to create different automobiles, buildings, energy infrastructures—and lots of things that have never existed."

Not surprisingly, the BioFuel Region vision has captivated people not only in Sweden but around the world. Carstedt now helps coordinate a €25 million global project sponsored by the EU, involving ten regions seeking to follow in northern Sweden's footsteps. "The purpose of this new endeavor is to try and speed up this transfer of knowledge and change, to try to get small fires going in those cities, which will then spread to others."

Carstedt's experience has also given him lots to think about regarding the profound changes that lie ahead. "Biofuels certainly will not solve the whole problem. We have to use transportation wisely; we cannot continue to transport vegetables around the world. We have to be dramatically more energy-efficient, regardless of the source of energy. If we come to reduce energy consumption as far as we can and we can only get 60 percent from sustainable sources, then we will have to live with more costly energy, or use less of it.

"We have come to regard cheap energy as a human right, and we've been prepared to do whatever is needed, in terms of politics and even military aggression, to guarantee 'free' access to it." Our dependence on cheap energy and ignoring the side effects of this belief is the defining feature of life in the Bubble. "Ultimately, this is about a shift in attitudes and in ways of living. I think seeing this shift actually occurring, as much as the technology, is what excites people about the BioFuel Region."

[6]

Aligning an Industry

When asked why he robbed banks, the infamous Willie Sutton responded simply, "Because that's where the money is."

If global carbon emissions were currency, most of the "money" could be found in our office buildings, malls, hotels, factories, apartment buildings, and private homes.

The greatest consumers of energy today—and, in turn, the largest contributors of greenhouse gases—are our commercial, industrial, and residential buildings. Heating, air-conditioning, and electricity for what the industry calls "the built environment" accounts for 40 percent of greenhouse gas emissions in the United States (almost 60 percent globally), almost twice the emissions of the automotive sector. Obviously, the built environment represents a high-leverage point for anyone looking to create energy systems suited for life beyond the Industrial Age Bubble.

And yet few sectors present more difficult challenges for change. The building industry is highly fragmented, and the competitiveness—and even suspicion—between different competing interests is, for most veterans in the industry, just part of the way the business works.

"There was often an adversarial relationship among the three main parties in any major project: the owner/developer, the architect, and the contractors," says Bob Berkebile, the founding chairperson for the Committee on the Environment, created in 1990 within the American Institute of Architects (AIA). Developers, for example, "tend to set their budget for total building costs as low as possible to maximize their profit on the project. Architects, engineers, and construction firms then compete to maximize their share of the fixed budget."

And so what you end up with is buildings that have the cheapest heating and air-conditioning systems, as opposed to the most efficient—despite the fact that a higher-priced, more efficient system would save the owner money in the long haul (and be better for the environment).

The net result is often a suboptimal conventional design that wastes resources and has double or triple the operating costs of green buildings—costs that are passed on to occupants indefinitely. Those occupants may have their own goals—including comfort, healthy workers, productivity, and lower operating costs—but typically they have no involvement in the development process and relatively little influence over these factors (and costs) once the building is completed.

Frustrated for several years by industry consensus processes that seemed to keep devolving to "lowest-common-denominator agreements," David Gottfried, a small-town developer, along with environmental litigator Michael Italiano, believed that there had to be a better way. They joined with Berkebile and his AIA committee to form a small group of like-minded people who were interested in genuinely addressing the total impact of buildings on the environment, human health and well-being, and communities.

In a story dissimilar in all the specifics but remarkably resonant with Per Carstedt's in terms of the core lessons, ten years later they had succeeded in establishing the U.S. Green Building Council (USGBC) and the Leadership in Energy and Environmental Design (LEED) certification system, which has now spread around the country and the world. Today, the USGBC—and its sister Green Building Councils in countries such as India, China, Brazil, and Mexico—has become a powerful and unifying force within the building industry.

Getting there wasn't easy. How these remarkable changes occurred is a saga of skillful networking and relentless dedication by a small group who, when they started, had no detailed plan but a fervent conviction that nothing would change unless they could find practical ways of fostering real thinking together among all the key parties.

GETTING THE "WHOLE SYSTEM IN THE ROOM"

The first USGBC meeting occurred in Washington, D.C., in 1993. About ten people were present. Most of them were already friends, and all had links back to companies that might support them. For example, Rick Fedrizzi, who became the founding chairperson of USGBC, was an executive with Carrier, a heating and air-conditioning equipment supplier. Although their backgrounds varied, the group members found that they shared a simple core vision: transforming how buildings get built.

Knowing that the competition and fragmentation within the industry thwarted real change, the founding group resolved to get representatives of the entire system involved from the outset. "That meant real estate owners, financiers, engineers, architects, construction companies, and all of the roles involved in the full life cycle of real estate, as well as people from environmental organizations, government, and the media," says Jim Hartzfeld of Interface, who later also became USGBC president. "Any plan that wasn't perceived to work for any key part of the industry would not work at all. It simply wouldn't happen. Unless the entire system was in the room, there was absolutely no chance to form a true consensus, and without that consensus nothing significant was likely to happen. This became our first founding idea." And it proved to be a pivotal one.

Though not easy. "Many of the meetings were pretty ugly," says Hartzfeld. "People would be cursing and throwing things at each other." Initially, the group limited its focus to large commercial office buildings. But even with a relatively narrow focus, finding common ground would require a change in the way they operated. Rather than try to resolve all the issues, the group sensed that they would need to go through many cycles of seeing the problem, clarifying their purpose, and "searching for things we could agree on," says Hartzfeld. "'Seek agreement and go' became our mantra. We didn't want to waste time fighting over all the pieces of the big puzzle that we disagreed on and spending all our time arguing over who was right.

"This proved to be a fundamental learning. It oriented us to action, based on what we could agree on, and to get going."

The bias to action also allowed the group to sidestep any pressure it may have felt to articulate a "grand vision" of green building early in the process. Agreeing on a complete picture was "premature given where we were as a working group," said Hartzfeld. This approach ultimately proved fortuitous because it made possible a more collaborative process of "learning through doing" as more and more people engaged themselves in the process. Hartzfeld and the others were discovering the first principle of building genuinely shared visions: It takes time, and along the way, engagement is worth much more than superficial agreement.

As more people became involved, the group discovered one important area of agreement early on: Market-based forces were much more powerful than legal or government action in spurring innovation and genuine commitment. "We realized that the voluntary response of the marketplace—generated by people's understanding that there were better ways to build buildings now, and it was in everyone's best interests to do it—was more powerful than imposing any kind of regulation," says Hartzfeld. "This idea of market-based transformation became a second key founding idea."

BRINGING THE EXPERTISE TOGETHER: THE LEED RATING SYSTEM

Even though they agreed they didn't need a grand vision, the early USGBC participants found themselves unable to answer, even in rudimentary ways, some important basic questions such as "What *is* a green building?"

"People would describe their building as 'Mine is kind of green,' or 'Mine is way green,' or 'Mine is somewhat brown,'" says Hartzfeld. Thus, their first collaborative project, launched in 1996, was to develop an initial set of objective criteria to determine the key characteristics of a green building.

Here, too, a guiding idea emerged early. "From the very beginning," notes Hartzfeld, "we saw the building as a whole system and articulated all the interacting attributes." For example, the mere use of recycled materials, while important, would not be enough in itself to designate a building as green. "You have to think about the whole system: the land, the site itself, how it uses water, how it uses energy, what materials are in it, what the indoor air quality is like, and the healthiness of the building for its occupants." This systems view became "vital and very different from prior attempts to reduce adverse environmental impact in architecture."

Looking at a building as a whole system, in turn, required tapping the expertise of all the different professions associated with design, architecture, construction, and building maintenance. This also required confidence, and a lot of humility, on the part of the organizers of this process. "Our contribution," says Hartzfeld, "wasn't in knowing the knowledge in any one expert's head, but in bringing the expertise distributed across the industry into the conversation."

This aim to tap collective intelligence and build collective ownership helped gradually to forge a strong, unified group. But it also took a long time. Agreeing on the initial LEED criteria turned out to be a four-year process. As it took shape, however, it catalyzed a collective learning process whose power surprised everyone. It became, like Per Carstedt's Green Zone, something tangible, something that, however imperfect, people could touch and use—and, in so doing, put their own handprint on.

"As the LEED rating system began to get articulated," says Hartzfeld, "people grabbed the system and said, 'Here are all the different ways you can gain points. The more points you gain, the greener the building.' That took the vague concept of green and created some objective steps so people could actually do something. It was never intended to be the ultimate guide to the green building. But it helped people make sense of an otherwise complex and amorphous concept. Even if they didn't know a lot about it, they could start taking steps in that common direction."

Meanwhile, during countless meetings and retreats, the founding group refined the rating system further. First they reached agreement on a basic five-part framework—sustainable sites (including erosion control, transportation, and pollution reduction), water efficiency, energy and atmospheric pollution, materials and resource use, and indoor environmental quality (including indoor chemical pollution and thermal comfort)—then broke it up into parts and found out who was interested in which part. Work was voluntary, and people focused on areas in which they had the most interest, expertise, and energy.

"There was tremendous passion and emotion associated even with the logical and technical discussions," recalls Hartzfeld. Gradually, members of the council were learning the first principle of dialogue: the ability to "hold" their passions—to express their varied perspectives, and the emotions associated with them, without fragmenting the group or causing anyone to feel threatened by their differences.[1] Doing this not only highlights the importance of respecting each individual but gradually builds a sense of momentum as different ideas start to come together and influence one another.

"People would advocate strongly where their energy and experience lay. One person might have spent a lifetime studying the effects of air in buildings on human health. They would look at everything from the perspective of ventilation and gas control." The discussions immersed everyone in a great deal of expertise that was foreign to them, which was, of course, challenging. But in the end, "Everyone benefited from that experience. People continually had their perspective expanded by everyone else's. And invariably people would say, 'There's more to this than I thought.'"

The capacity to talk through these disagreements without breaking apart didn't just happen by itself. It was fostered through a purposeful design of the group's dialogues, in ways that deliberately deepened relationships.

"Whenever we got together, we allowed time for people to introduce themselves, and we talked about what was important to us personally, why we were volunteering our time and energy to work on this together," says Berkebile. "When various people's views came into conflict, there was also some understanding of one another as individuals who cared deeply about real change. What linked us all was a common passion for changing the outcomes for our children."

"Throughout the whole process, we relied on the organizational learning concept of aspiration; people oriented themselves toward what mattered most to them, rather than just problems," says Hartzfeld. "In retrospect, it's crazy to think that a small group of people could think about transforming a whole industry that represents 8 percent of the U.S. GDP, but that's exactly what we had in mind."

MEETING A LATENT NEED

Once a working prototype of the LEED rating system was ready, the group tested it over nine months on a number of buildings that had already been built. But even during this prototype phase, others began using it as a design guide. "This was a huge discovery for us," says Hartzfeld. "There was an untapped hunger. Many people were trying to build greener buildings on their own. But they didn't know each other. In effect, they were waiting for something like this to pull them together."

With the introduction of the LEED certification system in 2000 came an explosive growth in the organization, and today it has become a cornerstone of green building. By mid-2007, over 7,500 buildings were registered with LEED worldwide, up from just 635 in 2002. The value of green building construction starts is expected to exceed $12 billion in 2008. In addition to the energy and cost savings, studies have documented improved employee productivity and health, decreased absenteeism, and improved morale from working in green buildings.

Although still voluntary, LEED certification is becoming an industry norm. In December 2006, the Washington, D.C., city council passed a bill requiring private developers to follow the LEED standard; the city of Boston similarly revised its building codes for all private buildings over 50,000 square feet. Other states and municipalities have followed suit.

From 2000 to 2006, membership in the USGBC grew tenfold, to more than 10,500 organizational members, with over 38,000 professionals certified in the LEED rating system and several hundred thousand people engaged in intense collaboration to design, build, and monitor green buildings in North America and globally. Today, the GBC has more than seventy regional chapters and projects in forty-one countries.

While criteria continue to evolve, the first LEED certification legitimated an idea whose time had come: It was possible to have an agreed-upon, voluntary certification system for more environmentally sound buildings, and this could be a powerful agent to spur innovation, ongoing learning, and community.

As the LEED program has become more popular, its requirements have become more stringent. Yet the cost of meeting these more-demanding standards is also falling with growing experience and know-how: The total cost of designing and building LEED-certified buildings now averages less than a 1.8 percent premium over conventional buildings, an up-front investment more than offset by significant savings in energy and other operating costs.

A wave of basic innovation is now transforming the building industry. New technologies—such as solar panels integrated into walls, window glass, and roof materials so that buildings' exterior surfaces can generate electricity—are reducing or eliminating the use of fossil fuel energy. Geothermal systems for heating and cooling are now being used extensively to radically reduce heating and air-conditioning costs. These systems make use of the earth's natural heating and cooling abilities; just a few feet below the surface, temperatures remain between 50 and 55 degrees Fahrenheit year-round, depending on the location's climate. These systems, many of which use a water-source pump to transfer heat between the earth and a building, can be used to heat buildings in cooler times and cool them in warmer ones.

Reflecting on these trends, Berkebile says, "The bar is continually being raised: Improvements in energy efficiency have gone from an average of 25 percent to over 70 percent reductions in energy use compared to conventional buildings. A next generation of 'living' (regenerative) buildings is coming—buildings that produce more energy and clean water than they use, and function more like trees and forests. The first of these will likely be designed and built in the next three to four years, as scores of design teams are now intent on achieving this 'living building' goal in projects that they are working on right now." For example, there is an enormous amount of solar energy that can be captured, used, and stored in well-designed structures, year-round in most settings. While many of the initial regenerative structures will be demonstration projects at universities, private foundations, and government sites and might not meet current economic criteria in diverse settings, they will show what is possible, and given the wave of innovation unfolding worldwide, they will undoubtedly move such bold ideas closer to broad application.

Perhaps most important, an integrative design process is becoming more and more common, where all key parties (developers, architects, engineers, contractors, suppliers, and end users) work together closely from the beginning of a project to ensure that the USGBC LEED standards are met or surpassed. Moreover, previously competing firms are helping each other to accelerate the innovation process. Exemplary buildings are being showcased by all firms as achievements of the green building design community, regardless of who built them. And firms are working together to develop new design tools, software, and innovative technical solutions that can and are being used by all.

For us, the story of the USGBC showed how organizational learning concepts could be used beyond company boundaries to help shift an entire industry. As Berkebile, Hartzfeld, and their colleagues learned, learning how to think together about the larger system and build shared visions that incorporate multiple perspectives is not limited to well-defined working teams or single organizations. Just as important, the USGBC established ongoing collaborative learning as a norm, so aspirations and daily practices continually evolve—abilities we will discuss further later in the book. When this happens, innovation begets innovation and genuine learning communities develop that are capable of realizing what may have seemed impossible before.

Today, the standards the USGBC has developed are being extended to a growing number of construction categories: retrofitting old buildings, rethinking home construction, commercial building operations and maintenance, neighborhood development, and a new emphasis on green schools. The USGBC now offers courses and online workshops and convenes an annual conference with more than 13,000 attendees, all of whom see this statement at the very front of their conference materials: "To lead the transformation of the building industry, we know that how we make our decisions is as important as the decisions themselves."

[7]

Unconventional Allies: Coke and WWF Partner for Sustainable Water

n early July 2007, CEO and Chairman E. Neville Isdell of the Coca-Cola Company, addressing the thousand-plus attendees of the triennial summit of the UN Global Compact, including the UN Secretary General and the world press, said that Coke's guiding principle in growing its business in the future must be "We should not cause more water to be removed from a watershed than we replenish."

At the same time, Isdell and Peter Brabeck-Letmathe, the CEO of rival Nestlé, announced the CEO Water Mandate and asked other CEOs to join them in confronting one of the world's greatest challenges—responsible management of the severely stressed resource.

For those who know Coca-Cola, one of the largest consumer goods companies in the world, this announcement represented a big step in a long journey to put water sustainability at the center of its business. "Coca-Cola has been focused on water management for about 120 years, really since the origin of the business," says Global Water Initiative director Dan Vermeer, a member of Coke's corporate water and environment staff. "But in the past, the emphasis has been on operational performance: efficiency, wastewater treatment, managing water within the plant."

Traditionally, little attention was paid to where or how plants got water for their bottling operations, or overall conditions of water availability for the larger community. "It took a real wake-up call," says Jeff Seabright, Coke's VP for Environment and Water Resources, "before we started to think beyond the four walls and pay attention to the larger system." As Vermeer adds, "It really doesn't matter how efficient you are if there's no water."

Behind Coke's new commitment lies a journey of awakening that has spanned years, led by internal corporate change agents and operational leaders throughout the company and its sister Coca-Cola bottling companies around the world, and that, more recently, was spurred on by a unique partnership with WWF, the global conservation organization.[1]

Indeed, the unusual partnership between one of the world's largest corporations and one of the largest and best-known non-profit environmental activist organizations represents a shift as significant, in a sense, as Coke's commitment to integrative water management.

Traditionally, leading activist non-governmental organizations (NGOs) have been far more likely to attack than work with huge global corporations. But times are changing, and a small number are recognizing that they must alter their strategies if they expect any real change to occur. As WWF US's chief operating officer Marcia Marsh says, "The simple fact is that we are failing relative to our larger goals. Despite our successes in raising public awareness and funding, species are disappearing at historic rates. Habitat continues to be destroyed. Working alone, NGOs are simply unable to reverse the tide of global change. To do this, we will have to develop new partnerships with businesses and governments, partnerships whose scale of impact is commensurate with the problems we face."

Moreover, today, a growing number of major corporations like Coke have come to the same conclusion: that the expertise, stature, and combined public and commercial influence of the two sectors working together may be crucial to fundamental sustainability challenges like water.

TWO JOURNEYS, ONE DESTINATION:
CONFRONTING OUR MOST BASIC NEED

But the partnership would never have come into being had it not been for deep changes in both organizations over the preceding years, changes brought about by the growing global water crisis.

People can live for weeks without food, for months without shelter, and forever without video games and television. But we cannot survive more than a few days without water. Nowhere is the need for working together more essential than when it comes to water, arguably the most pressing problem for the world today. As cited in Chapter 2, more than 1 billion of the world's people lack reliable access to safe drinking water.

Water shortages are widespread, especially in water-scarce areas like India, many parts of Africa and the Middle East, Eastern Asia, and increasingly many parts of the southern and western United States. The World Commission on Water, established by the World Water Council (an international multi-stakeholder platform) and co-sponsored by UNESCO, UNICEF, and the World Health Organization, estimates that in 2025 some 4 billion people, almost half the global population, will be living in areas that will be "severely water stressed."

The report notes:

> The arithmetic of water still does not add up. In the next two decades, it is estimated that water use by humans will increase by about 40 percent, and that 17 percent more water will be needed to grow food for a growing population. In addition, the water demand for industry and energy will increase rapidly.

Creating a truly comprehensive and responsible water management approach is not only essential for many organizations but crucial for the future in general.

For Coca-Cola, awakening to water as a strategic issue that would shape its future, as is often the case for very large and successful organizations, came about through a complex journey of internal change and external shocks. Simply by virtue of its size and presence around the world, Coke was sure to collide with water problems.

And this is exactly what happened in 2004 and 2005 in the state of Kerala in southern India. The region was going through a three-year drought. Many farmers were running out of water. All the while, Coca-Cola's local bottling plant was operating smoothly. "People drew the logical conclusion that Coke was taking their water," says Seabright. "Here they are struggling to make ends meet, and Coke's bright red trucks are pulling out of the plant with no apparent difficulty." In fact, Coke's plant was drawing water from a deep aquifer unrelated hydrologically to the surface water most of the farmers depended upon.

"But we missed the point," says Seabright. "Regardless of whether we were technically right, we should have realized that we were a big symbol of water use and we should have been more involved in helping the community solve its problems." The fallout from the incident was significant reputationally in that Coke became linked in many people's eyes with water scarcity. "It was a big issue on a lot of college campuses," says Seabright.

Fortunately for Coke, by the time this sort of incident was starting to occur, many inside the company had been working to understand water shortages and their implications for the business.

"We did a project on the future of freshwater in 2002," says Vermeer. "Soon, we and others in the company began to understand the state of freshwater resources and the depletion of aquifers, risks of costs rising, and the increasing competition for water. It was clear that this was one of the great sustainability issues."

Yet at that time water was not a strategic priority for many companies. Indeed, there was little global attention on water and it had not coalesced as a critical issue for any of the sectors—business, government, or civil society. Partly this was because water is a local issue, with conditions differing dramatically from one region to another, even in a country with hundreds of millions of chronically dehydrated people like India. Local conditions are also affected by many factors, including drought, floods, contamination of groundwater, and lack of infrastructure.

Finally, in late 2003, as part of a broader commitment to sustainability issues, Seabright, formerly of USAID, was hired into a new position as vice president for the environment and water.

"I asked right away about the company's water strategy," says Seabright, "and what I got back were several thick reports, each a detailed analysis in reaction to a different problem or crisis. They were informative, but they also, not surprisingly, had not had much impact strategically."

In order to develop a more strategic perspective, Seabright and Vermeer and their colleagues began conducting interviews with more than 250 people throughout the company about their perspectives on water issues, the challenges they saw, and "friction points in the local communities" around water issues.

As initiative members talked with people, says Vermeer, "We began to realize that there was a lot of concern around this issue, and people were eager to talk."

But just as members of the initiative realized that they had started to engage operations people around genuine concerns, they also discovered that the information they were developing was not yet that useful for them. Their "top-level view of water risk" in broad geographic regions was not getting close enough to the local realities that operational people faced. "Field people came back," according to Vermeer, "and said, 'You're telling me about water risk in Southeast Asia. I don't manage plants in Southeast Asia, I manage them in Rungsit, Thailand.' We had all this information about the broad context, but they couldn't do anything with that information. People needed information regarding water in specific locations and we didn't have that type of information."

The team decided to create a detailed local survey for bottling plants. The only problem was how to get people to do it. They discovered almost immediately that the survey evoked a basic problem with most corporate-led change efforts: suspicion as to why headquarters needed all this information. "We created a three-hundred-question survey," says Vermeer, "asking for all sorts of information that people had never been asked before. When people saw it, they told us that if we got 10 percent of the local bottlers to fill it out, we would be doing great."

Working with consultants and other Coke staff, the team focused on local operating people they knew from their interviews and got a few to complete the survey. The survey took ten hours per plant, and many questions explored areas where even experienced people had little operational knowledge.

Gradually, it became evident that the reality for the operating people was that if, for example, you were getting water from a municipality, that was assumed to be an ensured supply. Vermeer adds: "There was no transparency beyond the municipality, to where *they* got their water. That was a question that most people, in Coke and beyond, had not asked. So asking was important—even if there was no way to expect even experienced operational people to have all the answers."

It became apparent that, while many plant managers were aware of issues in the larger watershed they were part of, "they had no framework for addressing them, or clear support in doing so." But as local operating people became engaged in the survey, they wanted Vermeer and his colleagues to assure them that their efforts would be worthwhile. "People said, 'Look, we just worked really hard to provide this data for you. Don't be corporate.'"

In most big companies, local managers providing this sort of detailed and potentially important information to corporate headquarters have learned that one of two things usually happens. Either corporate staff do nothing with the information or there is a witch hunt. The first wastes everyone's time. The second is worse. Somebody writes a report and it goes to the CEO, pointing to divisions that have operational problems. The CEO then calls the division president, who then calls the technical people responsible, who will then typically say, "We don't know how they reached their conclusions."

To circumvent these concerns, the corporate water team created a two-day workshop for each business unit based on their facilities' survey responses. "The workshops were amazing," says Vermeer, "because people came together to study their own information, so it was grounded in the information they had given us, which we had analyzed to identify priority water issues for each site and geography."

People began to see connections between the data and the actual risks to their operations. "You could tell that it all started to become real to them when they stopped speaking English and started to talk to each other in their native language—Spanish, Thai, whatever. Suddenly, they would say, 'We need to discuss this among our team. When we've got this resolved, we'll come back to tell you what we've decided.'"

The water team conducted thirty workshops in six months, one in each of their twenty-three divisions worldwide, plus seven with key bottlers. The workshops started to build a critical mass of engagement, and more surveys started to come in. Soon they started to post practical insights and stories from different locations on their internal Web site, along with survey response rates, like which regions had 70 percent response rates and which had 10 percent. "We just published the information every day, and business units began to recognize that they were going through this process in parallel with other units around the world. Knowing that the whole global system was going through this process simultaneously created excitement, and some peer pressure too."

Eventually, they reached a 92 percent response rate from their 875 bottling plants around the world. "We figured at ten hours per plant for over eight hundred plants, that was a pretty significant investment in asking questions no had ever really asked before."

As this sphere of engagement grew, they were learning one other thing about systemic change. "Often, it's hard to get busy people to engage. We learned that sometimes you have to try to solve a bigger problem, create a bigger conversation that engages even more people—like how to get the whole Coca-Cola system to engage around water in a very short period of time. By doing this, many new connections among people who otherwise would have not been talking with one another happened and synergy effects started to emerge across the whole system. It was a pretty transformative experience watching this start to happen."

The process also served to develop the strategic perspective Seabright knew was needed for corporate management. "A strategic frame-work around four dimensions emerged," says Seabright. "It all starts with operational excellence, because if we are wasting water or polluting, we have no legitimacy to stand on. But we could also see that understanding watersheds was crucial, as was the social community context, and that, as a global brand, we have a responsibility to speak out on the global stage."

This also laid the foundation for expanding a relationship with WWF that had already existed for many years. "It became clear now that we needed expertise in understanding the broader systemic issues of ecosystems and watersheds," adds Seabright.

For WWF, being open to a long-term partnership with a multinational like the Coca-Cola Company was much less about identifying water as a common global issue and much more about rethinking its own mission and vision. Although WWF had long received significant donations from large corporations, says Suzanne Apple, the lead WWF coordinator of the partnership, "We had been in a traditional 'philanthropic' relationship with our corporate donors. We had to shift our thinking to focus on why we should work together and how we might really accomplish more together than separately." Apple, who previously worked on sustainable forest products at Home Depot, adds, "The established NGO model is about funding, not partnership. But this goes beyond money. You have to help people see the abundance of resources available, for example, the talent and knowledge within the corporate sector. We may know all about watersheds, but we discovered that they had some very sophisticated watershed analysis as well, and they know a lot more than we do about commercial decision-making, which can have impacts well beyond plants and facilities."

Apple also helped WWF staff appreciate the enormous potential impact of companies like Coca-Cola through their purchasing power. "Coke is a leading buyer of sugar in the world. They are a major buyer of aluminum cans, of citrus, and one of the largest purchasers of coffee, as well as glass. That doesn't include tea and cocoa and a lot of other things they buy. If we can work with a company like Coca-Cola and shift their purchasing to sustainable sources, it can have a huge impact."

But doing this effectively would require a lot of learning, on all sides, to see the larger systems of which they were a part.

SEEING THE LARGER BUSINESS SYSTEM

Finding how the Coke corporate giant and the WWF panda could actually start to dance together first required that each face stereotypes on both sides and then that they find a dance floor. WWF's broad knowledge of ecosystems could make Coke's focus on business performance seem narrow and pedestrian. Likewise, Coke's passion for operating detail and efficiency could cause WWF's scientific knowledge to seem academic and ivory tower. Fortunately, WWF had identified value chains as one strategic focus for its work going forward, which dovetailed with Coke's growing interest in a bigger-picture view of water.

"Very few companies have much of any idea of the social and environmental footprint of their value chains," says WWF's resident expert on food systems, Senior Vice President Jason Clay. "But it is not too hard to get them to see that they ought to."

Clay is right. Value chains are the glue that connects disparate businesses, whether they are local, regional, or global. Suppliers matter to any business because they determine cost, quality, and reliability of supply (the "upstream"), just as the "downstream" relationships with those who stand between you and your ultimate customers shape your success in the market.

Because value chains reach beyond the boundaries of individual businesses, they also present a window for seeing a company's ecological and social impact and its overall health. Working together to comprehensively assess the health of value chains creates a place where ecological, social, and business concerns meet.

This became evident to Coca-Cola in the first phases of the partnership. The company had been working for several years around specific targets to improve water efficiency in its bottling plants. "These were viewed as real stretch goals," says Vermeer, "in some cases, reducing water use 20 to 40 percent, including water contained in our products, water used for the cleaning and processing, and all the water usage for sinks, toilets, and watering systems on the plant grounds. But we were looking mostly just within our four walls."

Coke's targets for improved water efficiency were put into a new context when compared to the total water use, or "water footprint," embedded in the product's ingredients as well.[2] Though the exact size of this footprint is still being debated, and varies by region, Clay's measurements represented an order-of-magnitude shift in view.

While the company was working to bring down the average number of liters of water it takes to make a liter of Coke from about 3-plus liters to 2.5 or less, when Clay looked at the whole value chain, he concluded that it takes 200 liters of water or more to grow the ingredients that go into a liter of Coke, much of it for the sugar. "Sugarcane is one of the most water-intensive crops there is," says Clay.

While the validity of Clay's broad brush estimate was and still is debated internally within Coke (there is considerable variation in the "embedded water" in a crop like sugarcane based on geography and type of production, such as rain-fed versus irrigation), the point had been made: Looking at the total water footprint became a touchstone for thinking in the company, and solidified its budding commitment in campaigning for more integrated watershed management. It wasn't just that Coca-Cola didn't know their water footprint; no one else did either. Few of us, as individuals or companies, think of this in regard to products in general, like our cotton T-shirts, or food, or car tires, or ethanol from sugarcane. For example, a cup of coffee takes 140 liters of water to produce, a typical gallon of milk, 800 to 1,000 gallons. Looking at the total water requirements of a business requires suppliers and customers to see how they are all part of an integrated system whose total impacts must be measured and improved. It also points to the imperative to reach out to engage many partners in building political will for more comprehensive water management, through initiatives like the CEO Water Mandate.

The basic need is clear: Regions and municipalities must understand watersheds in truly comprehensive terms so that it might become possible to account for all the major uses of water relative to the rates at which water is replenished. This is a bigger goal than even Coke and WWF can accomplish, but they can point the way by showing how water can be managed more responsibly in particular areas and by becoming vocal advocates, locally and globally, for broader commitment. Water, after all, is the archetypal regenerative resource, but we cannot manage it as such without a truly systemic picture of how much water is being used, and by whom, and how rapidly it is being replenished. It is safe to say that few if any governments or regions in the world can do this today.

Getting to Know Your Neighbors

The Coke-WWF partnership transitioned from primarily a philanthropic relationship to a more collaborative partnership in late 2005, with a series of planning workshops in the field. These quickly led to important insights into the cultural barriers in both organizations to advancing their partnerships—and how to start working with and around them.

"Our first task was to find a way to connect productively with Coke's global presence," says Apple. "We identified seven major watersheds in the world, in very different but equally crucial locations. We then brought WWF and Coke field people together in organizing meetings in each region. We knew we couldn't do all the places that matter, so we picked these seven to see what it would take to bring in bottlers and our freshwater people and do some things together in a big way."[3]

As the first meeting, in the Mekong region in Southeast Asia, approached in January 2006, Apple quickly discovered a number of challenges, starting with convincing WWF staff why they should even participate in such meetings.

"Our people immediately thought this was about getting Coca-Cola money to do the work that they had already planned to do," says Apple. "We had to say, 'Not exactly. You need to think about what work you can plan to do together and how you shape a body of work that you can all agree to do. It's not just about Coke funding your existing plan to study catfish in one estuary of the Mekong.' People responded, 'We don't really want to work with the local Coke people. We just want their money.'

"It was an interesting process facilitating WWF people talking about what we're planning in the Mekong and Coke talking about its growth in the region, and then identifying certain things we could do together that were consistent with both of our missions."

These initial meetings proved just as much of a culture shock for the

Coke participants. Most had no history of working with an international NGO like WWF beyond corporate contributions. Moreover, many were uncertain how much latitude they actually had to engage in substantive discussions about conditions in their regions. "It was quite surprising," says Vermeer, "to see that something we took for granted—for example, the permission to engage transparently with international NGOs—was something that wasn't necessarily natural at the local level."

In a workshop in Guatemala, one of the bottlers was very excited about working with the WWF partnership on sustainable fishing and habitat protection in the Mesoamerican Reef. "This bottler commented," says Vermeer, " 'Wow, I've been a bottler for twenty-five years in the Coca-Cola Company. Let me tell you, we have not been encouraged by Coca-Cola in the past to engage with external public groups like WWF. Though it's not on paper anywhere, for people like me, "Did anyone notice me?" is always a question. You know, you keep your head down, stay under the radar, and if there's no press, you've had a good year—lots of visibility is not a good thing.

" 'But being encouraged to engage in a partnership like this—that is something new. Now, the company's telling me, "Get to know your neighbors. Get to know the NGOs. Get to know the local communities. Get to know their issues. Get to know where the tension points are, understand those issues, begin to deal with them." ' He said, 'It may not seem like it for you, but from where I sit, we haven't been given that permission till now.'

"When I heard this," adds Apple, "I knew the partnership was on the right track.

"One of the truly profound lessons that WWF has been learning over the past decades is that habitat protection and community protection are two sides of the same coin. People who are struggling to survive cannot be stewards for their environment. Yet most desperately want to do that. Their history and culture are bound up with the larger living world, and they usually feel a deep kinship with the animals, fish, plants, and trees of their homeland.

"If successful local businesspeople like the Coke bottlers, most of whom come from these local communities, can be freed up to engage with their communities around these issues, it can be a huge win-win for everyone."

Getting to What Really Matters

As the process has continued, it has unleashed "a lot of creative energy," according to Vermeer. But to make it work, he added, "Your bias should be toward engagement and understanding one another, not to trying to make all our objectives align too quickly. This takes patience. There is really a large gulf separating the reality of these two organizations and you need time to appreciate and start to bridge the gulf.

"People in the company understandably have a hard time seeing the business relevance of the biodiversity issue. They say: 'Okay, I may really care about the panda in China or the catfish in the Mekong. But I don't know why my business cares about that.'"

An issue like biodiversity can easily be polarizing. Because people in an organization like WWF can feel very strongly, they may naturally try to impose their passion on the other. As Vermeer points out, "If you get rigid and demand that people care, it will backfire. But if we build enough foundation in terms of why we care about water and why we care about the systems that renew water and regenerate water, and how biodiversity is part of a healthy larger watershed in which we operate, there is hope.

"The discussion has to unfold naturally. If we are patient enough, it will be very interesting to see how these paradigms begin to mingle into a fabric that makes a larger sense. It'll take a lot of constructive work."

WWF likewise has had to evolve its own views. "I think we are migrating from a focus on species protection and biodiversity to focusing on the broader context in which diversity can be sustained," says Apple. "But we, too, need to continue the conversation, so we can really learn about how to achieve this. One danger is to panic and think, 'There's just no time to get everyone on board—we have to do it by ourselves.'

"This is why experiences like we had in China are every bit as meaningful to us as to Coke team."

Apple is referring to a planned launch event for the Coke-WWF partnership work in the Yangtze River basin.

"The Yangtze was one of our big, iconic river basins that we were going to work in and it was a major part of our overall global plan."[4] But before she ever got started with serious planning, Apple says, "I heard from one of the Coke people that, 'There was just too much going on in China. There are too many other demands on their time. And the Olympics were coming.' And on it went." Greg Koch, senior water director at Coke, asked that Apple meet C. B. Chiu, the man who led the environmental work for the China business and was pushing Coke headquarters and WWF to focus more on the Yangtze.

But after a short initial meeting, Apple's uneasiness persisted. Although people seemed positive, there was no real time to get to know each other, and the two organizations had never worked together; it was clear their cultures were very different.

When WWF and Coke started to plan the meeting, Apple learned that there would be no bottlers there. "The message I took from that was that they didn't really want us talking to bottlers. So we went through this whole dance of how we get the right people there."

Still, Apple and the Coke people involved in the planning went ahead with their basic plans. Early on, they had decided that "this meeting was about getting outside of our comfort zones, getting outside of the corporate office, getting outside of the WWF office. So we decided the team would see our work in the headwaters of the Yangtze, in the Quiangy Nature Preserve, which is four hours north of Xian. So everybody had to fly to Beijing, fly to Xian, then take a bus for four and a half hours up into the mountains into this nature preserve. We would be holding the meeting and staying for three days at a Chinese 'summer camp' facility up in the mountains that had little cabins with outdoor plumbing."

As the group pulled out of Xian into the countryside, Apple was sitting with Chiu on the bus, and he told her he'd never been outside the cities in China. Born and raised in Hong Kong, he had worked for the Coca-Cola Company for twenty-seven years and now lives in Shanghai, but had never been this far outside of Xian or to the preserve. WWF has worked for years to help the people there support themselves in ways that allow them to protect the habitat, and C.B. was very impressed. "Wow," he said, "this is amazing. The way people here care so much for the environment is very new for me."

Over the next three days, the local residents who lived in the nature preserve cooked all the food for the group, food they grew on the preserve.

Apple says: "We had lunch with people and visited them in their homes. This is actually a sort of bed-and-breakfast program we established, to create income for the farmers so they can manage with their existing farmland and not need to cut more forest.

"One day, we hiked up this ridge and visited a family that had lived there for four generations; they served us lunch that afternoon in their front yard.

"Over the course of three days, we began to really relate to each other. We began to understand each other's work. Everyone developed a whole different sense of what it meant to preserve habitat and community. They began to understand where the water comes from and where it goes. And they saw firsthand some of the challenges.

"By the last night, after we'd done a little karaoke organized by the local Chinese people, C.B. stood up and offered a toast and said, 'The last forty-eight hours has helped us all understand our work and to understand China. I want Yangtze to be WWF's leading river basin project in the world. I want you all to come and meet with our Shanghai bottler and visit the largest bottling plant in China. It is also a good opportunity for us to discuss the whole issue around climate change and to work together with you on managing supply chain carbon footprints.'" (Coke recently joined WWF's Climate Savers program, a small group of corporations leading by example with carbon footprint reductions.)[5]

"Given my apprehensions leading up to the meeting, C.B.'s comments meant so much to me, and I think to everyone there. In the end, I could see it was our (WWF's) view that the bottlers had to be included in this first big meeting, but the Coke people were right. They know their culture and we don't—we needed to become a team first, to open up to each other. As I see more of these sorts of gatherings, I think the powerful learning is that we have to allow time for people to really enter into each other's lives, to walk in each other's shoes a little bit, and to allow their hearts as well as their minds to open.

"C.B. just reminded us that water really matters. The people who live in these delicate habitats near the sources of our water really matter. Even though we may have lived in ways that separated us from this reality, it is still possible to reconnect to it if we have half a chance."

As this work unfolds, so too does understanding of its purpose. "We don't need to force a superficial connection between what Coke would say is their business priority and what WWF would say," says Vermeer. "It may be more that we just need to see how our successes really depend on the same things. I think we are discovering that all we have to say is, 'Look, we don't have exactly the same set of objectives, but there's enough of a common ground if we think systemically about this that there really is a basis for working together.' This is in the interest of all of us."

THE RISKS

As promising as partnerships like this are, they are not without risks.

By merely teaming up with WWF, Coke acknowledges that the water crisis is real and could impact the soft drink industry. It is bringing attention to an issue—the amount of water used by soft drink companies in their entire supply chain—about which many people are unaware. As more people recognize this issue, they will want to know what percent of a country's water, especially for water-scarce countries like India, is being used for what purposes—and even though the percentage for soft drinks is quite low, it puts companies like Coke in the spotlight and could put them on the defensive.

Moreover, as part of their partnership, Coke has agreed that WWF will be able to report without interference on what it learns of Coke's present and future water footprint. Over the past two years, this has included, for example, the two organizations even working together to set targets for improved water efficiency and overall water use at Coke. "They are challenging us to set hard operational targets," says Coke's Greg Koch, who manages the partnership. Progress toward these targets will be reported publicly and, Koch says, "WWF will hold Coke accountable to meeting them."[6]

In many ways, WWF has just as much at risk—namely, its greatest asset: its public reputation and credibility as a leading environmental NGO.

In 2007, the Center for Media and Democracy, a "non-profit, non-partisan, public interest organization that strengthens participatory democracy by investigating and exposing public relations spin and propaganda," wrote:

WWF, the corporate-funded environmental giant often accused of taking greenbacks in return for greenwashing its corporate benefactors, has a new partner. WWF and the Coca-Cola Company proclaimed a "bold partnership" that has Coke paying WWF $20 million. WWF touts the deal on its website. A full-page *New York Times* advertisement announcing the deal is headlined "This is our drop," a phrase that Coke has trademarked. For Coke, $20 million is just a drop in the bucket, a cheap fee for the PR boost from its WWF partnership.

"We knew there were risks in approaching this partnership," says Carter Roberts, CEO of WWF, "but without taking risks nothing much will change."

For Seabright, partnerships like those with WWF go beyond gaining access to expertise: "A partnership is a different relationship from what you have with a consultant you hire. WWF has really stretched us to go outside our normal ways of seeing things. They've been real thought partners."

The two are embarked on a noble and undoubtedly treacherous venture. The upside of working together is considerable, combining WWF's expertise on water and sustainable supply chains and public credibility with Coke's understanding of the commercial system and a vast distribution network, political clout, and financial resources (and, of course, a deep incentive for good water management for both economic and public relations reasons). One thing is sure: The successes and stumbles of the budding partnership will be watched closely, including by those who understand that such partnerships will be crucial for our common future.

EITHER WE ALL HANG TOGETHER OR WE'LL HANG SEPARATELY

This famous line of Benjamin Franklin's was used to entreat squabbling American colonists to join in fighting for independence. But it describes equally well our situation today. No one entity alone—no individual government (local, state, regional, or national), corporation, or NGO—can address the sustainability issues we face. No one has sufficient resources.

No one has sufficient understanding. And no one has sufficient credibility and authority to connect the larger networks of people and organizations that real change must engage.

Partnering across sectors will be crucial in dealing creatively with all the core sustainability issues, including food, water, alternative energy and transportation, and climate change. Companies can offer market clout and financial resources. NGOs can offer not only their credibility but also knowledge of the larger system, and the ability to bring the right stakeholders to the table. Governments have regulatory power. All will be needed to make any real progress.

Recognizing this, similar collaborations are unfolding around the world: Unilever (another of the largest global food companies) and Oxfam have worked to assess Unilever's impact on poverty in Indonesia; Unilever and the Rainforest Alliance are now working on Unilever's Lipton tea business worldwide; American retailing giant Costco and local NGOs in Central American farming communities are building partnerships for sustainable farming; BP and Indian NGOs are working to bring heat and power to off-grid villages; IKEA and NGOs in Brazil are focusing on ways to ensure sustainable logging in the Amazon; Nike and NGOs in Thailand are trying to enable apparel makers to work in their homes rather than migrate to urban factories. We'll discuss many similar efforts throughout this book. But it is important to remember that all are in their infancy.

As our earlier stories illustrate, it is enormously difficult to actually build the capacity for successful collaboration. Mutual distrust runs rampant between NGOs and corporations. Most governments have little history of building such collaborative efforts with the other sectors, and most, sadly, still see little need. Typically, organizations from these three sectors have different technical know-how, speak different languages, and focus on different stakeholders. There is little to bring all of them together—other than the urgent need to do so.

Still, collaborations like these are also enormously encouraging. "If you look at the ranking of the most trusted brands in the United States, Coca-Cola is number two and WWF is number eight; in Europe, WWF is number two and Coca-Cola is number eight," says Apple. "What might these two brands do together? If we do the right substantive work and really focus on results, we could create a movement around water together that could really get the message out, not just to our own members and our own consumers, but much more broadly."

Time will tell. Where there is genuine intent to learn how to see larger systems and reflect together on taken-for-granted ways of thinking and acting, partnerships like this could become a cornerstone for life beyond the Bubble.

part III
GETTING STARTED

The most extraordinary thing about the people and organizations leading the way in creating life beyond the Bubble, such as those introduced in Part II, is that they are in fact quite ordinary. Some hold positions of power; some don't. Some work primarily with businesses, others with governmental and nongovernmental organizations, large-scale and regional. Some of these organizations are well established, while others have formed quite recently to tackle totally new problems. The people come from technical and nontechnical backgrounds. They include those with many years of formal education and those "educated by life." They are old, young, and in between. They are simply ordinary people who have made extraordinary choices.

But they do have ways of doing things that work. They are very skilled at seeing the larger systems within which they operate. They foster relationships and build creative teams and networks. They have extraordinary aspirations, but they do not take themselves too seriously. And they have high "organizational intelligence" as well as high emotional and intellectual intelligence: a knack for connecting with what matters most to people in an organization and unleashing the latent collective imagination and energy residing within and among them.

While there is no one way to get started, most change efforts start with seeing specific reasons for action. For businesses, this usually begins when people recognize the opportunities inherent in taking social and environmental issues seriously, and the risks of not doing so. Typically, this starts with realizing that there are significant short-term benefits from efforts such as basic waste reduction or improved energy efficiencies. But these short-term reactions will strand many companies in a me-too position of "being less bad" until they see opportunities to create new sources of value through new products, new processes, and new business models.

In this part of the book, we present in Chapters 8 and 9 a way to rethink strategy that moves beyond the typical one-dimensional view of sustainability that limits most organizations. Chapters 10 and 11 show how to get started in actually doing this in realistic settings, through engaging people and building a compelling case for change. Here we start to explore how enacting new strategies depends on skill in areas such as shifting the quality of strategic conversation and helping people clarify their deeper aspirations.

All great journeys start with small steps and meaningful questions. If you're reading this book, you are probably the sort of person who at some point has wondered: "What more can I do? How can I get my organization more engaged?" In the pages that follow, we hope to help you create your own answers to these questions.

[8]

Risks and Opportunities: The Business Rationale for Sustainability

U p until now, we've been looking at sustainability through an extremely broad lens: What are our actions doing to the planet as a whole? And how does that affect all of us? We titled this book *The Necessary Revolution* because these questions are now inescapable: The human community has caused a lot of harm to the planet, and things need to change. Doing nothing is no longer an option.

But true innovation requires thinking differently. Many businesses and organizations of all sorts have already come to this realization. Some, such as those whose stories we shared in Part II, have been acting on this understanding for years. Many others are working hard to catch up. And though plenty of organizations are still huddled in the throes of inaction and paralysis, more and more businesses in every industry sector are incorporating sustainability and social responsibility issues into their goals for the future. They've accepted that they must do so if they wish to survive and thrive in the tumultuous times ahead.

A NEW CONTEXT FOR BUSINESS

While all organizations face the same basic mandate for innovation, for-profit business is arguably the most influential institution in society today. Understanding how sustainability is becoming a corporate priority at the CEO and board levels is vital. The first step is perhaps the simplest and the hardest: seeing the entire Industrial Age system with fresh eyes. Recall the figure we introduced on page 36, which illustrated the difference between how Industrial Age systems work and how nature works. As Figure 8.1 shows, many executives still see the world from an Industrial Age point of view: They see the largest and most important circle as the economy, with society and the environment as much smaller domains within.

In fact, we believe that the only way to begin to effectively shift priorities and integrate sustainability into your organization is to reconsider

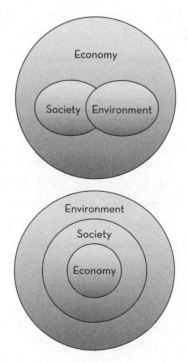

FIGURE 8.1 The "Real" Real World

that picture. In this new way of looking at the world and business's role in it, the biggest circle is the environment; within that circle is human society; the economy, industries, and individual businesses are much smaller circles that fit within both society and the environment. As Ray Anderson, CEO of Interface, puts it (quoting former U.S. senator Gaylord Nelson), businesses need to wake up to the simple fact that "the economy is the wholly owned subsidiary of nature, not the other way around." Similarly, there can be no healthy economy without a stable and vibrant social order—just ask businesspeople trying to do business in corrupt, lawless, or extremely poor societies.

Fortunately, many smart organizations understand the importance of this shift in perspective and practice, and are acting accordingly.

ALIGNING PRIORITIES WITH NEW REALITIES

In late 2007, Google announced plans to fund an internal research group with a mandate to develop cheaper renewable energy sources. Many industry and financial analysts believed the company was straying far from its business comfort zone. When the effort was announced in November, Jordan Rohan, an analyst with RBC Capital Markets who has recommended Google's high-flying stock in the past, was astonished. "What the heck are they doing? It boggles the mind," said Rohan to the press. "This makes me worry about Google's priorities."[1]

Rohan's quote gets to the heart of an important question: What are today's corporate priorities and how do they align with an organization's place in the larger business universe? Pressure for quarterly earnings growth from investment analysts such as Rohan has traditionally driven executive decision making, but when these choices butt up against the realities of global warming and sustainability requirements, their priorities must be reexamined. The status quo can no longer hold.

In fact, Google, which uses an enormous amount of power to operate the servers at the heart of its business, is simply following its motto ("Do no evil") and being pragmatic to boot. If the company succeeds in its quest, says co-founder Larry Page, "the world will have the option to meet a substantial portion of electricity needs from renewable sources and significantly reduce carbon emissions." Alternative energy is also vital for economic development in many places where there is "limited affordable energy of any kind," adds co-founder Sergey Brin. "We expect this would be good business for us as well."[2]

Google, like most other forward-looking companies, is not undertaking its mission alone. Part of understanding real-world systems, as we described in Chapter 2, is realizing how the larger, integrated environment—partners, suppliers, customers, shareholders, and competitors— has an impact upon every player. Besides funding its internal research, Google is providing grants to other companies, independent laboratories, and academia, knowing that unexpected synergies and innovation may be crucial to its success. Some companies are working with governments or NGOs; others are forming global partnerships and coalitions. The story of Coca-Cola teaming up with the World Wildlife Fund for integrated water management is just one example. Like GE, DuPont, BP, and many others who have been rethinking strategy by looking at the social and environmental realities of their businesses, Google appreciates the audaciousness of its goal and recognizes the need for partners in tackling problems that are much bigger than any one company can handle.

BUSINESS RISKS IN AN
INTERDEPENDENT WORLD

Most people accept the overwhelming evidence that the world has changed, and that business-as-usual global expansion can't continue. They are looking for answers—and leaders with solutions and the ability to get moving. Savvy executives have embraced the challenge amid the clear and growing evidence that companies that do little or nothing to address sustainability issues risk losing market share, cutting off their access to the best and brightest employees, and causing severe damage to corporate reputations and market capitalizations.

Survey after survey confirms that all corporate stakeholders—customers, employees, business partners, suppliers, and shareholders—care deeply and are making decisions about what to buy, where to work, and how to invest based on how companies are responding to the intertwined challenges of environmental and social well-being. In fact, customers and employees, perhaps the two most crucial constituencies, are telling companies that this matters a great deal. More important, they are holding businesses accountable. For example, in a recent survey of more than 25,000 people in twenty-five countries, GlobeScan, a highly respected and experienced research firm, found that 69 percent of respondents held companies "completely responsible" for not harming the environment.[3]

With this change, corporations are coming under heavy scrutiny from all sides regarding their environmental and social behavior. Knowledge on the subject is widely disseminated in the media and on the Internet's countless blogs and Web sites. Even companies that have worked hard to make change are not exempt: Nike, for example, still suffers image problems over its past connections to sweatshops and child labor in third world nations. Today, there is truly nowhere to hide.

Investors are at the forefront of the scrutiny, and so ignoring social and environmental issues is putting investment capital at serious risk. Consider, for example, the Carbon Disclosure Project (CDP), an organization that seeks information on business risks and opportunities presented by climate change as well as CO_2 and other greenhouse gas emissions data from the world's largest companies. In 2007, its database covered 2,400 companies and CDP issued a report on behalf of 315 institutional investors representing more than $41 trillion of assets under management. Paul Dickinson, CEO of CDP, says, "Increasingly, investors view good carbon management as a sign of good corporate management." Dickinson notes that as investors gain more and more information on a company's approach to climate change, "the pressure is increasing on companies to respond."

Many market leaders have struggled to get their arms around the issue. But when investors *and* customers speak, smart companies listen.

"As an executive, I was brought up to be totally suspicious of NGOs and the environmental movement," says Jeffrey Immelt, CEO of General Electric. "Five years ago, I started to see technology that I felt really, for the first time, didn't make this about compromise, it made it more about opportunity. If we made the right investments in renewable energy, conservation, water desalination, then we could earn money and solve a societal issue at the same time."

At GE, the changes were initiated and driven by customers telling individual business units that sustainability issues such as energy efficiency, renewable energy, and climate change mattered to them. And GE listened. In 2002, when Immelt began to see the opportunity in new, cost-effective technologies, crude oil was selling for $25 a barrel. Though this was a significant jump from the $11-a-barrel low in January 1999, it was hardly a blip compared to the $110-a-barrel price in March 2008. Yet Immelt wasn't waiting for disastrous economic conditions to initiate GE's environmental action plan.

"When society changes its mind, you better be in front of it and not behind it, and this is an issue in which society has changed its mind," Immelt said. "As a CEO, my job is to get out in front of it because if you are not out in front of it, you're going to get plowed under."

THE FINANCIAL INDUSTRY'S U-TURN

Compared to the big bad polluting manufacturing companies, industry sectors such as banks, financial institutions, and stock exchanges have traditionally had clean images. But the truth is, they are not environmental angels and never have been. They are just as involved in the current Industrial Age system as any manufacturer, and they face the same kinds of risks. Savvy, informed customers are now insisting that these businesses step up and lead the way.

In fact, the financial industry is making massive commitments to the environmental movement. Citigroup, which manages $2 trillion in assets, for example, has announced a $50 billion green initiative of its own, the largest single corporate commitment to date. About $10 billion has already been committed and another $10 billion is targeted to reducing Citi's own enormous carbon footprint in its 14,500 offices around the world. According to the London *Times,* Citi will invest another $31 billion over ten years to fund wind farms, biofuels, solar panels, and other eco-friendly technologies. "We believe very strongly that addressing climate change is one of the most important issues being faced by chief executives, investors and governments today," says Michael Klein, chairman, co-CEO, Citi Markets and Banking. "This is just the beginning."

Cynics may point out that to an institution with $2 trillion in assets, $50 billion spent over ten years is a drop in the bucket. If it is intended as nothing more than a PR campaign, however, it is unlikely to fool the NGOs, regulators, and activists who have come to understand the critical role banks play in the push to environmental responsibility.

As activists routinely began targeting big corporate polluters such as oil, chemical, timber, and steel manufacturers in the 1990s, it became clear that an even more effective strategy was to target the institutions that provided the money for these industries. Scrutinizing the lending portfolios of big banks and mounting widespread public campaigns to "out" the lenders who were funding ruinous social and environmental practices proved to be a highly effective tactic. In 2005, for example, protesters arrived wearing hazmat suits at the offices of JPMorgan Chase to let the world know that Chase was underwriting illegal logging in Indonesia and human-rights abuses connected with a mining operation in Peru. *Time* magazine reported that within two weeks, the company announced it would introduce policies to promote sustainable forestry, protect indigenous people's rights, and block funding that could be used for illegal logging.

"The private financial sector more than any other has the ability to begin the ecological U-turn modern society so desperately needs," Ilyse Hogue, director of the global finance campaign at Rainforest Action Network (RAN), told *Time*.[4]

Michael Brune, executive director of RAN, adds that his organization decided nearly a decade ago to "follow the money" and run market campaigns targeted at influential customers as well as investment institutions to try to dissuade corporations from continuing their destructive policies. RAN teaches its staff and campaign workers to think like a CEO. What, they ask themselves, will motivate a CEO to action?

"If you're the CEO of forest products company Boise Cascade, for example, you care about where you sell paper and wood, and where you get your financing," Brune says. "So to get Boise Cascade to adopt an environmental policy, we went to the marketplace—first to Boise Cascade's customers, like Home Depot. We convinced Home Depot to start phasing out wood products that were not certified as coming from well-managed forests. We went to 400 other companies in the Boise Cascade campaign. It took a few years, but Boise Cascade adopted a corporate environmental policy in 2003."[5] When a $90 billion customer such as Home Depot speaks, a $5.7 billion supplier such as Boise has to listen.

According to Brune, financial institutions now understand the issue from the perspective of their balance sheet. "Environmental liabilities add a risk factor when banks look at proposed transactions," he says. "Other risks that banks look at include shareholder litigation, reputational risk, or lack of insurance coverage. From a conceptual standpoint, we did the same thing with banks that we did with Home Depot. Slowly, banks are beginning to phase out loans and financing arrangements to companies that promote unsustainable projects."

While pressure tactics such as these have been useful to wake up many businesses to hitherto ignored risks, they only go so far in promoting real innovation. Understanding this, many NGOs and banks have come to a mutually beneficial détente, even coming together to form networks and alliances. One such alliance is a partnership between Banktrack (a network of civil society organizations and individuals tracking the operations of the private financial sector) and thirty of the world's largest private banks (including Citigroup, JPMorgan Chase, Bank of America, ABN AMRO, Barclays, HSBC, and ING), which formed in 2004. As Jon Williams, HSBC's head of sustainability risk management, told *Time*, "Everybody is interested in the balance between sustainability and economic development. We believe you can do well and do good."

OPPORTUNITY ON THE OTHER SIDE OF RISK

Scan any newspaper or business magazine and it's clear that the sustainability wave is breaking over the entire corporate shoreline; it's not just the financial sector that's making changes. And top-performing companies are leading the charge. For example, Goldman Sachs, one of the world's leading investment banks, recently examined six key industry sectors—energy, mining, steel, food, beverages, and media—and studied the companies within those sectors that are considered leaders in implementing environmental, social, and governance policies and strategies. Goldman Sachs found that these companies have outperformed the general stock market by 25 percent since August 2005. In addition, 72 percent of these companies have outperformed their peers over the same period.

For business leaders, such studies prime their boards to ask: What tangible financial benefits will accrue if we reorient our business? Can our company continue to be profitable, and even grow our profits and the value we provide, by committing to environmental issues?

When you ask questions concerning the business rationale for particular strategies, the issue always boils down to risk versus opportunity. While the short- and medium-term risks vary for each company and industry, the ultimate risks of ignoring sustainability issues are clear: If we continue to put more toxic waste into the environment and more CO_2 into the atmosphere than can be naturally disposed of, or if we insist on extracting and wasting more natural resources than can be replaced, business in the traditional sense will cease to exist. You can't have a fishing industry if there are no fish, or a soft-drink company without clean water.

What is required today is a new way of thinking about facing these business risks head-on—and finding the opportunities on the other side of those risks.

COMPETITIVE ADVANTAGE, INNOVATION, AND GROWTH

For organizations that are able to see the opportunities in this changed world, the future looks full of promise. But in order to justify the difficulty of making significant changes to the way a company does business, there must naturally be solid evidence of significant potential return on investment. Fortunately, in a world where corporate goodwill has become a tangible asset, a company's reputation in relation to the environment and related social issues is now a matter of competitive advantage.

Juergen H. Daum, a German management consultant and author of *Intangible Assets and Value Creation,* wrote, "The proportion of a company's total market value that exceeds its book value has increased from 40% in the early 1980s to over 80% at the end of the 1990s. This means that only 20% of a company's value is reflected in the accounting system."[6] The vast majority of the market value of a company, therefore, is based on brand and reputation, as opposed to the so-called hard assets. And brand and reputation are affected by a rapidly growing set of vocal, powerful external stakeholders, from NGOs to consumer activists and governments at all levels. As a result, corporate brands are rushing to embrace sustainable environmental efforts in unprecedented numbers—for good reason.

An October 2007 survey of 17,000 people in fifteen major global markets by Ipsos MORI, a British research firm, confirmed that customers put a high value on green brands. More than half of the survey's respondents said they prefer to buy products and services from companies with good environmental reputations.

In Britain, a report commissioned in 2005 by the Co-operative Bank revealed that "ethical consumerism" was up 11 percent from the previous year to nearly £30 billion, a figure that was higher than retail sales of beer and cigarettes. GlobeScan reported in 2007 that the "mainstream activist" segment in the U.S. population had grown significantly—from 38 percent of the population in 2005 to 45 percent in 2007. Mainstream activists are the people most likely to act on their expectations of companies through their behavior as consumers. This segment is also most likely to have high levels of education and income, as well as a high percentage of opinion leaders.[7] In the rush to join an obviously surging trend, many organizations are marketing small improvements and marginal efforts to make themselves look green to their customers and other constituents.

"Now I think there's a transition and it's only begun, and the grandstanding is ahead of the action," Joel Swisher, director of research at the Rocky Mountain Institute, told the *New York Times*. RMI is an influential non-profit organization, founded in 1983, that has made significant contributions at the levels of policy, strategy, and applied innovation that have brought sustainability into the mainstream, particularly in energy and transportation. But despite relatively small changes, Swisher believes it is all positive. "It is moving in the right direction," he said.

Producing environmentally friendly goods and services has become as much a brand attribute as quality and price. And once a corporate brand gains traction in this space, as with quality or innovation, the stakes and expectations remain high.

Just as consumers are making their preferences known with their purchases, employees are making career choices based on a company's reputation in corporate responsibility. Research shows that employees—especially young ones—want to work for a firm that understands what is going on outside the corporate offices. Monster Worldwide, the leading online jobs site, with a presence in twenty-three countries, revealed that 80 percent of those surveyed said they are interested in a job that has a positive impact on the environment and 92 percent would prefer to work for an environmentally friendly organization. The same Ipsos MORI survey found that nearly eight out of ten people in the fifteen global markets investigated said they prefer to work for "environmentally ethical" organizations.

"In my view, the successful companies of the future will be those that integrate business and employees' personal values. The best people want to do work that contributes to society with a company whose values they share, where their actions count and their views matter," said Jeroen van der Veer, chief executive of Royal Dutch Shell.

But brand issues and employee recruitment and retention are not the only reasons to embrace leadership in the regenerative economy. Here are just a few concrete benefits:

1. **There is significant money to be saved.** Companies in all sectors, from IBM to Alcoa to Wal-Mart, have achieved massive savings opportunities from reducing waste and energy usage. DuPont saved $3 billion thanks to their intense focus on slashing greenhouse gas emissions and associated energy use, while growing their business by 30 percent over the same fifteen-year period. GE Industrial saved $12.8 million per year just by upgrading the lighting in their plants to their own high-efficiency lights, and saved $70 million in their annual energy expenses as they worked across the company to reduce their energy use and greenhouse gases. Ford Motor Company has dramatically reduced the amount of time it takes to paint a new car as it comes down the assembly line by using a technology that applies three coats of paint simultaneously. This eliminates the need for costly, energy-intensive drying equipment. The change will allow Ford to reduce CO_2 emissions from production by 15 percent and volatile organic compound emissions by 10 percent. The process will also reduce painting time by 20 percent.[8]

Green buildings cut energy costs at least in half, and often much more—and according to Greg Kats, an industry financial analyst at Capital E, green building is a wave that has already broken. "The risks of going green a couple of years ago were material, and the risks of not going green were insignificant," Kats says. "Given that we are now beyond a billion square feet of green buildings, the risk of doing this has gone away, and the risk of not doing it is very substantial."

2. **There is significant money to be made.** Spending $100 a ton to dump waste in a landfill can quickly add up. But as *Fast Company* magazine reports, "General Mills has turned its solid waste into profits. Take its oat hulls, a Cheerios by-product. The company used to pay to have them hauled off, but realized they could be burned as fuel. Now customers compete to buy the stuff. In 2006, General Mills recycled 86% of its solid waste, earning more from that than it spent on disposal."[9]

And it's not just individual companies that are benefiting. The sustainability marketplace—companies formed to tackle sustainability issues—promises to be especially profitable. That's because the majority of preexisting organizations need their products or services as they shift to renewable energy, construct a new green building, or retrofit an existing one. According to a McGraw-Hill Construction Trends report, the value of green building construction starts will exceed $12 billion in 2008 and is projected to increase to $60 billion in 2010. As Greg Kats points out, the small additional capital investment (now less than 2 percent and shrinking) to build a green building instead of a conventional one typically has a return on investment (ROI) of 40 percent per year over the life of the building. This rate of return is rising steadily as energy costs escalate.

3. **You can provide your customers with a competitive edge.** As the price of computing power steadily falls, we are rapidly approaching the point—it could occur as early as 2009—where the cost of powering and cooling large computers and servers will be more than the cost of the hardware itself. IBM's Project Big Green, which seeks to dramatically reduce energy consumption in its own data centers and those of its custom-

ers, could save its customers about 40 percent in IT costs and increase IBM's share of the market.

4. Sustainability is a point of differentiation. About half the fleet at Enterprise Rent-a-Car—more than 334,000 vehicles—gets more than 28 miles per gallon (nearly ten times the number of fuel-efficient vehicles offered by its closest competitor, Enterprise asserts). The company is currently adding thousands of hybrids and flexi-fuel cars and is making investments in research for alternative fuels.[10]

5. You can shape the future of your industry. Years before car firms in the United States caught on, BMW and other European automakers realized that enlightened self-interest is a good thing and can allow companies to shape the direction of future regulations (we discuss this story further in Chapter 15). Sony Europe has played a similar leadership role in the EU in helping to build a cost-effective system for the take-back of electronic equipment at the end of its life. BP and Shell, because of their leadership stance on climate change, have had similar influence on policy developments affecting the energy industry.

6. You can become a preferred supplier. Costco and other food retailers focus on long-term, reliable suppliers who can meet their quality targets; when these targets include higher social and environmental standards, it can lead to unique supply partnerships. The world's best companies know that for their supply chains to be truly robust and sustainable, all players in their entire chain must be leaders in radically reducing their environmental impact and meeting stringent demands for social responsibility globally. They are setting this as a condition of doing business with them, and will accept nothing less than consistently demonstrated leadership. This represents an enormous opportunity for suppliers who can commit to meeting these standards.

7. You can change your image and brand. Companies in every industry, from small firms to large global enterprises such as GE and Shell, can

successfully remake their reputations and brands through serious investments in environmental initiatives. Giant retailer Wal-Mart, for example,
is using "going green" as the vanguard effort to offset the negative press it
has received for treatment of its employees and its impact on small local
businesses. GE initially committed to doubling their annual investment in
R&D to $1.5 billion on their suite of environmentally friendly ecomagi-
nation products, and has since increased those investments substantially.
They are well ahead of their plan to double annual revenues from $10 bil-
lion to $20 billion for that growing product category over five years. (See
Chapter 9 for more on this story.)

FROM COMPLIANCE TO INNOVATION

No matter what the reason, more and more companies are moving to take
advantage of the new realities of business. And as with every trend, for all
the early adopters, there are the laggards who wait to see how the prevailing winds are blowing before jumping in. Many people wonder who is
walking the talk and who is just paying lip service and avoiding the hard
work of integrating sustainable practices into the fabric of their business.
In truth, we're not sure this matters anymore: You've got to start somewhere. Wal-Mart CEO Lee Scott openly admitted that the company's early
conservation efforts were part of a campaign to clean up its sullied image.
Once organizations make this commitment, however, customers and employees will hold them to it. If they don't deliver, these same customers
and employees will go elsewhere, to others who are demonstrating a serious commitment to moving forward.

Whether an organization is reacting to a changed business environment, such as Wal-Mart, or proactively seeking a new opportunity, such
as IBM and GE were, it starts in one of five stages along the path to full
integration of sustainability into its strategy and purpose, as shown in the
figure on the next page.

Many get stuck near the bottom, in non-compliance or compliance
stages. These initial stages often involve reacting to external pressures—
such as a regulator giving you thirty days' notice to fix large-scale illegal
air emissions before they shut your plant down, or an aggressive NGO

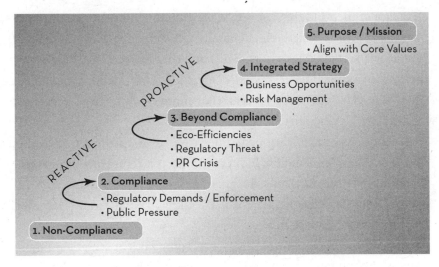

FIGURE 8.2 Five Stages and Emerging Drivers[11]

picketing your corporate offices with global media at their side. As this is a very expensive way to change, executives often assume that making the leap beyond compliance will cost even more, and so they miss the benefits and substantial savings of a proactive approach.

Momentum for change starts to build when people see the cost-effectiveness of going further than compliance in stage 2—which is just trying to meet minimum legal requirements in areas such as air emissions, toxic waste, and wastewater. As they move beyond compliance to stage 3, they find that savings and payoffs begin to far outweigh their initial investments. This can become a self-reinforcing snowball, as the reinvestment of initial savings leads to more and more gains, including an improvement in reputation and brand value.

The move to stage 4, where sustainability is fully integrated into strategy, often occurs when companies discover that a much broader set of business opportunities is available—but only if they proactively integrate sustainability factors into every dimension of their business strategy and into the core of their investment and decision-making processes across the organization. For example, Wal-Mart, GE, DuPont, Alcoa, and scores of leading firms in every industry have made the move to stage 4. One clear sign of their progression is that the accountability for sustainability has shifted. It is no longer the domain of a director or VP who is focused primarily on stakeholder management and communications. This is now the domain of their business unit leaders, CEOs, chief technology officers, CFOs, and chief operating officers. (For more on this shift, see Part VI, Chapter 24: "Redesigning for the Future.")

At stage 4, sustainability penetrates right to the heart of corporate strategy and implementation. It directly impacts internal capital and budget allocations, supply chains, the pursuit of major new markets, core operations, and R&D. People are regularly asking, "What's in our lab now, and how can we get it to market?"

Many of the best-known examples of companies at stage 5 are those founded by individuals who saw the opportunities sustainability challenges presented long before most companies started aiming for compliance. They placed their companies squarely in stage 5 without passing through the other stages by boldly declaring that the mission or purpose of the company was to contribute to society and be regenerative. This was the case with The Body Shop, Patagonia, Seventh Generation, and Husky Injection Molding Systems, among others. Others came to a realization of the harm they were doing and shifted direction. In the summer of 1994, Interface CEO Ray Anderson was asked to give the sales force at Interface, the carpet tile company he founded, some talking points about the company's approach to the environment. "That's simple," Anderson recalls thinking. "We comply with the law." But as a sales tool, compliance lacked inspirational verve. So he started reading about environmental issues and thinking about them, until pretty soon it hit him: "I was running a company that was plundering the earth." So instead of talking about environmental regulation and compliance, he focused on his realization that "only one institution was powerful enough and pervasive enough to turn these problems around . . . and it was the institution that was causing them in the first place: 'Business. Industry. People like us. Us!'"

He challenged his colleagues to set a deadline for Interface to become a "restorative enterprise," a sustainable operation that takes nothing out of the earth that cannot be recycled or quickly regenerated, and that does no harm to the biosphere.[12]

More and more organizations are moving toward stage 5, many from SMEs, which are defined in most Western nations as those with fewer than 500 employees. They represent over 98 percent of all businesses in the United States, Canada, and Europe. The BALLE network (Business Alliance for Local Living Economies; see Chapter 26 for more on BALLE and other mission-based businesses) is one of countless international networks of small and midsized businesses that have contributing to sustainability as their primary mission and purpose.

Yet we believe that the shift to stage 5 can also occur as part of a natural progression from stage 4 as leaders learn from their experience of launching new initiatives and getting positive feedback from their employees. They discover for themselves that enormous additional energy can be unleashed by taking steps to align their purpose and mission with the core values their people hold.

For public companies, moving to stage 5 means taking on the challenge of continually demonstrating that they can and must be profitable and successful as a business in order to make a sustained positive contribution to a regenerative society and environment.

As we reach a critical mass of companies in stages 4 and 5, their strategic commitments and actions make it self-evident that these are not static categories. As these proactive companies make strategic moves in their industries and markets, customers, suppliers, investors, and competitors sit up and take notice. These leaders change the game for everyone else by raising the expectations of customers, the public, NGOs, and governments alike. Compliance does not mean just meeting the minimum requirements of regulators—it means meeting the rising expectations of all stakeholders.

While many organizations start out at stage 1 or 2, many others are already operating at stage 3. They've accepted that things need to change, whether for the survival of their own company or because they see the benefits of operating more sustainably, such as reduced costs or an improved brand image. But the most significant jump is to move beyond stage 3. Once companies enter stage 4 or 5, they step into the role of influencing not just their own future but the futures of others in the larger systems in which they operate. They see the connection between their survival, opportunities to prosper, and the health of the environment they operate in. As Bob Willard, author of *The Sustainability Advantage* and *The Next Sustainability Wave,* rightly observes, the difference in motivations between stage 4 and stage 5 organizations doesn't necessarily matter at this point. Their behaviors are essentially the same.[13] In both stages they're crossing the line from merely reacting to risks to recognizing the opportunities that result from actively creating a world in which they can thrive for years to come.

[9]

Positioning for the Future *and* the Present

While most businesspeople understand that the landscape of risks and opportunities is changing rapidly, many are unsure of how to act on that knowledge. Leaders want to learn how to ride the wave of sustainability innovation into the future while still maintaining a healthy and viable business in the present. Those leading their industries today are doing so because they have recognized the new reality of business and positioned themselves accordingly. Yet many leaders have found that the challenge of embracing broader issues of sustainability leads to conflict, confusion, "analysis paralysis," and inaction. And as diverse and passionate external stakeholders get involved (including non-governmental organizations, consumer activists, community groups, and leaders in government), frustration and perceived misalignment can escalate.

Fortunately, this doesn't need to be the case. Not only is it possible to bridge daunting gaps between stakeholders, but you can create focus and unleash enormous energy for progress in the process. When you align business priorities with the new forces at play in the world (as Google did), you create long-term sustainable value for all stakeholders, beginning with shareholders.

Doing this starts with stepping back and thinking about value creation (your contribution to both shareholders and society) along two dimensions. In "The Four Elements of Shareholder Value" (Figure 9.1), originally developed by Stuart Hart and Mark Milstein, the vertical axis (time) reflects an organization's need to manage business in the present while simultaneously creating technology and markets for the future.[1] The horizontal axis (space) reflects the firm's need to grow and protect internal organizational capabilities while simultaneously incorporating new perspectives and knowledge from the outside. This dimension reflects the tension between staying focused on core operations and at the same time remaining open to fresh perspectives and new, disruptive models and technologies.

Juxtaposing the time and space dimensions produces a matrix of four distinct areas—risk reduction, reputation, innovation, and growth—each of which is absolutely crucial when it comes to generating shareholder value.

Companies that perform well in all four quadrants maximize shareholder value over time by thinking more comprehensively about their business, which also enables them to attend to all stakeholders more effectively. Focusing on only one or two quadrants can spell poor perfor-

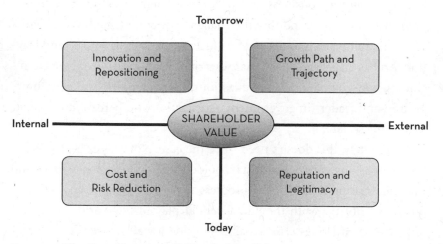

FIGURE 9.1 The Four Elements of Shareholder Value

mance—or, at the very least, can lead to many missed opportunities and a failure to build long-term future value. Companies such as Kodak, for instance, which failed to adequately invest in digital technology, illustrate how overemphasis on today's business (to the exclusion of tomorrow's technology and markets) may generate wealth for a time but will eventually erode shareholder value as competitors flood the market with superior products and services. An overemphasis on the present, of course, is not the only pitfall facing an organization. The experience of many Internet companies early in the dot-com era stands as testimony to how a preoccupation with tomorrow's business (to the exclusion of current performance) may be exciting and challenging but short-lived. Furthermore, focusing too much on internal aspects of a business (such as pouring too many resources into a key product) may enable short-term execution but ultimately blind the company to the competition. And, of course, an overemphasis on external forces can hamper an organization's ability to get things done.

SUSTAINABLE VALUE CREATION

Sustainability, like shareholder value creation, is also a multidimensional challenge. Yet most managers (particularly those operating at the noncompliance or compliance stages of the five-stage model we introduced on page 115) frame sustainability "not as a multidimensional opportunity, but as a one-dimensional nuisance," as Hart and Milstein note. The Sustainable Value Framework they originated addresses this in a simple and elegant way.

It is built around the same two dimensions—time and space—described earlier but this time includes the social and environmental challenges businesses now face. It's been used by companies of all sizes in many industries, and by broader coalitions of business and non-business leaders. The city of Sarnia, Ontario, for example, in the heart of Canada's "Chemical Valley," brought together leaders from government, business, and civil society to look at both the current state of each of their sectors and possible opportunities for the future. During a period of intensive work, they used the matrix to create a plan for achieving their vision of evolving to a cleaner "bio-hybrid" economy, in which bio-based inputs or feedstocks replace conventional oil and gas feedstocks.

The framework demonstrates the connection between sustainability and the core functions of any business. As Hart and Milstein point out, many executives look at this model and realize that *this connection simply has not been made before.* If managers and employees are apathetic about their organization's sustainability efforts, it is most likely because they don't see how it ties in to business goals. As a result, efforts are generally piecemeal, reactive, and poorly integrated into the company's core mission and business plans.

The framework helps people place their organization's activities in perspective, and shows how they can work together to create and maintain value and simplify strategic decision making.[2]

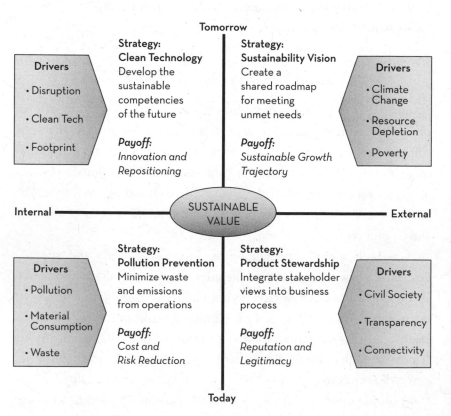

FIGURE 9.2 Sustainable Value Framework[3]

Sustainability Drivers

There are many distinct forces compelling businesses toward the regenerative economy, but the Sustainable Value Framework helps us categorize them into four broad groupings—and allows us to better understand how sustainable practices are directly related to a company's core strategies.

The first, and perhaps most obvious, relates to the increasing industrialization of the last two centuries and its side effects, material consumption, pollution, and waste generation among them. Firms can create immediate value by reducing the level of material consumption and pollution associated with their activities.

A second set of forces concerns the proliferation of "civil society stakeholders." As the power of national governments has eroded in the wake of global trade regimes, non-governmental organizations (NGOs) and other civil society groups have stepped into the breach, assuming the role of monitor (and, in some cases, enforcer) of social and environmental standards. At the same time, the spread of the Internet and information technology has enabled these groups to communicate with members and with each other in ways that were unimaginable even a decade ago. Internet-connected coalitions of NGOs—such as Banktrack, Rainforest Action Network, and others—are making it increasingly difficult for governments, corporations, or any other large institution to operate in secrecy. Moreover, companies that operate at greater levels of transparency and responsiveness to the public's desire for sustainable practices will see the direct impact of improved brand image on their bottom line.

Another set of trends includes emerging "disruptive" technologies that challenge the status quo and could render many of today's energy- and material-intensive industries obsolete. Genomics, biomimicry, nanotechnology, information technology, and renewable energy all hold the potential to drastically change both the way we do business and our effect on the planet. There are few more effective ways for companies to invest in the future than by developing new, potentially game-changing technologies.

Finally, a fourth set of drivers relates to gobal problems like resource depletion, deteriorating ecosystems, and climate change; poverty and inequity in the developing world; and an equally broad set of sustainability drivers in the developed world, including global security issues and their close links to climate, resource consumption, and energy supply and security. Social development and wealth creation on a massive scale, especially among the world's poorest 4 billion, are essential to sustainable development. However, development everywhere must follow a fundamentally new course if it is not to result in ecological meltdown. But not only is responding to this final set of drivers essential for the health of the planet; firms can also create value by pursuing sustainability-related opportunities that are rapidly emerging in all industries. One example is meeting the basic needs, including food, sanitation, and health, of those at the bottom of the world income pyramid in a way that facilitates wealth creation and distribution.

Global sustainability is so complex that it cannot be addressed by any single corporate action. Therefore, companies that hope to thrive in the years to come must address each of the four broad sets of drivers. Deciding how much to invest in each quadrant and over what period of time will differ for every organization; insight into this process is one of the real values of using this framework. Ultimately, a balanced portfolio of investments in all four quadrants is necessary to maximize value creation.

TRANSFORMING DUPONT

Few companies of any size and scope have done as comprehensive a job of reinventing themselves as the $29 billion, 206-year-old chemical giant DuPont. The company's story offers important lessons for how best to use the Sustainable Value Framework and translate it into action.

Despite DuPont's countless breakthrough products—many of which are emblematic of the exploding growth and prosperity of post–World War II America, such as nylon, Lycra, cellophane, and Teflon—the Wilmington, Delaware-based company's reputation for innovation eventually soured. In 1989, Greenpeace demonstrators infiltrated a DuPont manufacturing plant site in Deepwater, New Jersey, climbed the plant's 180-foot-high water tower, and hung a huge banner across it that declared DuPont, the developer of the refrigerant gas Freon, the world's number one polluter.[4]

Responding to that claim and others like it became a top priority for the new chairman and CEO, Edgar Woolard, who announced shortly after that incident: "I don't know what color this company is going to be in the future, but I can assure you it will be some shade of green." In the future, he said, his CEO title would stand for "chief environmental officer" in addition to "chief executive officer." He coined the phrase "corporate environmentalism" to indicate his belief that public trust, not just legal compliance, would be DuPont's environmental focus. Twenty years and many changes later, environmentalism has proved to be, as Woolard described it, "the most empowering and unifying initiative I've ever seen in this company."

Well before their public "outing" by Greenpeace, however, DuPont executives had begun to seriously rethink the company's entire value proposition. They made a strategic decision to strike out in a new direction from their petrochemical-based past into a new position as a world leader in plant-based chemicals and new, environmentally friendly products. The move was prompted in part because that's where DuPont's executives and scientists envisioned future growth, and also because they recognized that the company's existing chemicals and polymers business would, over time, become commoditized and far less profitable. Today DuPont is focused on biotechnology, chemistry, and natural systems, as opposed to synthetic ones. "It clearly is a transformational change," says Paul Tebo, now retired from his position as vice president of Health, Safety, and Environment. DuPont's reputation has also improved significantly. In 2005, *BusinessWeek* ranked it number one on their list of "The Top Green Companies." And Ceres, a well-respected environmental watchdog, ranked DuPont number one in the United States and number two globally for meeting the business challenges associated with climate change.

DuPont's Approach to Sustainable Value Creation

When he describes DuPont's efforts, Tebo uses the sustainable value matrix to shed light on the strategic thinking behind the company's actions and to explain how he and others achieved widespread buy-in from stakeholders for their efforts. Those involved in the march toward sustainability began with meeting basic requirements in the lower left quadrant—by addressing current issues of cost, risk, and footprint reduction—and turned them into transformative business initiatives and technologies that not only have led to innovation but promise growth and profitability far into the future.

Cost and Risk Reduction: The Lower Left Quadrant

Given the pressure on companies to meet quarterly targets and Wall Street's expectations, it is difficult for many to get past focusing on the here and now.

For DuPont, the first step toward sustainable growth focused on reducing risks and cutting costs. That meant reductions in waste, air emissions, and energy usage. What such industry leaders come to understand quickly is that their sustainability efforts will end if they don't demonstrate a viable commitment to cutting their environmental footprint and reducing risks today. In other words, it is within the lower quadrant of risk and cost reduction that a company gains credibility for all future sustainability efforts. After all, as soon as you start making statements about the future (the above-the-line quadrants in the matrix), stakeholders will declare, "Show us what you are doing today! Don't talk to us about grand visions of the future until we see proof of your engagement and commitment today."

DuPont set out a series of aggressive reduction goals in 1990, and Edgar Woolard charged Paul Tebo with ensuring that managers across the company made the commitment to meet them. By 2004, global air carcinogens were down over 90 percent, global hazardous waste by over 40 percent, global greenhouse gas emissions by over 70 percent, and total energy use by over 5 percent. Tebo calls these "footprint reduction goals" and points out that they were able to calculate what DuPont had saved by keeping energy costs flat while production increased by 40 percent. The number was a stunning *$3 billion,* and it quickly was embraced by the media and began to appear everywhere in reports or discussions about the impact of going green. "A few simple numbers like that make the case very, very clearly," Tebo says. Interventions to reduce the internal carbon footprint carry a low risk—paybacks can be calculated in advance, and they represent real cash, not just an optimistic sales forecast for some new green product.

This became a virtuous, self-reinforcing cycle. The money DuPont saved could be reinvested in the innovative new options they viewed as most important. In 2005, the company extended their cost and risk reduction goals to 2015. These included:

- Further reduce greenhouse gas emissions by at least 15 percent from a 2004 base.
- Reduce water consumption by 30 percent at sites where freshwater supply is either scarce or stressed. For all other sites, hold water consumption flat.
- Ensure that 100 percent of DuPont's off-site fleet of cars and light trucks represent leading technologies for fuel efficiency and fossil fuel alternatives.
- Further reduce air carcinogens by at least 50 percent.
- Ensure that 100 percent of global manufacturing sites have successfully completed an independent third-party verification of the effectiveness of their environmental management goals and systems.

Demonstrating significant progress on reducing waste and emissions was crucial for external credibility, but seeing the numbers was equally powerful inside the company. Anything that reduces costs goes straight to the bottom line, improving competitive edge and reducing risks. It's also empowering: There is no need to convince customers or count on any outside forces. And as Tebo says, "It's a powerful motivator, particularly for younger employees today, to know your company is working in the right areas and doing the right things. Clearly, when you move from being a laggard to a leader, that's important to employees. The focus on sustainable growth and innovative products has built on this, creating a new level of excitement and commitment for everyone."

Reputation and Legitimacy: The Lower Right Quadrant

Reaching out beyond internal borders to engage outside stakeholders, including powerful community groups, NGOs, and regulators, is unusual for most companies. For a company such as DuPont, that type of engagement had often been defensive and combative. Tebo and many others, however, saw the need to reach out and talk with these groups, including Greenpeace, which had spent decades aggressively attacking the company.

In spite of some discomfort, Tebo defined this work as "an extraordinary learning opportunity" and sought advice on how to address the reduction challenges that had been set, as well as ideas about the future direction of the company. He went so far as to engage Paul Gilding, the former executive director of Greenpeace International, as a direct advisor. He eventually brought Gilding inside DuPont to meet with the CEO and other senior executives about sustainability issues. By engaging hundreds of "outsiders" such as Gilding, they eliminated destructive sparring and focused on simply fixing problems (especially environmental problems), creating shared goals for the future, and collaborating in the quest toward achieving them.

Real engagement with outsiders can be a cathartic experience for executives. Listening to many people with whom they don't usually interact and taking their input seriously are crucial to the process. But chief executive officers such as DuPont's current CEO, Chad Holliday, are starting to change their thinking and, as a result, see a very different landscape.

"The view of scientists locked away in a laboratory inventing something new and wonderful to spring on the world has given way to a market-back approach," says Holliday. "For innovation to be successfully introduced into the marketplace and accepted by society, it must be based on many forms of partnership and continuous dialogue with stakeholders, including governments, NGOs, and academia. Science and innovation that do not address pressing human needs will not advance sustainability. Likewise, a vision of sustainability detached from science and technology will not succeed. We need both the commitment to sustainability and the accomplishments of science."

The urgency of these revolutionary new partnerships can't be overstated. As Hart and Milstein point out, "Engaged diverse stakeholders are an essential source of feedback, direction, vision, and innovative new ideas."

"If you are thinking about addressing societal issues, that probably includes helping the 4 billion people in the world who are on the edge of survival meet their needs for protein and nutrition. There's no way the business community understands or knows that population," Tebo says. "Yet many local NGOs know it very well. Unless you have a way to reach these people, you really can't bring them the products and services that businesses can create."

In other words, even if a business such as DuPont wants to commit to sustainable practices, partnerships with non-governmental organizations are essential to make any real progress. Because of its sullied reputation, DuPont had to form these partnerships from scratch in most cases. And that proved to be difficult initially, given the inherent mistrust both sides had when they started. Many business executives are convinced that people who don't have profit-and-loss responsibility just can't understand the pressures companies, and the people who work inside them, are under. And people who work for government or non-profits just don't believe businesspeople have a serious commitment to improving the environment and addressing the needs of people in developing countries.

Nonetheless, companies are starting to realize that positive relationships with thought leaders in society can be extremely useful. In order for these relationships to bear meaningful fruit, NGOs must be involved in developing your business strategy. Engaging public groups is starting to become well accepted within modern multinational corporations. For Tebo, this activity is key. He believes it directly impacts a company's ability to innovate, reposition itself, and grow into the future.

Innovation and Repositioning: The Upper Left Quadrant

When a company begins to look toward the future, the shift in focus is transformational. DuPont, for example, is really reinventing itself for the second time—having already shifted from its origins as a maker of explosives to a petrochemical company. The next century will involve a focus on the combination of biotechnology and chemistry, as the company embraces organic chemistry and natural systems that mimic real life. These efforts to move from fossil fuels to biofuels and from chemical feedstocks to more natural materials represent a transformation of the highest order. Current chairman Chad Holliday refers to this as moving from synthetic systems to natural systems, toward the way nature does things. Moreover,

DuPont is focused on three "mega sustainability trends" that they believe will shape the markets of the future: the drive for renewable energy and materials, the demand for greater safety and security, and the need for increased food production.

Currently, DuPont makes eight of the products necessary for the manufacture of solar panels. It's also led the efforts on the Integrated Corn-Based Bioproducts Refinery, and along with BP is introducing biobutanol, a biofuel that has many advantages over ethanol as a gasoline substitute. Tyvek, one of its signature products, along with the newer AtticWrap helps consumers save enormous energy costs by improving the insulating capacity of buildings. Among the company's most recent innovations is a new polymer, Sorona, based on a starch found in the kernels of corn. It is being used to create carpet and to make cloth for apparel that is soft, durable, and absorbs color well.

One of DuPont's more ambitious goals is to double investment in R&D programs with direct, quantifiable environmental benefits for customers and consumers. There is a great deal of internal dialogue at DuPont about modeling its processes on natural systems. For example, scientists there have been working for years on trying to produce Kevlar by learning how silkworms make silk.

In order to create these ambitious, higher-value, higher-margin products, companies must collaborate with all the stakeholders identified in the "reputation and legitimacy" lower right quadrant—non-governmental organizations and local civic leaders—as well with other companies, large and small, to lay out investments over different time horizons.

Growth Path and Trajectory: The Upper Right Quadrant

A company's growth trajectory is what will propel it to create sustainable value and provide it with the ability to make a significant positive difference in the world.

It is here that companies ask questions like: "How are we going to bring our products and services to a larger world and shift our way of thinking about global social and environmental issues? How are we going to reach people who want and need to improve their quality of life and standard of living?" Many of the advancements pertaining to sustainability work to date have been achieved within manufacturing plants. But as companies reach out to new markets, they may realize that their products have far greater impact than their manufacturing facilities. At DuPont, for example, as part of a broad nature-inspired strategy, the company has set and publicized bold goals to be achieved by 2015. Among them, the company has promised to:

- Grow annual revenues by at least $2 billion from products that create energy efficiency and/or significant greenhouse gas reduction for customers.
- Nearly double revenues from non-depletable resources to at least $8 billion.

The ability to reach out to underserved populations—the 4 billion people who live on less than $4 per day—begins with products that meet basic human needs. DuPont is now fast on the track of introducing a wide variety of products and services that address basic Industrial Age imbalances in energy, food, water, and other areas.

These new products are essential to its growth strategy: DuPont recently announced a goal of achieving 35 percent of revenues from products introduced in the past five years—up from 20 percent—and many of those new products with the highest growth potential will be bio-based. Astute outside observers of DuPont's progress over time say it's unlikely the company will stop when they meet these goals; this is just the beginning. The introduction of new products at such a rapid rate is not surprising given the company's history of innovation; what is surprising is the approach the company is now taking. The shift to bio-based feedstocks, including crop and other waste streams, signals a dramatic change in their scientific focus from polymer chemistry to biology.

Through the work of catalysts such as Tebo and other passionate people inside DuPont, the commitment has clearly reached the executive suite and is transforming the core of the business.

"Sustainable growth is not a distant goal but an immediate reality," Holliday says. "For DuPont, 2015 begins today. Sustainable growth is about products and services we are working on right now. Our 2015 Sustainability Goals are our investment in the future of our business, the future of our customers, and the future of families around the world. They are also about the future of our planet—the one we live on today and the better, safer, and healthier planet we aspire to leave for tomorrow." The sustainability drivers create a whole set of unmet needs, and it is in this growth quadrant that leaders such as Holliday can set the strategies for meeting those needs.

Sustainable Growth as a High-Margin Strategy

For DuPont and many other companies, the sustainable value model is a useful tool to break sustainability issues into understandable, "actionable" areas. It broadens the concept of sustainability beyond the traditional view of environmental impact, risk, and cost reduction. It gives companies a way to see the benefits of making value creation through sustainability a central goal, not simply an add-on. The more quadrants a company chooses to build strategies in, the more stakeholder value is created. And it was an invaluable tool for bringing sustainable value onto the corporate agenda at DuPont. "Sustainable growth became adopted as the corporate mission," Tebo says. "Not the *sustainability* mission but the *core corporate mission* for DuPont for the twenty-first century."

One of the biggest challenges is to provide specific ways for every part of the company to embrace the mission. Everybody, after all, can figure out ways to reduce waste. But with sustainable growth, the challenge is more difficult. "How do you really orient your products and services to more closely match societal needs?" Tebo asks. Because this is still an emerging concept at so many companies, the effort is still considered a fringe activity performed by someone outside the core business. But in the long run, those who recognize the alignment between sustainability and value creation understand that sustainable growth is truly *a high-margin strategy*. If environmental and societal good come at the expense of a company's financial performance, then it is not practicing a sustainable business strategy. The sustainability effort has to provide an enhanced financial bottom line, and the way to do this is through increasing market share, reducing cost of product, and improving value for the customer.

Savvy CEOs such as DuPont's Holliday have made sure this future-facing work has not been relegated to the corporate extremities. "We never forget that we are a business and our first job is to create value for our shareholders," Holliday points out. "Sustainable growth means creating value for our shareholders and for society by developing products that the market demands—and which also are good for the environment and for the health, safety, and well-being of people everywhere. Many companies say that what's good for the environment can also be good for business. We have the view that what's good for business *must* be good for the environment and for people worldwide or you are not moving toward sustainable growth."

INVESTING IN THE FUTURE

Corporate giants such as DuPont are not the only organizations that are investing in the future. Venture capital (VC) trends in "above-the-line" investments have been posting remarkable growth rates in the last few years. Since VC typically provides financing for smaller, entrepreneurial enterprises, often at the start-up stage, it's natural to assume these external investments have little in common with the significant internal investments of large corporations. But venture capital has long been viewed as an important lead indicator of the future flows of mainstream capital investments, and frequently predicts rapid growth in entirely new sectors and industries. One of the unique talents of the best venture capitalists is to spot high-growth industries—such as telecom, semiconductors, and biotech—early. So it's not surprising to learn about the emergence of "cleantech VC," a category that was barely visible in 2001.

The Cleantech Venture Network was instrumental in defining this investment category and acting as a catalyst for its growth. Now part of the Cleantech Group, it was launched in 2001, in the early days of investing in "clean technology." Co-founder Nicholas Parker had experience investing in environmental funds in the 1990s but was concerned about where a lot of the money was going. "I particularly disliked that the more pollution that occurred, the more money there was to be made in that industry," he says. "The more soil that was contaminated, the more remediation projects there were. The more coal-fired plants built, the more scrubbers had to be put on smokestacks. I didn't want to be part of that; I wanted to leapfrog past it."

With partner Keith Raab, Parker decided to build a "community of entrepreneurs and their financial backers" who could learn together how to grow businesses in these rapidly growing markets. They started by collecting data that had never been organized—showing, for example, that, in 2002, 4 percent to 5 percent of venture capital flows were already going into cleantech investments, and that many of these investments were being made by large and reputable companies such as Intel and Coca-Cola. Then they organized large forums bringing investors and entrepreneurs together, created a membership service so people could get online access to deal flows, and put information packages together for large pension funds to show that investing in this category made sense.

Since then, VC investments in cleantech have been growing at an annual rate of over 50 percent, the highest growth rate of all investment categories. And momentum continues to build: VC investments in cleantech companies more than doubled in the fourth quarter of 2007 compared to the fourth quarter of 2006. From its small beginnings, the Cleantech Venture Network has grown to a membership organization of 8,000 cleantech investors, 9,500 companies and professional services organizations worldwide, and a core group of 1,300 elite members with assets exceeding $6 trillion. They include venture capital firms, investment banks, governments, and major corporations.[5]

From Mercenaries to Missionaries

Now many of the most credible, successful leaders in the venture capital field are calling cleantech the greatest investment opportunity in the twenty-first century. These include John Doerr of Kleiner Perkins, one of Silicon Valley's most respected and influential figures; Vinod Khosla, founding CEO of Sun Microsystems; Steve Case, co-founder of AOL; and

Richard Branson of the Virgin Group. As Parker points out, "Whether you are a missionary or a mercenary, there is room for everyone here. People who come in for mercenary reasons end up as missionaries, because they can't help but get informed about the bigger issues."

Yet venture capital is now a small part of a much larger influx of mainstream investment capital into cleantech; pension funds such as CalPERS, insurers including Swiss Re and AIG, and major investment bankers such as Goldman Sachs, JPMorgan Chase, and Citigroup are all building multibillion-dollar portfolios.

And increasingly, connections are building between small companies and large ones. The Cleantech Venture Network has formed explicit "accelerator projects" with Wal-Mart and Microsoft to encourage small firms to bring forward innovative cleantech solutions. But for almost all large companies, participating in venture capital networks can be a window on innovation that they otherwise wouldn't have. Many are coming to realize they can't innovate their way out of unsustainable boxes; they need access to new technologies, business models, and market opportunities. Moreover, big companies bring more than just money to the table: things such as large-scale market access, logistics, a big fleet of vehicles, a regional or global set of plants, or refineries that they want to clean up and redesign.

Big and Small Can Work Together to Provoke Innovation

General Electric, the $173 billion global conglomerate, is just one example of a large firm proactively exploring this synergy with smaller entrepreneurial companies. GE Energy Financial Services, a capital and financing division of GE, announced in early 2008 that it had raised its 2010 renewable energy investing target by 50 percent to $6 billion, a major acceleration of a previously announced target of $4 billion.

It's notable that many of the investments from GE Energy Financial are for projects that don't use GE wind turbines or other GE equipment. They have recently invested directly in other companies for projects in solar, landfill gas, electricity grid efficiency, and lithium-ion batteries. Their placement of capital in a wide range of small and midsized companies is clearly improving the growth prospects for the entire renewable energy and cleantech sector.

This business unit of GE crossed the $3 billion mark in early 2008 with its single highest-value wind deal, a $300 million investment in wind projects spanning four U.S. states—Oregon, Minnesota, Illinois, and Texas. By 2010 the company expects clean investments will comprise 20–25 percent of its overall energy and water portfolio, up from about 10 percent in 2006.

GE'S INVESTMENTS IN THE FUTURE

In addition to these external capital commitments to other growing companies, GE has also been successful at developing an internal culture that bears some important similarities to the "vibrant, creative community" that Nicholas Parker sees building among entrepreneurs and investors in the cleantech venture capital field. Mark Little, GE's director of global research and development, describes it this way: "In the 26 years I have been at this company, there has never been a more exciting time to be at GE. The kind of impact our innovations could have on the well-being of the planet is vast and incredibly motivating—I can't tell you what that does for the morale of our engineers, marketers, financers, and leadership team. . . . These technological moves are big, they're expensive, and they take being able to make some mistakes and being able to recover from them. This is not for the faint of heart. It requires staying power."[6]

His comment raises an important question about the source of this staying power and how GE started down this path. The answer lies in embracing a new way of thinking about investments in innovation and growth.

GE's CEO, Jeff Immelt, does an annual strategic review of every business in the company—the products they're funding, how each will fit into the market, and how that market is going to grow and change. In some cases, this means redefining the market. What he observed, beginning in 2003, was that every one of the businesses had an emerging imperative from their customers to improve efficiencies and reduce emissions. This was true for GE's big infrastructure businesses such as energy, water, aviation, and rail, as well as its appliance and lighting businesses—there were no exceptions. As fuel prices were starting to rise, so too did interest in alternative energy.

A New Way of Thinking Emerges

Lorraine Bolsinger, VP of GE's ecomagination initiative, describes what happened this way: "Jeff's a student of all kinds of trends, and saw the importance of thinking about these issues very differently. Our chief marketing officer at the time, Beth Comstock, was also a very keen observer of trends. She did a lot of work bringing outside firms in—which was a first for us—to talk about megatrends: everything from demographics and changing population trends, energy, water scarcity, to the building of megacities. We began to think differently about these issues, and not just read about them in *Newsweek*. We brought experts in to talk to our marketing people, our product leaders across the company, and leaders of our global research centers. We began to redefine our long-range strategic planning, particularly resource scarcity. We asked ourselves, 'What if we actually used this as a rallying cry to our colleagues within the company to think creatively about this, to be able to use it as an inspiration for new product ideas, because we know these trends are coming?'"

To validate this internal rethinking, leaders from the company saw the importance of listening to all parts of the larger community surrounding GE, including customers. They hosted a number of two-day "dreaming sessions"—asking customers where they thought their industries were going to go and what they and their own customers would want well into the future. Given that many of these customers were making twenty-, thirty-, and forty-year decisions, GE leaders challenged them to think about what their world was going to look like in 2015 and well beyond that. They also met with governments and NGOs to ask how they saw future regulations and legislation evolving and how they could work together to align GE's interest in innovation and growth with their interest in reducing environmental footprints.

Bolsinger points to one of the most powerful forces they saw in their rethinking of the future: "We saw early on—and still see—that the trend with the biggest impact is economic growth in the emerging markets, in the emerging economies of the developing world. Trends will have the most impact in those markets because they're big, they're growing fast, and they need solutions quickly. We see it as crucial to get the future technology out there. If it doesn't get deployed right now, that means they continue to buy older technology; that just proliferates the amount of greenhouse gas emissions, energy consumption, and environmental contamination. If we can't forestall the continued use of old dirty technology, then we're going to get more of what we already have."

A Commitment to Investing in the Future

As their internal rethinking process and the feedback from external stakeholders around the world came together, GE developed the confidence to launch their bold ecomagination initiative. The four commitments that frame this initiative match the four quadrants of the sustainable value matrix. Their first two address the "below-the-line" quadrants—reducing their internal greenhouse gas footprint while growing, and maintaining proactive communications with all external stakeholders. Their second two commitments focus on innovation and their growth trajectory—the "above-the-line" quadrants.

Launched in May 2005, ecomagination is GE's company-wide platform to "imagine and build innovative technologies to help customers solve their toughest environmental problems." It is based on the belief that "financial and environmental performance can come together to drive GE's growth, while taking on some of the world's biggest challenges." Now in its third year, GE's ecomagination portfolio has grown from seventeen to more than sixty energy-efficient and environmentally advantageous products and services. Their offerings include renewable energy (wind, solar, biomass, and geothermal); high-efficiency power generation (including advanced gasification systems that support carbon capture and storage); next-generation jet engines for aviation and hybrid systems for locomotives, buses, and other vehicles; advanced lighting systems such as organic light-emitting diodes (OLEDs); and solutions for water use, purification, and reuse around the world.

GE invested $1 billion in cleaner technology research and development in 2007 and plans to invest $1.5 billion annually in ecomagination R&D by 2010, more than doubling their baseline annual investment. R&D investment in sustainable products, one of four areas GE committed to focusing on in 2005, has reached a total of more than $2.5 billion since the program's inception.

And they are well on their way to overshooting their initial growth target, which was to double revenues to $20 billion by 2010. Revenues reached $14 billion in 2007, and their total orders and commitments since launch had soared past $70 billion by the first quarter of 2008. The company continues to demonstrate that they understand the powerful reinforcing cycle between innovation and growth—the two most enduring dimensions of GE's corporate DNA—to ensure that they are well positioned in the present and for the future.

[10]

Getting People Engaged

The preceding chapters told the stories of many organizations and people who have made a difference in moving us toward life beyond the Bubble. The chapters that follow are intended to help you, the reader, focus on creating your story: the story that, in effect, you are about to write as you go into the world to act. Since everyone takes action in their own setting or context, we have written the next chapters to help you tailor your actions to your unique situation. We don't pretend that the ideas, tools, and methods we offer are anywhere near comprehensive, so we often point you to other resources to help you learn as you go forward.[1]

Taking the next steps, at whatever level, puts you in the company of many other passionate change agents around the world. Like them, you know something needs to be done, and you are willing to devote time and attention to doing it. You know that to make progress you need to be resourceful and open-minded, draw methods from different ideas, and look for allies and capabilities wherever you can find them. You probably know some of the things that need to be done. But you do not know them all. How could you? What you are about to undertake has probably never been done before, certainly not in exactly the same way or under the exact same circumstances. But like others before you, you will discover much of the plot as you invent it, which is what will make this story—your story—exciting.

While learning how to live beyond the Bubble involves changes at many levels—within organizations, larger networks of organizations, and society at large—it always starts with how we talk with one another. Often, unfortunately, it ends there as well. The following hypothetical story, set in a business context, mirrors conversational patterns that recur in organizations and groups of all sorts when people encounter profoundly different realities and find themselves, naturally, holding very different opinions about them. What seems obvious to one person is far from it for another, and one group's urgent necessities present questionable premises for others. Given the immense uncertainties and risks involved, the only thing surprising about such communication breakdowns is that we still *view* them as surprising. Sustainability innovators can ill afford to be unprepared or unskillful when it comes to fostering engaging conversations that build mutual understanding and the ability to work together.

THE FIRST CONVERSATION

Imagine for a moment that you are the CFO of a major electric utility that is rapidly expanding into a global company, with important investments in developing countries. You are attending a management team meeting early Monday morning. During a relatively routine discussion on the last agenda item about next year's capital budget for the company's coal-, oil-, and gas-fired generating facilities, this heated skirmish occurs:

> **Ted** *(VP, Environment, Health, and Safety):* "I think this is the year we need to completely rethink our approach to capital budgets. It's becoming increasingly clear to me that global oil and gas production is going to peak and begin to decline within the next five years. This heightens the risk of major disruptions in supply, and rapidly escalating prices for oil, gas, coal, uranium and all other conventional fuels. We're not really prepared for this. We'll have to swing at least 30 percent of our future capital allocations to renewables, beginning next year, or else we're taking a big chance."

Joanne *(VP, Operations)*: "But there's still plenty of coal, and break-throughs in technologies for oil and gas exploration and clean-burning coal will surely extend the lifetime of these fuels. We've seen oil and gas prices go up before, but that doesn't mean that demand disappears. The world will be living off fossil fuels for a long time. Plus, oil was half its current price only two years ago. Price fluctuations are inevitable in this business and can be devastating to companies that make risky bets—"

Stan *(VP, Public Affairs)* (interrupting Joanne): "But even with ample supplies of coal, oil, and gas, we may still get clobbered by carbon taxes in many of our markets. Public pressure for action on climate change is growing exponentially around the world. And pollution from coal-fired power plants in China is causing riots and widespread social unrest. I know they're doing all this work on clean coal, but the country is expanding so fast, I wonder how much real impact it will have. With the international pressures mounting, I wonder if there won't be more unrest and challenges in other places."

Robert *(CEO)*: "Energy has always been about politics, and the politics today are very complex. Sure, politicians are stumbling all over themselves to appear as if they're doing something about climate change, but one more terrorist incident and they'll also be doing everything possible to assure people that our energy supplies are secure. We may find ourselves with major new markets for coal gasification and generating liquid fuels to replace imported gasoline. Given the time horizon of our commitments and responsibilities, we can't let ourselves overreact to media attention on just one issue. I have had issues like this come and go many times in my career here. Don't get me wrong, I think climate change is important, but the market and political signals are still very mixed. When it dawns on people that government policies that overreact to climate change will damage our economy and global competitiveness, they'll think more broadly about keeping all our options on the table. I agree with Joanne—I don't believe there is any way we are going to run out of coal, or oil and gas for that matter, in our lifetimes. I think it may be premature to worry about radical shifts in our strategy until the market signals are clearer."

Anthony *(VP, Strategy)*: "Robert, I respect your opinions about the politics of climate change and the supply of fossil fuels, but what are the implications for the future of our company if you are wrong on one or both of these issues?"

Robert *(CEO)*: "I don't think I'm wrong, but I'm certain I'm late for my next meeting. It sounds like these issues warrant further discussion by us here, but it will have to be at another time."

As others get up and leave, you reflect on this conversation. You ask yourself, "How could I intervene effectively here so that our whole team can address the uneasiness that many of us feel about the issue?" You know that several other members of the team have voiced similar fears outside of your meetings, but there is no forum to raise them together.

The Perils of Advocacy

As we noted in the previous chapter, sustainability is rarely incorporated into the heart of most companies' business strategies. But why? Clues can be found in the management team's exchange. Both Ted and Stan set the course of the conversation by predicting and advocating that specific driving forces (peak oil production and climate change) are going to cause big problems for the company in the future. They attempted to convince the others that the team should agree to a big financial bet based on their personal convictions, and take immediate action. Joanne and Robert argued for very different predictions about the future. Neither side inquired into why the others saw the future differently.

Conflicts like this arise frequently when discussing strategy, but they are especially pernicious around emotionally charged issues such as sustainability. People who believe strongly in the need to address sustainability issues often unleash their pent-up energy in direct attempts to convince others of their views. They predict dire consequences unless there is a significant change in course. They forcefully advocate for their preferred strategies—often "big bets" based on their own assumptions about the future. They might call for investing in new technologies, building new production facilities, developing materials or processes that would leave a smaller environmental footprint, entering new markets, or initiating "green" marketing campaigns to try to force a commitment from the rest of the enterprise or industry. Their intent is to provoke immediate and large-scale change. But that rarely happens. Instead, senior leaders discount dire predictions and resist making any significant changes. Often they won't even make a small bet on an exploratory pilot venture. And more important, the advocates have missed an opportunity to engage in meaningful conversation about the future with people in key leadership positions.

Although this example was inspired by management team exchanges we have lived through, similar conversations play out in all kinds of teams, whether inside companies, government agencies, or non-profit organizations—and not just at the senior management level. Just like the impasse this group reached, the issues are real and the intensity of the arguments is increasing. As we said earlier, stakeholders now expect their organization to do the *right* thing, not just something. But new strategies require new conversations, and chances are you have participated in a meeting similar to the one above—whether about climate change or another significant issue—and left feeling frustrated. Most people already know (or think they know) how each individual in a conversation feels. What they don't know is how to help people shift their views and feelings.

Getting Unstuck

The result is that people tend to get stuck into one position or another. Some are cast as advocates. Having read about the challenge of climate change, they feel it is their responsibility to raise questions. They may even have a sense of moral imperative— if they do not get their organization to shift direction, this represents a personal failure on their part. Therefore, they become perennial advocates. Chances are the company in this story has not heard the last of Ted on this subject. He will raise it again and again, and the more resistance and opposition he receives, the harder he may push.

Nor has the company heard the last of Joanne. If Ted is an advocate, then Joanne from operations is an "opposer"—someone cast in the role of saying no on behalf of the larger firm. People like Joanne are usually passionate opposers because they feel they must protect something that would otherwise be rendered vulnerable—the company's profitability, its financial stability, or even the livelihood of its employees. If Joanne falters, she might reasonably wonder—especially if Robert, the CEO, changes his mind—who will look out for the firm's existing business.

Conversations like this can easily polarize. The harder the advocate pushes, the more diligent the opposition. Some, like Stan from public affairs, may join one or the other camp. As Joanne pushes back, Ted and Stan will become only more stubborn and more convinced that they are right. "They just don't get it," Ted and Stan will say to themselves. Meanwhile, Robert the CEO and Joanne (and others) may come to see Ted and Stan as one-issue advocates who have lost their perspective and who are no longer looking out for the welfare of the business as a whole. "They're acting like a cult!" the CEO may say to himself. Ted and Stan, for their part, may perceive that the whole problem lies with the CEO: "He just doesn't see the big picture." Their job, as they see it, is to convince the opposition.

Meanwhile, others find themselves caught in a dilemma of either getting drawn into the shouting match or withdrawing. But there is another option, one that occurs far too rarely. If you look back at the exchange, the most crucial part of this conversation may have been the question that Anthony, the strategy VP, voiced: "If Robert is wrong, what are the implications for the future of our company?" This is an example of neither advocating nor opposing but asking a *genuine question* that could lead to fresh perspectives on the issues. Such actions, though simple, can bring crucial balance to the debate.

That question, and the CEO's willingness to come back to the conversation later, are valuable inflection points that many miss—they're an opportunity to begin a very different dialogue. You don't have to believe that catastrophic climate change is inevitable to find Anthony's question meaningful—you simply have to believe the risks are plausible and inquire into the implications together with others. And you have to be willing to look for the opportunities that it might create, to anticipate the kinds of capabilities that could be gained as you pursue those opportunities, as well as the ways in which the enterprise could thrive as a result. (See "The Four-Player Model Toolbox" on page 276 for more on productive team conversation.)

Developing teams that can think together more productively is not a marginal issue; too often the so-called "soft stuff" of business, such as deeper listening skills and consciously shifting perspectives on issues, seems to matter less than "hard" investments and organizational strategies. But working together effectively is essential to meeting hard goals. As we have seen in the stories in Part II, it's crucial to build effective teams and larger leadership groups, often incorporating members of other organizations and communities. Individuals simply operate at too small a scale. But individuals can move companies and organizations, and even larger communities, if they join in creating inspired teams or groups as the starting point.

How, then, can you act effectively in your unique situation—here and now—to help move your organization forward in this crucial effort?

BECOMING AN ANIMATEUR: YOUR ROLE AS A LEADER

Over the last twenty-five years, the field of organizational learning has consisted largely of people trying to find and test answers to questions such as these, drawing on a wide range of ideas, tools, and experience. In the next few parts of the book, you will be able to explore some of the ways that people have applied those tools in the service of sustainability.

The suggestions that follow are not only for those in leadership positions but also for those who may be starting from zero, with no particular position of authority at this moment, at least not in relation to the organizations or groups they seek to influence. These steps can be taken by those in companies, non-governmental organizations, governmental agencies, or communities as well as by those looking to switch sectors: people working in business who see themselves at an NGO five years from now, and those who have moved from government to private enterprise. But all of them, no matter what they are doing now or where they are going, have one thing in common. They all want to get results: to help move the world's industrial system past the limits of the Bubble, and thus to help build a sustainable future.

The French word for people who seek to create systemic change in this manner is *animateur*. An animateur (from the root *animer*) is someone who "brings to life" a new way of thinking, seeing, or interacting that creates focus and energy. While few non-French-speakers may be familiar with this word, in fact it expresses the essence of leadership. Leadership is strongly associated with inspiration, but few appreciate how important that association is. *Inspire*—from the Latin root *inspirare*—means "to breathe life into." In this sense, leadership is inspiration, the creation of new life and energy in organizations.

Animateurs are professionals who create revolutions that legitimize the kind of thinking and acting needed to live beyond the Bubble. They do so by making that behavior part of their daily routine. Conversations and actions become more productive. As animateurs deal with practical problems, accomplish tangible goals, and reflect on the results, people move from concept to action. Doing so builds confidence and a stronger sense of purpose that's not bogged down by self-importance. Often it is only when people look back, when the larger scope of their journey is evident, that they see just how deep and far-reaching their achievements have been and how much they have developed personally on the journey.

Animateurs also learn to step into the shoes of others—to recognize and comprehend the reasons others feel strongly about particular views and goals—without getting stuck in their own (or someone else's) perspective. For example, consider the challenge facing Ted and Stan, the advocates for change in the electric utility company management team conversation. It would be very easy for them to respond to their CEO, Robert, with feelings of frustration and determination: "He is blocking us, and we have to convince him somehow." Those feelings would tend to lead them to push their case harder, to try to get Robert to change his mind, and to enlist others in the company in persuading him—or else to give up, abandon hope of change, and perhaps even look for another job (the classic fight-or-flight instincts programmed in us all).

But if Ted and Stan could bring themselves to stand in the shoes of the other people in the room—particularly Robert and Joanne—and understand their points of view and assumptions, then they might respond differently. For example, they might learn that there is, in fact, a back story that underlies Robert's attitudes. After all, he has had an exemplary thirty-year career with the company. Perhaps one of the reasons his decade as CEO was one of the most successful in the eighty-year history of the company was that he maintained a steady course when others overreacted. Maybe he succeeded by insisting that the company focus on one best prediction of the future, ignoring the noise of other variables and forces that distract people from "driving the business forward for growth."

If that's the case, then the views that Robert expressed at this meeting are consistent with his personal beliefs, assumptions, and experience. His worldview is made up of variables with which he is familiar and comfortable. He has high confidence in his ability to control his company's future. The way to reach him, and others in this organization, is not to challenge his views but to find questions that he is ready to ask, as Anthony did at the end: Has the world changed since he formed his views? Is his confidence as well founded now as it was in the past?

This type of inquiry starts with the recognition that no one has the full picture. Ted and Stan need to embrace the possibility that they are only seeing one slice of the possible future, and that Joanne and Robert see other important dimensions. At the same time, Robert's strategy may involve far greater risks than he realizes. Can anyone dispassionately present the risks and uncertainties in a way that makes the underlying complexity clearer? Yes, and developing that capability is essential to progress.

As Ted, Stan, the CEO, and others learn how to work with their team on their shared future, in a very real sense they will be breathing life into a part of the organization that had been, if not lifeless, at least dormant until now.

FIRST STEPS TOWARD IMPROVING DIALOGUE

Based on the experience of successful animateurs and leaders in a wide range of roles, here is a summary of the steps that you can take if you want to fundamentally improve the dialogue in your organization. You may change the order to fit your unique situation, but take note of the overall evolution and avoid jumping ahead too quickly.

1. Do some personal reflection to determine which sustainability issues are most central to you, and create a rough prioritization of these issues based on what you personally think is most important. Once you've decided which of the steps below you want to take, let your boss know and get his or her support.

2. Choose a few other like-minded people to talk with, people who you believe may have similar concerns. As you have these initial conversations, discuss whom else you might talk to, and add them to your list.

3. Based on these one-on-one discussions, choose and convene an informal team that has some common concerns, a diversity of perspectives on the issues, and a desire to act. Ask for support from your manager and other managers/executives for the time you think you will need to do this work—assure them some of this work will be done on your own time.

4. Think of your informal team as an advance "scouting party" working to explore issues, develop your aspirations, and create a proposed plan for change. Strive for a balance of perspectives that take both the present and the future into account, those that are both practical and strategic.

5. Develop an initial draft of a case for change to take to your management team (whether for the whole organization or just for your business unit/division) and a proposed plan for how that team could become fully engaged in the dialogue. This helps to connect the work of your team to the whole of the organization in the most productive way. Plan to meet

with the management team within a month or two of your informal team's first meeting—or longer, if necessary, to fit with the normal cycle of meetings of the management team.

Making Your Role Productive

How these steps play out depends on the different types of settings in which you might find yourself, what your role is, and how well you connect with others. Understanding how these leadership roles relate to one another in a web of interdependence will help you establish and sustain an open, generative stance—here different people can lead in different ways and complement each other. Leaders are people who "walk ahead" and are committed to making deep changes in themselves and in their organizations. They naturally influence others through their credibility, capability, and commitment. And they have different responsibilities, titles, and areas of expertise. The following four kinds of leaders are especially essential when it comes to tackling sustainability issues: local line leaders, internal network leaders, managers of specialist functions, and executive leaders.

1. **Local line leaders.** Virtually all successful change initiatives involve imaginative, committed local line leaders—plant managers, engineering team leaders, or sales or regional managers—people who are accountable for results and who possess sufficient authority to make changes in the way that work is carried out and priorities are set at the local level. Their reach may be limited to a small team of direct reports, or they may manage a few thousand people. Such leaders are vital because they, along with their colleagues, can invent, commission, and support meaningful organizational experiments to test the practical impact of new ideas and approaches.

2. **Internal network leaders and community builders.** Internal networkers may include staff members, consultants, or those in training or management development departments. These leaders may also be front-line people in sales, marketing, production, or engineering positions. Internal networks serve as a natural counterbalance to local leadership, where the focus will be much narrower and more provincial. The strength

of these network leaders is their ability to move about the larger organization, nurture broader alliances with other like-minded individuals, and put local line leaders in contact with others who share their passions and who can teach them and help them to innovate. It is often their connection to the informal social networks of the organization, combined with their lack of hierarchical authority, that makes internal network leaders effective.

3. **Managers of specialist functions with the capability to initiate or work with key cross-organizational processes.** Many managers of functional groups (such as strategy; environment, health, and safety; or organizational development) have the opportunity to convene a group of people from many areas of the larger business to begin the process of thinking freshly about strategy. For example, such managers can often influence the agenda of meetings and forums in which managers and executives consider potential alternative futures and the risks and opportunities inherent in each. These functional initiatives often involve young next-generation leaders, which can be critical for the long term success of your initiatives.

4. **Executive leaders.** In outlining the above roles, we don't mean to imply that executive management is unimportant. If anything, leadership at the executive level is more essential today than ever before, as the changes that organizations must confront are long-term and deep. They will require fundamental shifts in the assumptions and norms of the past, and a rethinking of conventional strategies, structures, and practices. Leaders must become capable of asking questions that do not have easy answers. And they must realize they cannot do this alone.

Take Stock Personally

A good place to begin is to build your own awareness of the situation around you and your role in it. What are some of the issues that bother you, or some things that you would like to change? What keeps surfacing when you ask what's important to you, and where do you want to direct your energy? Reflect on the issues and concerns that you have, and think about how they relate to your organization. What are the points of connection between what you care about and what your organization does?

If you feel irritation, impatience, or discomfort with any of these issues, give yourself permission to rant. But also tell the truth. Turn the irritation into a rough initial positive statement of what you want—such a mandate may be useful later. For instance, your frustration with "the unbelievable amount of stuff we throw out" could be turned into a desire to "reduce solid waste 80 percent in two years and fully implement a lean manufacturing system." Do some broad scanning and diagnostic work around your organization or industry related to what bugs you and look for links to the organization's issues, goals, and imperatives. Assess your role and your connections to these issues, based on your exploration thus far. Are you in a line role directly connected to these issues? A support role? A consulting role?

How much freedom do you have, given your existing accountabilities, to further explore these issues? How much are you prepared to do on your own time if you don't have time at work?

As you gain clarity, your aspirations will grow: You will become more and more focused on what you want to accomplish and why that change is necessary. When you have some initial idea regarding what you are trying to create, then you can begin to see who your initial collaborators might be, and what actions can be taken to move toward your goals. Of course, all this may change as you begin talking with others, so stay open to that possibility, and don't spend too long thinking about these issues alone—it's easy to feel overwhelmed.

FORMING YOUR INITIAL TEAM

Richard Beckhard, one of the founders of the organizational development field, used to say, "One person seeking to change an organization will get killed; it doesn't matter what position the person is in. Two can commiserate. Three can become a full-fledged conspiracy." Making a case for change within an organization is extremely difficult to do alone, regardless of your seniority or influence. For something as big and complex as sustainability, making the effort a team exercise is crucial. You can begin by searching for like-minded people in the organization who share your concerns and are also seeking to make a case for change.

For example, if you work in marketing, consider ways to bring in people from R&D, operations, finance, production, sales, and strategy. Who else might be interested in the same goals and actions that you are? If you work in customer support, could some of your most progressive customers become allies and help provoke the interest of your boss? Do you know people in new-product development who share your outlook and would talk to your customers about their unmet needs?

Anticipate whom you will need to engage in your internal marketing initiatives before responding to current customers or reaching new customers. Leaders of new-product teams in world-class marketing organizations such as Procter and Gamble have demonstrated the power of this tactic for decades. They have built their success on brand and product leaders who can enroll and inspire the entire "supply chain" within their company to successfully create and launch a new product—taking it all the way from a vague concept through R&D, prototyping, manufacturing, and test markets to earning a substantial market share.

If you were the CFO who listened silently to that conversation on pages 141–43, you might seek out Ted and Anthony, both proponents of action on the company's part, and enlist them in your plan. It may be worth including the vice president of communication in this group as well. Consider meeting one-on-one with each of them initially to have a brief conversation, establish some common ground, translate your frustration and theirs into larger visions and goals, and build a case for change. And of course your team would want to reach out to all the other members of the executive team and draw out their issues and concerns fully.

Already, you can probably create a list in your mind of a potential team. As soon as you begin talking about what matters to you, you will probably attract people who have real energy and commitment. They may not be inspired by the exact same issues, but as you listen and inquire into their interests and concerns, you will immediately begin to fill in a broader picture of the system you are members of. This shared discovery can form the basis for early alignment around bold changes.

Keep in mind that people don't need to agree on everything when they

meet; a broad goal, interest, or point of common frustration is often sufficient. Indeed, disagreements can help generate energy and momentum
if you talk openly. The conversations that take place among your team
members may be the first ones in your organization in which a number of
difficult but essential questions and issues come to the surface in a productive way. It is very helpful to think of your small group as a "container"—a group of people who consciously set themselves up to unearth
and address the unresolved tensions that inevitably exist in the larger system. If your organization is going to change its ways of operating, you will
most certainly encounter disagreements.

Such partnerships start to model the kind of collaborative leadership
that will be foundational going forward. Though the numbers involved
will almost always grow over time to include a broader cross section of
players, your initial meetings with a circle of partners is a key first stage.
Your team can serve as a model for the kind of working environment in
which people raise difficult issues without getting stopped by anger, cynicism, or conflicting passions—not by pretending these strong emotions
don't exist but by acknowledging and moving past them.

Regardless of how long it takes, soon you will find yourself connecting
people from a variety of backgrounds and groups. Many of them will neither know nor necessarily trust one another initially. Even if your team
consists of people from a single organization or department, they should
be sufficiently diverse in terms of experiences and points of view. Even
though the group might be relatively large, they will need to get to know
and appreciate one another over time, and recognize not only that they
can depend upon one another but that they must do so in order to be successful. The foundational learning capacities we discuss throughout the
book—understanding systems, working collaboratively, and fostering individual and collective aspiration—will be crucial in this process.

PUT YOUR ASPIRATIONS ON THE TABLE

Nothing will happen unless you and your team have a clear sense of the
importance of what you are doing, even if all you begin with is a broad,
high-level vision.

The high-level vision of the founders of the U.S. Green Building Council, for example, was to transform the building industry. And the initiators of new endeavors in BP, GE, DuPont, and Alcoa talked of leading their respective companies through the next wave of change, eventually redefining the boundaries—as well as inventing a compelling new future—for their industries.

Make time early on to look ahead together, perhaps with a time frame of twenty-five years in mind so that you are unconstrained by present-day realities. What would you like to have accomplished by then? What might your sustainable subsystem look like? How would it be aligned with natural systems? Share the collective hopes that led you to start talking together in the first place.

Be patient with your initial vision. Your aspirations will change—indeed, some of the specific practices of organizational learning will help them deepen and evolve. Truly shared visions are a continual work in process. They get stronger and more powerful, and a reinforcing process starts to take root—as you create more visions, you'll simultaneously get better at assessing the current reality, taking action, and reflecting on progress, all the while building stronger relationships with your collaborators through each part of this cycle.

Among other benefits, articulating an initial vision will help you attract more people. As Lorraine Bolsinger, the vice president in charge of GE's ecomagination initiative, puts it: "People are flocking to work on these kinds of issues for two reasons. First, very smart, technical people often have a bias toward environmentalism and sustainability. Their intellectual curiosity and problem-solving nature predispose them to solving issues on multiple fronts: environmental, technical, societal, and economic. That's their nature. They care about the world and see the longer-term interdependencies. Second, they relish the opportunity to work on the most advanced technology. They're naturally drawn to doing this work."

You may not get representatives of every part of the system to join you at first, but proceed with this end in mind. As your small team meets, consider together whom you can invite to join. Who can contribute to building a "chain of influence" to those people you will want to engage in later decisions? For example, if you realize that in order to make progress, there will need to be changes in plants and equipment in the future, then you will want to enroll someone in finance who works on capital budgeting. Ask that new team member to help you anticipate the chains of influence to your CFO and the VP of Operations, as both of them will be key decision makers in approving capital expenditures for plant and equipment. You'll also want to engage someone from Sales and Marketing, as that group may be the first to see new market segments, create pull for new products, and enroll key players from Finance, R&D, and Production.

MOVING FORWARD

At some point your core team will become fairly stable, and team members will begin to build good working relationships with each other. As you continue to hone your ideas and your understanding of what it will take to realize your goals, you'll naturally shift your focus to coming up with effective ways of communicating with the rest of your organization. Building your case for change will be a constant balancing act between creating new ideas and engaging the essential players in your organization who can make them happen.

[11]

Building Your Case for Change

n Chapter 9, we introduced the sustainable value matrix and used it to make sense of how one company, DuPont, charted their course into life beyond the Bubble. By using the sustainable value matrix, your team can plot your own organization's issues and opportunities. This tool can help you see new potential pathways for innovation while you're simultaneously addressing pressing current issues.

As explained earlier, the matrix also helps to frame issues in ways that allow senior management teams and company boards to make decisions that preserve the financial value of the company and the "sustainability" of that value over time. Senior leaders, after all, have a stake in this kind of value creation. If your team attempts to engage these leaders with focused advocacy about the environment or social responsibility, they will tend to see such issues as a narrow slice of the future—and, traditionally, one that is only marginally relevant to the core of the business and its viability. Their beliefs that these issues should be delegated to specialists who will "take care of them and keep them out of our hair so we can get on with business" reinforce this perception.

You may recall from Chapter 9 that the matrix introduced four sets of "drivers" or forces related to global sustainability. A first set relates to increasing pollution, material consumption, and waste. Focusing on this lower left quadrant means looking at how addressing these issues today reduces costs and risk. The drivers in the lower right quadrant relate to the growing number of civil stakeholders who are quick to hold organizations responsible for their actions in an increasingly transparent world. The top left quadrant focuses on new emerging technologies that challenge an organization to innovate and reposition itself as it develops sustainable competencies for the future. And the top right quadrant focuses on increasing global and local pressures that require including both global sustainability issues like climate change, resource depletion, and the growing imbalances between the rich and the poor, as well as how companies can find growth, opportunities, and a sustainable vision while addressing these global issues.

Once your initial team is formed, you can map out the quadrants where your collective frustrations and goals for change best fit. Learning how to place different initiatives in these four quadrants can help you make the connection between sustainable practices and your company's goals. Doing so can also guide you to the right partners throughout your organization, those who have a stake in these issues.

Many start and build momentum through waste-reduction initiatives aimed at the lower left quadrant of the matrix. People are often frustrated initially with the amount of waste in the system and want to reduce energy use and related emissions, such as greenhouse gases. This can be an ideal starting point. Once the wastes are made more visible, many people can be actively engaged in reducing them, and cutting costs as they do. Actions in this quadrant are often both practical and symbolic: practical because they cut costs and wastes, and symbolic because they are visible and send a signal that the organization is committed to reducing its own internal footprint. Significant cuts in energy use reduce not only greenhouse gases but costs as well. And the cash from reduced costs can be used to fund investments for the future.

Fred Ware, of the famous Canadian retailer Hudson's Bay Company (HBC), began his work to dramatically cut wastes with a quiet start in 2001, when he conducted an audit of all the waste at their corporate headquarters in order to make everyone aware of how much waste they were creating.[1] At the time, he summarized the current situation this way: "It's disgusting how much stuff we throw away. As a society, it is unsustainable to continue the way we are going." All this waste obviously bothered him a lot. It was also very costly. By mid-2007, the corporate headquarters building, which holds 1,500 workers and includes employers not affiliated with HBC, had achieved a 96.5 percent waste diversion rate. In the early transition period, cleaning staff left unsorted trash, and reminder notes, in employees' offices until everyone learned to separate their own waste properly for recycling.

Once waste reduction efforts start to pay back their investment, they can become a bridge to initiatives in other areas. People can begin to think about the larger field of possibilities—such as taking external stakeholders' needs more seriously and investing in cleaner technologies. For example, HBC now air-conditions its downtown store and office in Toronto during the summer using water piped from Lake Ontario—part of the EnWave collaborative of building owners who "borrow" the enormous natural cooling power of the very cold lake water as it travels from the filtration plant to end users of potable water in Toronto.

The majority of sustainability initiatives today are in the lower left quadrant—they're internal and focused on today. Some organizations have made substantial external forays into the lower right corner, but the overall pattern remains—most initiatives are "below the line," with few investments in the future. The larger goal of your work is to create a balanced portfolio of options and investments across all four quadrants.

At some point it often helps to consider what other admired firms in your industry, as well as other industries, are doing and how their focus has broadened and become more balanced. Recall that DuPont began their journey out of necessity with a focus on major reductions in emissions of all kinds. They and their industry had a reputation for producing toxic chemicals and wastes, and changing that was a clear corporate imperative. At the same time, however, they were making substantial investments in bio-based clean technologies and reaching out to a wide range of external stakeholders for feedback, guidance, and ideas for future innovation. This in turn has led them to identify major new growth markets.

Executives at GE started by asking questions about what it would take to grow their various businesses in the long term, a move that was closely tied to their traditional emphasis on growth and innovation. After asking current and potential customers about their vision and needs for clean energy and clean water fifteen years or more out into the future, they saw that meeting these needs represented significant growth opportunities for GE. But to realize these opportunities, GE would have to make bold investments in clean technologies and be prepared to use those technologies themselves. They found they had no credibility in attempting to sell high-efficiency electric motors, lighting systems, and equipment to customers unless they could answer with a resounding yes the question most customers asked: "Are you using these products in your own facilities?"

Large retailers, especially in the United Kingdom (Marks and Spencer and Tesco are two examples), realized that their customers and other stakeholders want them to reduce their footprint in all aspects of their business. But they also found ways to give customers the option to do the same, as well as to provide the healthiest and most responsible options for food and other products—two "above-the-line strategies" (upper right and upper left, respectively). And it's not only general consumers interested in green options. When it comes to the goods and services they buy from their supply chain, from computers and IT services to all the materials and equipment that end up in their facilities, business customers are demanding sustainable options.

TOOLBOX
Using the Sustainable Value Matrix to Build the Case for Change

Step one: Paper an area of the wall or use a whiteboard to re-create the matrix on a large scale. Using Post-its or other sticky labels, begin by placing the initiatives that are important to members of your team in the quadrant where they seem to best fit. You may notice that some issues naturally belong in one quadrant, while others may quickly bridge to a second quadrant as early goals are achieved.

Step two: Reflect on the matrix at this point, and use it as a tool for identifying which groups within your organization you want to engage. While you know that many people will want to join you in the lower left quadrant, don't stop there. You can naturally extend your focus on reducing the internal footprint of your company to thinking about the full life cycle impact of your product or service (we'll discuss how to do this in greater depth in Chapter 14).

At this stage, you'll already have a better understanding of what various stakeholders in the lower right quadrant, including customers, really want and are willing to pay for. This will help you identify people in marketing, market research, sales, and new-product development to include as members of your team or to add to your network.

Similarly, consider links to breakthrough innovations in clean technologies for the future, such as renewable energy and bio-based inputs, that could fundamentally change your way of doing business. Whom might you want to talk to in engineering, R&D, and other groups exploring these options? Begin to imagine how these breakthroughs in the way you do business could open up opportunities with new customers and new markets in the top right quadrant. Which people within your company are most interested in that territory and could become members of your team?

Step three: Using a different color of Post-its, add other initiatives that are either already under way or being considered within your company. Then, using a third color, post as many initiatives as you can that have been launched by other leaders in your industry, in adjacent industries, or even in new industries that could be relevant to your business in the future. This will help you open your thinking about the future even further.

Step four: Notice the balance among the four quadrants of both your initiatives and other initiatives in your company, compared to those of industry leaders. Be particularly aware of the balance in the number of initiatives that are below the line—those focused on your current business or extensions of it—and those that are above the line, representing investments in the future.

Step five: With all of these Post-its displayed, stand back as a team and ask, "What are the broader forces in each of these four quadrants that connect to our initiatives and those of industry leaders? What assumptions about these dynamics have we been using to make decisions and investments up to this point? How do we think the assumptions of industry leaders differ from our assumptions? How are they thinking differently than we are? What are the particular driving forces that could move our company above the line, to make investments in the future in the top left and right quadrants? Do any of those drivers connect to the interests or aspirations of individual members of the management team?"

Step six: Your team can go further with this exploration by looking at other examples of companies thinking differently and making different assumptions about drivers in each of the quadrants.

CONNECTING YOUR EFFORTS WITH YOUR MANAGEMENT TEAM

Your team can accomplish a few very important things: You can explore, research, and build a case for change that you can use with confidence to engage the management team of a particular business unit or the corporate management team.

Know that, as with all scouting parties, your success is not measured by how much new territory you've explored. It is ultimately measured by how well you communicate with the full community (the wagon train) and what choices you make together. While you may have explored the territory ahead and can report back to the rest of the community selected aspects of what you learned, they have to find their own path forward, taking into account your experience as a scouting party as they see fit. You may want to consciously introduce them to "outsiders" you met along the way—as Paul Tebo did with Greenpeace—who challenged and inspired you, and could do the same for them.

When approaching your management team, consciously retrace your steps from the first meeting of your team. Avoid the assumption that you can skip any of those key steps as you actively engage the management team. You may be able to anticipate some of the concerns of individual members of the management team, but be creative about providing opportunities for them to speak for themselves.

Help the management team use the sustainable value matrix as you did, as an active tool to grapple with. You can seed the conversation with some examples, but encourage other examples as well; don't fall into the trap of presenting your work as a fait accompli.

A simple goal for your first meeting could be to use the sustainable value matrix to engage the management team in identifying all the assumptions they hold, individually and collectively, about external driving forces that could impact their strategies and investments for the future.

Perhaps in a second meeting, once all assumptions about the forces driving the future have been posted and distilled, the second question might be: "How do our current strategies serve us if these assumptions change?" A third question could be: "What options could we create and invest in over time that would improve the robustness of our overall port-folio of strategies in the event that these assumptions change?"

You'll find that members of the management team naturally gravitate to questions such as these, as the prior exploration of assumptions gener-ates a lot of creative tension that they will want to resolve through further work together. Once your management team sees how their current strat-egies could be disrupted by inevitable changes in the way the business or the industry works, they will want to examine how significant those im-pacts might be and what areas may be affected.

That exploration, in turn, creates energy for tackling the question "What should we be doing now so that we are more prepared if our as-sumptions change?" You can later focus the team's attention on generat-ing ideas about how they will respond to shifts in the market, technology, and overall public or industry norms and expectations (one easy way to do so is to become more knowledgeable about particular areas of vulner-ability). You will likely want to use a more open, creative process here, going for quantity of ideas first, then beginning to narrow down to a set of initial options that each have an owner or sponsor from the manage-ment team. Executive sponsors often take ownership for working with a new team, fleshing out the actions needed to develop each option, and monitoring changing external business drivers relevant to that option.

A NEW PERSPECTIVE ON CHANGE

The next three parts of the book will further describe tools and strategies to help you make progress on the unique path forward that you, your core team, and others who join you are navigating together. At heart, this sec-tion of the book is a guide to creating profound change.

There are no clear rules that will fit everyone's progress. You have to choose your own path. That means you and your core team will need to repeatedly ask, "What's important to us now?" and use the energy and direction that come from your answers to create a future that flourishes beyond the Bubble.

part IV
SEEING SYSTEMS

The innovators creating tomorrow's regenerative economy have all, in their own ways, learned how to *see the larger systems* in which they live and work. They look beyond events and superficial fixes to see deeper structures and forces at play, they don't allow boundaries (either organizational or culturally imposed) to limit their thinking, they make strategic choices that take into account natural and social limits, and they work to create self-reinforcing cycles of innovation—change strategies that mimic how growth occurs in the natural world.

They have learned to see systems by cultivating an intelligence that we all possess. Human beings are natural systems thinkers, but like any innate capacity, this talent must be understood and cultivated. Organizations committed to building the capacity to see the larger systems in which they operate not only create powerful learning environments within but begin to be a positive force for systems intelligence to flourish on a larger scale.

[12]

The Tragedy and Opportunity
of the Commons

n its fourth and final report on climate change, released in November 2007, the Intergovernmental Panel on Climate Change (IPCC) warned of a global collapse of all species being fished commercially by 2050 if fishing around the world continued at its present pace. The report revealed that 250 percent more fish are being caught than the oceans can produce in a sustainable manner, and that the number of fish stocks classified as "collapsed" (defined as 10 percent of historic highs) had doubled to 30 percent globally over the past 20 years, with 70 percent of all commercial fisheries on the IPCC's endangered list. Overfishing is hardly a recent problem—the annual catch in the Pacific sardine fishery off the California coast declined from 800,000 tons in 1936 to less than 100 tons in 1952, and the annual catch in the Georges Bank in the northwest Atlantic, once considered one of the most fertile and productive fisheries in the world, declined over 95 percent between 1965 and 1992, from which it has recovered a mere 10 percent. But, as the IPCC shows, the scope and scale of the problem are now unprecedented.[1]

Fisheries can recover—in fact, many have done just that. Pull back the boats, limit the catches to sustainable levels, and nature will often rebound. The Alaskan salmon and king crab fisheries have been sustainably managed through quotas and limits on harvests for decades. Similarly, five years after the establishment of marine reserves in the Egyptian Red Sea, catches increased by 66 percent in neighboring areas. Still, these success stories are the exceptions that prove how difficult it has been to build the shared understanding, collective will, and effective infrastructures to extend sustainable fishing practices worldwide.

Why is this so difficult? Why, when people know the devastating effects of overfishing on local economies and communities, not to mention ecologies, is it still so hard to prevent?

The answer, to paraphrase Shakespeare, is not in our stars . . . but in our failures to see the systems we create.

People frequently use the word *system* when they want to imply that something is outside their control—"It's not my fault, it's *the system*." The sustainability arena is no exception. People blame greedy corporations, corrupt governments, or shortsighted investors for creating systems that deplete natural resources, destroy species, and generate poverty and waste. While all of these institutions do, indeed, need to change, it is unlikely they will do so as long as everyone is blaming someone else.

One of the fundamental differences between social systems (like a business or supply chain) and natural systems (like a rainforest) is that social systems are created by human beings. There can be no "system" without the human actors who inhabit it and take the actions that bring it to life. Put differently, how the system works arises from how we work; how people think and act shapes how the system as a whole operates.

In turn, to understand our actions, we must understand our "mental models," the internal images of the world we all carry. That we have mental models is not good or bad. It is human. None of us has a company, or a city, or a family in our heads. But these internal worldviews are often fragmented, leading us to enact systems that produce outcomes that no one seeks.

Seeing systems and understanding our role in shaping those systems are two sides of the same coin. It is easy to acknowledge this philosophically; it is far more difficult to see how this connection occurs in practice. So let's take a deeper look into the plight of fisheries.

"GIVE A MAN A FISH . . ." BUT BEWARE
A FISHING BUSINESS

When scientists want to better understand a complex phenomenon, they create experiments where they control a number of factors so that they can focus on a few key causal relationships. When systems educators want to help people understand how their own actions shape larger systems, they do the same: They create simulations, such as Fish Banks, Ltd., a simplified world of commercial fishing where there are no foreign competitors, no money-hungry investors, and no corrupt or incompetent government regulators—just people like you and me trying to grow their fishing businesses.[2]

The Fish Banks simulation is a computer-supported board game that looks a bit like Monopoly. But instead of real estate companies, teams of six to ten members apiece run fishing companies. Each company begins with a small fleet of boats, a bank account with a positive balance, a set of options regarding where and under what conditions they can fish (deep water, shallow water), and information on each fishery, like how rapidly fish stocks regenerate. They can buy new boats or sell off old ones. Every team understands that the sea's potential bounty is substantial but not unlimited. Each has the simple goal of making profits by maximizing their fish catch and minimizing their costs. In the hour or so it takes to play the game, ten years of simulated time pass.

After more than two decades of running the simulation with thousands of people around the world, the results are sobering. Almost every game results in early overfishing, continued overfishing, catastrophic overfishing, and eventual collapse. Even teams that start out fishing wisely and sustainably usually yield to competitive urges, as they assume they must add boats and fish harder in order to keep up with other fishing businesses that are growing. Players from the public sector overfish. Players from the private sector overfish. Even teams staffed by environmental advocates and watchdog organizations have overfished, although sometimes more slowly. Once a group from a major state environmental protection agency played Fish Banks—and overfished. It seems that we should add a clause to the old axiom: Give a man a fish and he will be fed; teach him how to fish and he will feed himself; give him a fishing business and he will overfish.

Ecologists call this phenomenon "The Tragedy of the Commons," using the title of a 1968 essay by Garrett Hardin that appeared in *Science*. "Commons" refers to an old custom of grazing livestock on a common pasture-land. The "tragedy" refers to what happens next. Specifically, each farmer has the incentive to expand, but if they all do, the total herd size eventually exceeds what the commons can bear. If overexpansion continues, at a certain point the animals graze their shared pastureland into dust.

No community-shared resource—fish, land, water, oil—is immune to this tragedy, and it doesn't matter whether the resource in question is local, such as a watershed, or global, such as the atmosphere. The forces at play are the same.

But collapse is not inevitable. Fisheries, in Fish Banks and in real life, can flourish in spite of limits. Once, in a workshop hosted by Harley-Davidson, the Harley team refused to go ahead with the game until every team agreed to share information on fish catches.[3] They reasoned that this basic information was necessary to monitor overall supply. Though no one knew exactly how big a catch was too big in any given year, everyone would see if the total fish catch was starting to decline. The Harley team elected also to announce to the others each year whether or not they were going to expand their fleet, even though no such disclosure was required. Gradually, this prompted many others to do the same.

The result was that the fishery never collapsed. The entire industry regulated itself. Moreover, profit and total assets for all teams were higher than for any other game; the least profitable team (everyone still competed) made more money than the most profitable teams in games that resulted in collapse! The fish stocks present at the beginning of the game were not only still there at the end, they had increased to the full carrying capacity of the fishery.

Why was this game so different? Perhaps it had something to do with Harley's culture, which has long valued organizational learning, systems thinking, and conversation between and among groups as core business practices.[4] In fact, in the 1980s when the company faced "extinction" themselves, a group of employees literally bought themselves back from the brink through a collective buyout of the company. Working together to create conditions for healthy competition was a mental model they shared.

What happened at Harley can happen anywhere. Stewarding healthy commons starts with thinking about the larger system your team or organization is part of and recognizing that business-as-usual practices could easily end up causing everyone to lose. As the Harley team proved with their risky move, competition and collaboration are not either-or options; in fact, the very word *compete* comes from the Latin *competere*, which means "striving together." This sharing of basic information ensures that all players know the health of the commons upon which all ultimately depend, the essential condition for healthy competition.

Tragedies of the commons can be averted by players in industries accepting "rules of the game" that recognize underlying limits. Such limits can come in the form of government regulations, like the EU's end-of-product-lifetime regulations, which we discuss in Chapter 15. But they can also come from that same combination of industry-wide peer pressure and sharing of basic information demonstrated by the Harley team, as evident in a number of other industry leaders in real-life versions of the game. For example, Unilever, the largest seller of fish products in the world, became so concerned about the problem of overfishing that they instigated the formation of the Marine Stewardship Council (MSC), with the aim of certifying sustainably fished products around the world. Time will tell whether enough of the key players in this industry can come to share mental models based on stewarding resources rather than only intensely competing—and depleting the resources to everyone's loss.

THE SYSTEMS-THINKING ICEBERG

The mistake most Fish Banks players make, like their counterparts in real industries, is that they fail to step back and, together with their competitors, think more deeply about threats to their industry as a whole.

Specifically, they fail to realize the assumptions that put them in danger. They adopt a limited worldview that consists of "our boats," "our fish catches," and "our profits." Of course, they pay attention to the other fishing companies—namely, to their boats, catches, and profits. They know that there is a limit, ultimately, to the size of the fishery, but they consider it a peripheral piece of information; once the competition heats up, players are consumed with keeping up with or doing better than their competitors—after all, they are not sure what, as one of many competitors, they can do about the limit anyhow.

Were they willing to step back, they would realize that figuring out how to respect the limited capacity is the key to long-term success, because once this limit is exceeded, their catches will inevitably dwindle. Furthermore, if such a limit is reached, their intense competitiveness can make it impossible to work together to undo the damage. Clearly, some degree of collaboration is essential and the sooner it happens, the better for everyone.

The recurring failures of fisheries and other commons are not the result of bad luck or a few villains but rather stem from the all-out competition that blinds individual players to the larger threat. It is folly to think that we will see different outcomes without fundamentally transforming this tendency. Succeeding in Fish Banks, and in any real-life industry facing limits to resources, is difficult because it requires the ability to see the larger reality in which you are operating. One way to do this is to learn how to look at situations at the four levels, as illustrated in the Systems-Thinking Iceberg in Figure 12.1. Like real icebergs, most of these levels are "below the waterline" or invisible to anyone looking at things "normally." But focusing only on what is visible makes it impossible to understand what is really happening and how the forces at play arise, and can change.

What's required in order to thrive in Fish Banks is a shared understanding of the following four factors that influence any situation: events, patterns or trends, deeper systemic structures or forces, and the mental models or assumptions that shape these structures and forces.

Events. The first level of the iceberg can be summed up in the question "What just happened?" Think of it as the "Six O'Clock News" version of reality. Immediate events are tangible, they catch our attention—much like a loud noise that suddenly causes us to drop everything and look up. The problem is that events can so dominate our attention that we get stuck here and, as a result, miss the bigger picture entirely. In the Fish Banks game, an

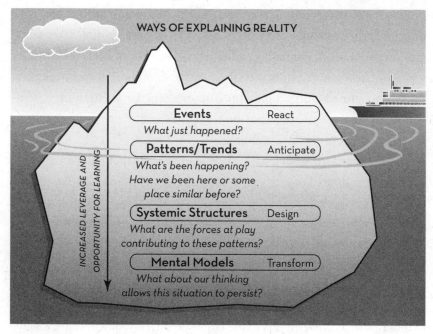

FIGURE 12.1

event might be a sudden drop in catches or the purchase of more boats by a competitor. When people are stuck at this level, they see only the tip of the iceberg and can do little except react as new circumstances arise.

Patterns/Trends. We move beyond immediate events when we ask, "What is happening over time?" Answering this question takes us a little deeper into the system, a little below the typical water surface. Figure 12.2 shows what happens in Fish Banks when overfishing occurs: Overall fish stocks drop, and eventually so too do the sizes of the catches. But unless players decide to share information with other teams, they'll never see the curves and will only know their own catches, and perhaps those of a few competitors.

Once teams know the total annual catch, however, they can also see when the total catch starts to peak (see arrow in Figure 12.2). Usually, this coincides with events like a leveling off or drop in profits. But most players react to falling profits by fishing harder to maintain their revenues. If they do so, however, the fishery will collapse. If they start to cut back, on

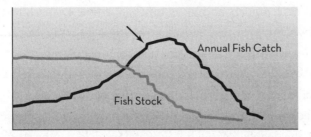

Annual Fish Catch

Fish Stock

FIGURE 12.2

the other hand, the fish stock will begin to recover. But few do so because they are not paying attention to this pattern *and* because they do not understand the underlying systemic structures at play.

Systemic Structures or Forces. Ask, "What are the deeper forces driving these patterns or trends and how do they arise?" For example, if each Fish Banks team thought about how the fishery becomes depleted and how it regenerates, they could start to understand these deeper forces. A key "structural" question is, "When are the fish stocks falling most rapidly and why?" The answer is, When the fish catch is at its maximum, because this is when the number of fish being taken most exceeds regeneration. In other words, when the fish companies are experiencing their greatest revenues, the fishery is most stressed. On the surface, profits are high, but below the surface (literally and metaphorically in the systems thinking iceberg) the fish population is collapsing.

Few realize this, however, because most people fail to think about the underlying population dynamics. To see exactly why this is so important, it's helpful to return to the image of the CO_2 bathtub we shared in Chapter 2, page 29. In this case, think of the fish stocks as the level of a bathtub, where the amount of fish caught is the outflow and the regeneration of the overall stocks the inflow. The fish stocks are falling most rapidly when the outflow, total fish caught, is greatest.[5] So in order to avert disaster, companies must cut back their fishing at the very moment when the pressures to keep growing are greatest!

You can understand why companies without a systemic understanding of what is happening and how it will affect them in the long run are unlikely to cut back at this point; this, of course, is why collapse occurs so often.[6] Yet such understanding is quite intuitive: Even children under-stand inflows, outflows, and bathtubs. So why is it so rare for people to pull back before collapse? Because it contradicts most players' mental models.

Mental Models. Our mental models are reflected in core beliefs, such as nationalist sentiments, patriotism, or religious convictions. "Free mar-kets!" reflects a powerful mental model held by many businesspeople. So does "Free the people!" We all hold mental models—some shared across a society, others across a social class, a political party, an industry, a particu-lar company, or even within our own family. What is often less clear is how these models affect, even dictate, our thoughts and actions and the thinking of those around us.

The first challenge is recognizing the assumptions we might be cling-ing to. Because mental models frequently live "below the surface" and may even contradict the politically correct views that people express (such as "We all care about the health of the fishery"), they are usually invisible, and may even be actively denied. Not surprisingly, it often takes children to say what adults do not, as sustainability educator Jaimie Cloud has discovered. She asked hundreds of students who played Fish Banks, from eight-year-olds to teenagers, about why they acted in ways that led their fisheries to collapse. Here are some of their responses:

- Extrapolationist: "Our actions won't affect the future; there will al-ways be fish."
- Win at All Costs: "You've got to win; it's that simple."
- *Titanic* Syndrome: "There isn't enough to go around, so if we're going down, we might as well go first class."
- Bummer: "Things are the way they are and there's nothing we can do about it."
- Social Trap: "If others do it, I'd be stupid not to do it also."
- Maximizing Gains for Self: "My responsibility is to myself and my family."
- Invisible Hand: "The market or technology or someone/something will take care of it."
- Greed: "I want a lot, and I don't care about the consequences."
- "It's just a game."

Why is it so important to look beneath the surface at the deeper levels of reality? Because in our experience it is often the key to lasting change. When people or organizations pay attention only to the visible tip of the iceberg, they can only react to change as it happens—so at best, they survive the crisis. They often try to compensate for their lack of analysis of a problem with aggressive and "proactive" strategies. But being "proactive" from a reactive mind-set is reactive just the same. With a long enough lever, boasted Archimedes, "I can move the world." In this case, the lever is our willingness to go below the surface of what's visible so we can better recognize and understand the mental models and the systems and forces, like tragedies of the commons, they shape.

ECONOMY *AND* ECOLOGY

The challenges posed by global systems such as the "Big Three" we introduced in Part I (food and water; energy and transportation; and material, waste, and toxicity) can seem overwhelming. But we have a compass to guide the journey in systems thinking. Once people start to practice seeing systems, they begin to understand basic flaws in prevailing mental models and alternative futures that are possible.

For example, Fish Banks illustrates a key point that many business leaders have misunderstood for years: There is *no* ultimate trade-off between the economy and the environment. In the short run, of course, businesses can make more money by ignoring environmental and societal side effects. But the short term ends. As in so many situations today, when underlying environmental (and social) limits come into play, all three aspects of the so-called "triple bottom line" of profit, natural resources, and human community align. Economic, environmental, and societal health become tightly coupled. Either all flourish or all suffer. In failed fisheries, the fishing companies that survive are poorer, fish stocks are depleted and larger marine ecosystems may decline, and local communities suffer and often collapse.

Businesspeople with traditional competitive win-lose mind-sets are closing their eyes to the fact that there are really only two long-term options when it comes to dealing with sustainability issues: win-win or lose-lose. To avoid the lose-lose path, we all must be able to (1) break free of established mental models and the arbitrary boundaries on thinking such assumptions impose; (2) step back, expand our boundaries, and see the larger limits on natural resources and what they mean for our businesses; and (3) when needed, work to build a stewardship ethic in our industries, helping other key players realize that we all share a "commons" that will support us only so long as we learn what it takes to support it.

[13]

Spaceship Earth

uckminster Fuller once likened our planet to a spaceship hurtling through the universe. Noting that no instruction book came with "Spaceship Earth," he cautioned that if we intend to survive, we need to learn how to look at the planet as one system, as a whole, and steward all its resources accordingly. "If it is true that the bigger the thinking becomes, the more lastingly effective it is," he wrote in his 1963 treatise, "we must ask, 'How big can we think?'"

"Thinking big" means consciously stepping back and expanding the boundaries of our own awareness. Most of us have a certain comfort zone within which we live and work. We operate within the boundaries of our own small system and ignore the larger systems upon which our lives and work depend. But once we begin to look beyond the mental fence lines that keep us thinking small—about the daily tasks of our job, perhaps, rather than our place in the larger organization, industry, or world—we begin to discover things that desperately need our attention.

Take, for example, the phenomenal growth of the Internet over the past years; many of us spend hours a day plugged in. Between 2000 and 2007, global Internet usage grew by over 250 percent, but few of us have thought about how much electricity it takes to power all this interconnectivity, and the implications that raises.

Today, estimates of the electricity needed to support the Internet range from 3 percent to 5 percent of the total electricity load in the United States, and in the same range for the world as a whole. This includes all our PCs, all the data centers and servers, all the electronic commerce, all the search engines—in short, all the myriad ways we access and share information and communication online. That may not seem like a lot, but when you consider the rate of growth of Internet use, doubling worldwide every four to five years, conservatively, think again. A 2007 report by the U.S. Environmental Protection Agency confirms that the energy usage of servers and data centers alone doubled between 2000 and 2006, and it's poised to double again by 2011.[1] Researchers had previously calculated that U.S. servers and data centers already use more electricity than all the TVs in the country combined.[2] That means that, within ten to fifteen years, if this growth continues, electricity to support the Internet will exceed the electricity used to light all the homes in the world.[3]

Obviously, something has to give. In a world where we need to shift as rapidly as possible to low-carbon, non-fossil-fuel sources of power, the extraordinary growth of the Internet poses a huge challenge. And we, as users, are all part of this challenge. Either it will catapult people and countries into intense competition for limited electricity supplies or it will lead us into thinking in radically new ways about how our power is generated. Google's major investments in alternative energy research are a result of seeing the larger system within which their business prospers or suffers and understanding they can't ignore the limits of that system. And Google is not alone.

"WHAT WOULD WE DO IF . . . ?"

To see how expanding your boundaries can lead to longer-term change, consider Alcoa. In 1997, Pat Atkins, head of the company's Corporate Environment Department, brought together a group of about thirty managers representing most of the firm's businesses around the world. For two days, they tried to envision what their commercial and social environment would look like over the next quarter century.

They set one ground rule: Whatever problems they might encounter when thinking about this potential future—limited resources, hostile interest groups, major climate shifts—would be the company's problems to solve. There would be no foisting responsibility upon governments, societies, or other companies; no blame games or passing the buck.

Once they set this rule, the group began asking themselves: "What would we do if . . ."

". . . there were no more waste dumps?" When the group looked out to 2020, "We talked about things like landfills," says Atkins. " 'If the world has any sense at all,' we said, 'we won't be allowed to dump stuff in landfills for future generations to deal with. So that's one of the things that we ought to be thinking about in terms of our vision.'

". . . water became increasingly scarce?" Water quickly went to the top of the agenda because aluminum production is very water-intensive. Even ten years ago, it was starting to become a problem for Alcoa, and the company's leaders knew it would only get worse. "California had already denied an expansion permit because the facility used too much water," says Atkins. "We were told to relocate the facility somewhere else. That told us that water would probably be the limiting resource for a lot of our plants around the world, including many places where we thought water was never going to be a problem." The group also envisioned a continual increase in the public's sophistication about discharges such as "chlorine, mercury, and the buildup of soluble materials in water. A lot of people don't trust the quality of tap water anymore."

". . . a range of problematic emissions had to be curtailed or eliminated entirely?" Similarly, the Alcoa team recognized that emissions that had long been part of the business—such as sulfur dioxide, oxides of nitrogen, organic emissions, and carbon dioxide—would have to be dramatically cut back. When they imagined a future without these emissions, they realized it made sense economically as well as environmentally, and in the short and intermediate term, as well. Cutting many emissions saves energy, and saving energy saves money.

Eventually they came to two conclusions: Industry leadership was needed to show that real change was possible, and effective strategies around problems such as climate change would make business sense. As Atkins recalls, they reported to the company's Executive Council, saying, "We can do this and stay in business. In fact, we'll be better off."

Alcoa's exercise in thinking out over the next quarter century not only opened many minds, but led also to formal targets and significant changes. They set a company target of zero process water discharge from their aluminum plants. "That was radical then and it is now," says Atkins. "People still raise their eyebrows." Water usage fell 17 percent (relative to 2000 levels) by 2005; the company recently set new targets of 70 percent reductions by 2010 and zero discharge of process water by 2020. Other "stretch goals" included a 25 percent reduction in greenhouse gas emissions by 2010, and a 50 percent reduction in landfilled waste by 2005. The company reached its greenhouse gas reduction target seven years ahead of schedule, in 2003, and managed to cut landfilled solid waste by two thirds by 2005—leading them to set a new goal for 100 percent reduction of their year 2000 levels of landfilled solid waste by 2015.

How did they accomplish this? By engaging thousands of people. One strategy was to approach their operations people with their targets for dramatic reductions in water use and ask for their help. Eventually, people came up with lots of ideas for water reduction, including many small ones and a few big ones. For example, in 2005, through the installation of closed-loop rinsing and cooling circuits (where the same water is used repeatedly within a self-contained system), Alcoa's Saint Cosme facility in France achieved an 85 percent water consumption and discharge reduction, leading to a $40,000-a-year reduction in operating costs.

Ideas traveled fast throughout the company. In Fusina, Italy, Alcoa's European Mill Products (EMP) business reduced water consumption by 95 percent by installing a closed-loop system that recycles and recirculates all process water. Alcoa has already achieved their 2020 goal of zero process water discharge in some refineries, such as those in western Australia and Jamaica.

Just as important, as the group looked to the future, their fundamental perspectives shifted, and previously marginal issues became crucial parts of the company's strategy. In particular, in 1997 climate change was far from a primary concern of most businesses. Still, the team concluded that it was "the real deal." "At best, we're running a worldwide experiment that will prove not to be a problem," said Atkins. "But at worst, we're running a worldwide experiment that could drastically change the character of the planet. We think we'd better err on the side of conservatism and do something." Looking back, Randy Overbey, president of Alcoa Primary Metals Development at the time, observed, "We turned a corner when we said, 'We're not going to debate the science of climate change any longer.' We're going to believe that it is an issue requiring a response from Alcoa globally, and that hopefully we can provide some leadership."

SUGGESTIONS FOR RETHINKING BOUNDARIES

When you rethink boundaries, you will almost always encounter resistance. People will say things like "We should stick to what we know best," or, as they did about Google, "They should focus on their core competency of securing advertising."

Attempts to convince people that they are wrong and that they need to rethink boundaries will almost always be met with resistance; few people appreciate being told that their thinking is too limited. Instead, a more effective approach is simply to help people reflect on the assumptions that they are making.

Before Roger Saillant, the CEO of fuel cell manufacturer Plug Power, and a former Ford executive, met with the management team of a large jet engine manufacturer a couple of years ago, he had been told to avoid a lecture about greenhouse gases and other environmental matters. He learned that these managers had hosted several previous visitors who spoke about these issues, quite unsuccessfully.

"These are technically savvy, hardheaded executives who do not enjoy hearing that their business model is somehow part of the problem of global warming." But Saillant was undaunted by the challenge.

He began by asking the managers to talk about their business strategy.

After a while, he asked them what key assumptions were underlying their strategy. Soon they had identified one key assumption: They believed that governments around the world were, for the most part, tolerant of greenhouse gas emissions. "We are assuming that there will be no tax on emissions, or that if there were, airlines would be exempt," the managers said.

"What would happen if that assumption turned out to be wrong?" Saillant asked. With no further prompting, the group then launched into an extended conversation about different technological options, fuel choices, overall aircraft design, and even alternative modes of transport where their know-how could be valuable. Before long, they were having the very conversation about air transport "beyond the Bubble" that so many "outsiders" had tried to force upon them. This time, however, Saillant was asking them to reflect on how they were thinking now, rather than trying to force them to think differently.

As this story shows, in general, inquiry is a far more effective strategy than advocacy in expanding the boundaries of people's thinking. When teams see how they are limiting their current efforts by embracing questionable assumptions, they naturally start to challenge those assumptions, as Alcoa did.

Here's a simple way to start. Take a real problem that your organization or team is wrestling with and begin to make the current boundaries in thinking explicit:

- What are the key factors in the problem we are facing?
- What is going on right now, and what forces are likely to shape the future?
- Who are the key actors or decision makers in the system, including those with less authority?

While this process sounds simple, in fact, we rarely ask these kinds of questions explicitly. Problems are often defined based on pre-established and fragmented mental models that embody arbitrary or convenient boundaries. For example, we *define* a problem as an operations problem, or a forecasting problem, or a marketing problem, or an environmental problem. Or we predetermine who the key experts or decision makers are and define the problem accordingly, saying something like "This is the logistics team's problem, or the VP of sales' problem." Or we define a problem by only paying attention to what can be measured ("The problem is the slump in last month's sales results") or by implicitly stating our favored solution: "The problem is that we have not implemented our new quality program."

As you consider the problem you are focusing on, ask,

- "In what ways are we imposing arbitrary boundaries?"
- "Why do we assume that a certain person is the decision maker? Is it because the most obvious problem symptoms are in her or his organization?"

Finally, expanding time horizons is a great way to discover any limited boundaries you are imposing, as Alcoa did by looking out to 2020. When you expand time horizons, spatial boundaries shift as well—who and what is included in the system you are considering. It is easy to ignore larger systems if your time horizon spans only months and quarters; your perspective shifts when you think about consequences of your decisions over decades.

- What is the implicit time horizon built into the current definition of the problem you're facing?
- How would this shift if you doubled that time frame, or made it ten or twenty years longer?
- Pick an expanded time horizon and re-ask the questions you started with, and see how any new responses reflect assumed boundaries you had not noticed initially.

Boundaries are inescapable; all thinking and, consequently, all management is based on boundaries—you can never think about everything. The problems come not because we have boundaries in our thinking but because we forget there are boundaries. Groups forget the assumptions they are making and get frozen in taken-for-granted worldviews. Then, when pushed by people or events to think more broadly, they can get paralyzed trying to consider too many options or get overwhelmed by issues beyond their direct spheres of influence. When pushed to cross boundaries, they often grow frustrated, throw up their hands, and declare, "We can't take on problems of this magnitude. It's too big for us. Shouldn't the government or the UN be handling this issue?"

This often results in retreating to assumed boundaries that do not match the reality of the problems with which people are wrestling. When this is so, the first step is to help people see these self-imposed boundaries and inquire into why they are there and what better alternatives might look like. Do not try to do too much at once. Help people get a feeling for challenging their own assumed boundaries and they will usually start doing it on their own more regularly—even if this requires occasional prodding.

PRINCIPLES FOR A 1,000-ACRE ISLAND

Let's return to Buckminster Fuller's suggestion for the development of an operating manual for Spaceship Earth. A number of people and organizations have developed principles that could form the basis of such a manual, and the most well-known (including The Natural Step and Natural Capitalism) have been included in the Appendix to this book.[4]

But the following exercise can help your group to begin thinking on its own about some of the basic principles such a manual might include. Many groups find that this exercise is a useful first step before they go deeper into what others have said about sustainability principles.

In *Collapse,* Jared Diamond describes an island named Tikopia located in the South Pacific. Though only 1.8 miles square (roughly 1,000 acres), it supports 1,200 inhabitants. And despite a population density of 800 people per square mile of arable farmland, Tikopia has sustained its population for almost 3,000 years.

On this small island, the phrases "to seaward" and "inland" are common reference points; a native might even point out to a visitor that there is a mosquito on their "inland" shoulder. The sea is always present, always audible; the awareness of islandhood is constant and real. Other islands in the area are far off, and journeying by sea in the cyclone-prone region is dangerous, often deadly.

As it turns out, the Tikopians have survived thanks to an intensive knowledge and management of their environment. To ensure continuous and varied food production, they practice sustainable forestry and use of freshwater swamps, they limit seafood catches by means of tribal taboos, and they forgo the slash-and-burn agriculture practiced elsewhere. In addition, for centuries the Tikopians have been limiting population through various methods of birth control (they were preaching zero population growth long before Western organizations ever did). Tikopians also practice a high degree of collective decision making, have a networked power structure, and are among the least stratified by Polynesian standards. Indeed, they think of themselves as a single people, usually referring to themselves as "Matou nga Tikopia"—We the Tikopia, reminiscent of the "We the People" of the U.S. Constitution.

Just as playing Fish Banks can help people re-create the dynamics of the fishing industry, imagining that we live on an island like Tikopia can help us grasp the reality of living on Bucky Fuller's Spaceship Earth. What kinds of principles must island residents follow in order to thrive over such a long period? What can we learn from the basic "truths" of the Tikopia? If you were charged with the task of governing this island, ensuring that human society continued indefinitely, maximizing health and prosperity for all, what principles would you adopt as a base for the laws, policies, and practices of your island?

TOOLBOX
Creating Principles for a 1,000-Acre Island

Imagine yourselves living on a 1,000-acre island like Tikopia that possesses a variety of habitats. Imagine further that you live there with your family, friends, and an extended community of about 1,000. You cannot leave the island—at least, not easily or for long. The island gets plenty of sunlight, which can be used as a renewable energy source, but has a finite amount of materials such as metals, forests, fish and game, soils for food production, and water. All material goods must come from the island, and all wastes must remain on the island, forever and always.

Consider the basic laws of physics, of thermodynamics, of biology: Matter and energy are neither created nor destroyed; things tend to move from areas of higher concentration to areas of lower concentration, from higher-energy states to lower-energy states (i.e., gases tend to disperse, a snowball rolls downhill but must be pushed up); the primary producers of energy and structure are green cells, which use photosynthesis to turn sunlight and inert materials into sugars and starches, stored energy, living structures, and life itself.

Brainstorm together what principles you would like to use to govern this island. Principles should be distinguished from policies. For example, "to protect all water sources and keep them pristine" is a principle. A policy based on this principle might require all industries to use their effluent water as their influent source. It's important to get to the root principle behind each policy.

Using flip charts or Post-its, write down all the principles you can come up with. Group them by theme as appropriate. What principles do you come up with? If you followed these principles regularly, would you be able to sustain yourselves indefinitely? If you have the opportunity to do this exercise with several groups simultaneously, compare notes. What principles have others focused on that you've overlooked? Are you accounting for the whole system? How can your principles be applied to the systems you are part of now?

SEEING LIMITS TO GROWTH

When you begin to expand boundaries, you will start to see underlying limits and new forces at play, such as the increasing costs and risks of oil-based feedstocks (DuPont) or the need to reduce waste (Alcoa) or to conserve water (Coke and Alcoa). Many of the limits were there all along but have been obscured by previously assumed mental models, such as "We're in the oil and gas production and marketing business, not the energy business, and certainly not in the renewable energy business." Additionally, the day when we'd need to take these limits into account seemed far enough in the future that they were easy to ignore, and most companies did just that. But that day is here or rapidly approaching for many, often more quickly than people's mental models are changing.

Developing an instinct for seeing deeper forces at play comes when you move "down the iceberg," seeing beyond events and symptoms to underlying patterns and forces. When you do this, the patterns you see are often not unique. In fact, they arise from underlying structures and mental models that recur over and over; that's why we call them "system archetypes."[5] Developing our natural systems intelligence starts with recognizing patterns that are part of our everyday experience but that often go unnoticed because we lack the ability to recognize them and the language to talk about them.

By looking ahead and considering the larger systems that supported their businesses, Alcoa saw that water was a limit that might encroach on their future. Whereas many other companies would have responded to the denial of the plant's expansion permit in California by seeking out another site, Alcoa took it as a sign of an emerging pattern and probed the deeper causes. Previously, the company had a business model that was largely oblivious to water as a limit to growth, just as they were oblivious to the limit overfilled landfills would present down the line. But they could see that these limits were starting to become more pressing and needed to be taken into account.

Figure 13.1 is one way to depict Alcoa's shift in thinking and strategy. They had always operated with a business model based on a basic self-reinforcing growth engine: As production expanded, so too did demand,

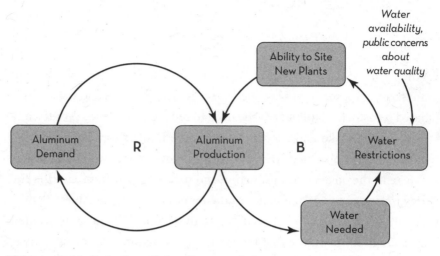

FIGURE 13.1 Limits to Growth for Aluminum Industry

leading to further expansion in production (the self-reinforcing circle to the left, R). At a certain point, however, they began to encounter a set of limiting or "balancing" forces in the circle to the right, B. Further expansion of production required more water, which led to more water restrictions and increasing difficulties in siting new plants, circling back to limit growth in production. Water availability, along with increasing public concerns about the quality of water, represented fundamental limits in the external system—limits that began driving this balancing process.

Seeing such systemic forces can have significant strategic benefits. In effect, teams such as those at Alcoa that develop the capacity to see limits to growth also develop a capacity to see into the future. You do not have to wait for these impending forces to manifest as urgent problems that demand immediate action. In this way, limits can act as a kind of crystal ball; businesses that see them can adapt a lot faster than their competitors and can strategize much more effectively. For instance, early investors in small to midsize cleantech ventures—businesses dedicated to bringing clean energy and new materials to market—recognized the opportunities inherent in industries' desire for green processes, and the public's increasing demands for renewable energy and green products. GE took a similar long-term view of the limits on their customers' fuel costs and emissions and decided to double their investments in R&D. They were able to do this early enough to reap the benefits in sales growth from a suite of new products—from nano-photovoltaics for solar cells to next-generation jet engines—developed to respond to those limits.

Because they could see a deeper pattern, Alcoa managers did not assume that the refusal of a plant-siting request was the result of local politics or a mismanaging of the formal application process for a plant expansion. They did not wait for five more such setbacks to take action. Seeing that the underlying limits on both water and landfills were not going to go away, they asked, "How can we turn this to our advantage?" By designing aluminum plants that don't require water, and completely recycling their water, they could continue to grow and be successful.

DuPont, too, looked ahead: They did not wait for oil prices to hit $100 a barrel to see that higher prices and growing concerns about the effects of carbon emissions on climate change and elsewhere would drive their businesses in the future. They saw these forces building in the early 1990s and began shifting toward bio-based feedstocks before virtually all their competitors.

Not all limits are driven by external forces; sometimes they are self-imposed. For example, the auto industry has missed the opportunity to achieve significant improvements in fuel economy by assuming that cars had to get heavier. In recent years, even U.S. automakers have realized that many consumers want cars with greater fuel efficiency and that meeting that demand can spur sales. But automakers have felt that achieving higher fuel efficiency meant significant sacrifices in performance. In this case, the reinforcing R circle to the left in Figure 13.2 shows the potential for consumer demand to favor cars with higher fuel efficiency, leading to enhanced sales of those cars and more satisfied customers helping create further demand. The balancing forces in the B circle to the right arise from greater fuel efficiency (with smaller engines) leading to poor performance, which circles back to limit demand. Of course, this is true only if car weight is unchanged.

For years, few auto companies recognized and reconsidered the limit imposed by car weight because no one questioned the norm of heavier cars. The average weight of the total automotive fleet in the United States

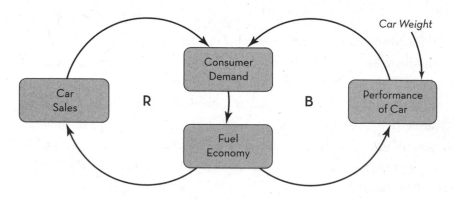

FIGURE 13.2 Limits to Growth for Auto Industry

has increased substantially in the last twenty years. The weight of pickup trucks has increased by almost 50 percent, and the weight of many models of cars, especially smaller ones, has nearly doubled. (For example, a Honda Civic sedan weighed nearly 1,500 pounds in 1990; in 2000, it weighed 2,800 pounds.) In addition, many drivers who used to drive sedans now drive SUVs, vans, and trucks, which are much heavier than the cars they would otherwise have been driving.[6]

A few companies have woken up to the fact that this is a self-imposed limit. Toyota and Honda are now both planning cars made from lightweight composites, and Ford recently announced a new line of aluminum vehicles. Ford's target is a 30 to 50 percent improvement in mileage without a sacrifice in performance. The key insight driving this new wave of innovation came from recognizing this limit (the unquestioned assumption that heavier is safer and cars must be made of steel) and seeing ways to get around it.

Seeing the forces that arise from underlying limits also enables seeing into the future. Pierre Wack, one of the pioneers of scenario planning, used to say, "When it rains for a week in the foothills of the Himalayas, within a week the Ganges will flood." This kind of specific prediction is only possible based on an understanding of the underlying system of water, limits to ground absorption, evaporation, and tributaries. Large amounts of rain in the Himalayan foothills end up in the Ganges because there is nowhere else for the water to go.

The discipline of seeing systems is an ongoing process of stepping back to see a bigger picture, appreciating the deeper forces underlying a problem or situation, seeing new opportunities these forces might also create, and then focusing on these opportunities. But the intellectual insight this generates will only take you so far. Ultimately, we need to reflect on the mental models or assumptions driving the systems we belong to and make the choice to move in new directions.

TOOLBOX
Using the Limits-to-Growth Model to See Deeper Forces at Play in Your Organization

Identify a key challenge your organization is currently facing. It could be, the need for significant growth in sales, reach, and profit, or your desire to have a greater impact in the world—or both. To work on this, form a team that incorporates multiple perspectives—for example, including people from Sales, R&D, Manufacturing, Materials Procurement, and Marketing.

1. Identify a key self-reinforcing process that could produce this growth (the R loop in Figure 13.3). For example, more demand for a particular product leads to more sales, which, through positive word of mouth among customers or boosting product development resources, leads to still more demand.

2. Identify a limiting or balancing process that is offsetting the growth process by asking yourself: (a) What limiting force (such as the ability to

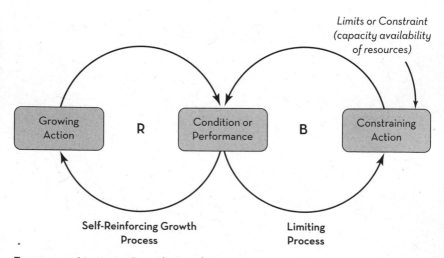

Figure 13.3 Limits-to-Growth Template

site new plants or declining car performance) arises as a side effect of our growth? and (b) What is the underlying limit, either external (such as water availability) or self-imposed (such as assumptions about the ideal car weight)?

3. With your team, draw the model shown in Figure 13.3 and identify the reinforcing process, balancing process, and underlying limit(s) that you're experiencing. People may have different views of how to do this; this can lead to a fruitful conversation about the assumptions behind your differing views. Either try to converge on a single best diagram or consider a couple of options. There is *no* single right answer; the aim is to get everyone thinking together about the basic elements of this structure and how the forces play out over time.

4. How does your organization usually respond to the effects of these forces? Consider, for example, what happens when a problematic event generated by the balancing process occurs—such as the failure of a plant-siting application, or disappointing sales from a more fuel-efficient but poorer-performing car. How does your organization react? Most respond by trying to push the reinforcing process harder: They work harder to get plants sited or pour more money into marketing even modest improvements in fuel efficiency.

5. Alternatively, what would be a higher-leverage strategy—such as creating lighter cars? And what would need to happen to enable people to follow such a strategy? The greatest leverage is usually found in addressing the limits in the balancing loop, rather than pushing harder on the reinforcing process.

6. After completing the first five steps, reflect on the following questions: What is different about this way of thinking compared to how we usually think? What are the benefits and limitations? If the strategies we've discussed are useful and potentially profitable, why are they not more common? What would we have to change to make them part of our core strategy?

[14]

Seeing Our Choices

For years, Nike, like most of its direct competitors, ignored the labor practices of the Asian manufacturers that supplied their products, believing the issue was not really core to their business since they were not a manufacturer. They discovered otherwise when several organizations mounted a major campaign that severely damaged their corporate image in the mid-1990s.

Within a year, Nike reversed a tradition of neglect and began to establish better labor policies and oversight to ensure compliance. Today, they have one of the best reputations in their industry for social and environmental practices, and are led by one of the business world's more active and influential internal corporate responsibility staff groups (the VP of Corporate Responsibility reports directly to the CEO).[1] They not only work on improving labor practices but have pursued a variety of innovations, ranging from establishing dedicated suppliers who work with Nike alone and who are committed to sustainability innovations to developing distributed production networks in countries such as Thailand so that workers can stay in their own villages rather than face a long commute. They've also introduced a host of new green products, many of which we'll discuss later in the book. "We realized we faced a choice," says former Corporate

Sustainable Development head Sarah Severn, "of either complying and trying to stay out of trouble or becoming a leader in our industry."

Back in the early 1990s, Toyota faced a similar choice: continue doing what most other automotive companies were doing and base their future on the internal combustion engine, or strike out in a different direction, one that acknowledged the looming limits to cheap, accessible oil and the unsustainablity of greenhouse gas emissions. The gas-electric hybrid Prius was the product of intensive innovation and investment in a new platform combining smaller gas engines and electric motors. It was widely viewed in the U.S. auto industry as a money-loser for several years after it was first introduced—and in fact, for a time it was. But it gradually captured a consumer market that had been waiting for someone bold enough to do something different. Now the sales and profits generated by the Prius give Toyota the ability to invest in next-generation vehicles that are primarily electric, as well as fuel cell vehicles.

Once companies see clearly that have a simple choice to make— either take the lead on sustainability issues or shift the burden to someone else—they can start to make serious investments.

The shifting-the-burden dynamic we first introduced in Chapter 2 can help companies see the very different outcomes of these two choices. You may recall that one set of choices involves addressing a problem with short-term, symptomatic solutions (taking an aspirin for a headache). The other looks at fundamental, long-term solutions (addressing the root cause of the headache). The key insight here is that opting for quick fixes and avoiding fundamental solutions tends to set up a reinforcing set of pressures for more quick fixes over time.

Figure 14.1 represents the choices facing so many companies today. The upper loop represents the decision to do as little as possible and externalize the impact of your choices by shifting the burden to nature. This tactic will certainly be familiar to you, as will its results, in which one symptomatic solution leads to another. Companies try ignoring the potential limit, whatever it is, believing that damage to a watershed, greenhouse gas emissions, or increasing waste is not their problem. Because this may give the organization a negative public image, companies often also try "greenwashing," or improving their image through public relations campaigns,

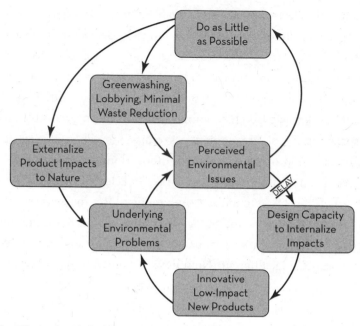

FIGURE 14.1 Choice to Shift the Burden or Innovate

lobbying, minimal waste reduction programs, or making minor product changes (such as introducing hybrid SUVs that get poorer gas mileage than conventional sedans of a decade ago). They continue to choose to operate in the upper loop because they think it will be easier, cheaper, and faster. But all the while the real problems are growing—as are the risks associated with unsustainable business practices.

But there is another choice. The lower loop, in which we create fundamental solutions, means investing in sustainable solutions that are regenerative. In this "innovation loop" you take responsibility for your impact on the larger world.

Ultimately, as Sarah Severn says, the choice to lead becomes crucial. While it may seem defensible to argue that no one organization can be justly accused of causing climate change or any similar large-scale damage, in reality—as Figure 14.2 illustrates—the additive effects of many individual companies choosing the upper loop have exactly that cumulative impact. On the other hand, when one or more companies in an industry

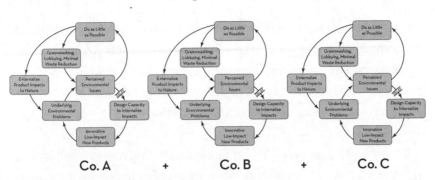

FIGURE 14.2 Sliding the Burden to Nature or to Innovation: Collective Impact of Individual Company Choices

stops blaming others or "the system" and takes responsibility for being part of the problem, they can play a pivotal role in becoming part of the solution, and influencing others to do likewise.

SEEING COMMON LIMITS

When you ask yourself what measures you can take so that your capacity to handle your limits grows, you may find that others in your industry, or in your geographic region, are asking the same questions. When businesses in Kalundborg, Denmark, realized they all faced a potential water shortage, managers worked together to build a system of pipes from a nearby lake to their plants to save dwindling groundwater supplies. They would then reuse that water between plants, cutting overall water use in an industrial park significantly.

Similarly, as shown above, many data centers and software and computer companies have realized that they are likely facing limits in electricity supplies in the near future. In fact, all technology companies are now recognizing that they are in the energy business, and many are planning accordingly. While few have started to make major investments in alternative energy, such as Google is doing, more and more are realizing that they have a big energy footprint and need to extend the boundaries of their business models to address it. If they invest in innovation now, they will ultimately reap the rewards down the road.

It makes sense; the computer industry is, by nature, forward-thinking, and companies would not survive without expanding boundaries, creating markets, and sustaining innovation. Most have embraced the idea that if they don't figure out how to dramatically reduce energy consumption, recycle products, and move to alternative energy, some competitor will.

But in the long run, every player in the computing universe will butt up against a set of common limiters. Working together to face these common limits is likely to drive innovation faster and more successfully. For decades, technology companies struggled to agree upon de facto industry standards for communications, packet switching, Ethernet connections, file sharing, networking, and so on. But eventually they did and everyone benefited. Building on this historical cooperation, these companies now have a chance to take on even more daunting challenges.

CHOOSING TO STEWARD THE COMMONS

When we interrupt the shifting-the-burden pattern, we begin stewarding the restoration of shared commons. Organizations will inevitably discover that many of the limits they face are in fact "commons," shared by others in their industry or by society itself. Building on their own efforts, they can then reach out with credibility to collaborate with others.

The eleven companies in Kalundborg's industrial park that began by finding a solution for limited water supplies, for example, then started working together to turn one company's waste into another's "food"—or in many cases revenue. There are dozens of examples of this kind of stewardship within the complex and between the park and the town itself. Waste heat from the power plant, for example, provides heat for residences as well as for an oil refinery and a pharmaceutical plant; the waste fly ash from the power plant is sold to cement plants to significantly reduce the amount of raw materials used and greenhouse gases generated in their cement production process. Surplus yeast from insulin production at the pharmaceutical company goes to local farmers who use it for pig food. Gas from the oil refinery, which used to be flared off, now goes to the power station, saving about 30,000 tons of coal a year.[2]

A number of companies are recognizing other ways to steward the commons they are a part of.

Companies often begin by developing an "internal commons" across the organization, using it to reduce their environmental footprint, realize cost savings, or develop new products. DuPont began by building powerful internal networks that focused on slashing their energy costs and toxic emissions, and later played a key leadership role in developing the Responsible Care program for the entire chemical industry. BP achieved major reductions in emissions by connecting and leveraging innovations in its operations around the world. They then developed a company-wide internal carbon trading system as a tool for learning, and used that experience to contribute to the development of the EU carbon trading system.

Alcoa has invested heavily over time to develop its global technical capabilities for aluminum recycling, based on the economic reality that recycled aluminum requires 95 percent less energy to produce than virgin aluminum and can be recycled a multitude of times. They've also broadened their thinking to focus on the aluminum industry as a whole, and continually challenge themselves to take a proactive leadership role in building a global "commons" for recycling in the industry.

For example, in early 2008 Alcoa announced a goal to raise the industry's used beverage can (UBC) recycling rate in North America from its current 52 percent rate to 75 percent by 2015. "The aluminum industry must work together for common sustainability goals that transcend individual commercial objectives, and we must approach this with a sense of urgency. It's all about recapturing this pool of energy before it is lost to the landfill," said Greg Wittbecker, Alcoa's Director of Corporate Metal Recycling Strategy, in a call-for-action presentation to aluminum industry leaders during the Platt's Aluminum Symposium. In the U.S. aluminum beverage can market of over 1.5 million metric tons per year in the United States, about 800,000 tons of UBCs are currently being recycled. Wittbecker added that the U.S. recycling rate has fallen steadily from its high of 68 percent in 1992. In comparison, Brazil and Japan report phenomenal recycling rates of nearly 95 percent and 92 percent, respectively, and the global average is 60 percent.

Wittbecker cited several reasons why recycling has fallen in North America, including inconvenient collection systems, technology stagnation in coated scrap processing, and commercial objectives that have not been aligned with recycling. All of these areas represent significant opportunities for change.

Similarly, Sony Europe, for example, led the way toward creating a common extended producer responsibility system that requires manufacturers to take back all electronic equipment at the end of its lifetime. The European Recycling Platform for electronic equipment has made it possible for all companies in the industry to organize and manage product takeback collectively, with significant cost savings. For example, the average costs for packaging takeback in Germany fell from €350 per ton in 2000, to €80 per ton in 2004. Similarly, the costs for recycling IT products in Austria fell from a high of €0.60 per kilogram in January 2005, to a low of €0.11 per kilogram in June 2006. Sony itself saved over €400,000 in 2005.

The savings Sony and the electronics industry as a whole achieved are typical of the significant cost savings possible when commons are managed well. These cash flows can then be reinvested in further progress and expansion improvements that will bring more benefits as virgin raw materials, currently mined or extracted, become more and more costly. This also illustrates the positive self-reinforcing or "snowballing" characteristic of the most successful sustainability strategies.

CREATING POSITIVE CHANGE SNOWBALLS

All too often, change advocates fall into a trap of needing to pour increasing amounts of time and energy into their efforts just to maintain forward motion and, as a result, "burning out," as Per Carstedt put it. Fortunately, through his networking among truly committed people, Carstedt eventually found ways for positive change to feed on itself. So too did the founders of the USGBC, once the LEED system started to take shape. Catalyzing self-reinforcing change turns out to be a common strategy of sustainability for innovators who see not only the systems that are currently operating but those that might in the future.

Malcolm Gladwell popularized these snowball effects in his bestselling book *The Tipping Point: How Little Things Can Make a Big Difference*. Tipping points, says Gladwell, are "the levels at which the momentum for change becomes unstoppable . . . the moment of critical mass . . . when ideas and products and messages and behaviors spread like viruses do."[3]

For example, the successful initiatives starting to shift how organizations collectively steward commons are distinguished by their moving beyond one-time interventions to self-reinforcing change. By reinvesting the benefits from successful initiatives to better manage commons, a virtuous cycle of improvement can ensue: Cost savings become investment capital for further building the commons, reducing system costs still further.

Nurturing self-reinforcing snowballs is an intuitive strategy for successful sustainability innovators because it is a natural model. Everything that grows in nature does so because of underlying self-reinforcing structures. One cell divides to produce two, which produce four, which produce eight, and on and on. The first fuzzy shoot starts to poke out from the seedling, which draws in more water and nutrients and extends farther. Animals move to a new bioregion with ample food and start to reproduce, leading to still larger populations and more reproduction. Snowballs arise from an

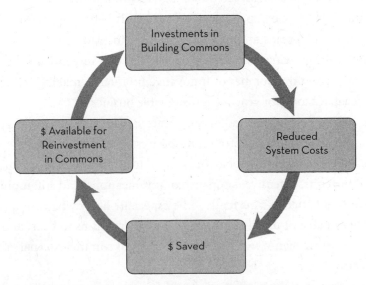

FIGURE 14.3 Harnessing the "Snowball Effect" of Cost Savings and Reinvestment

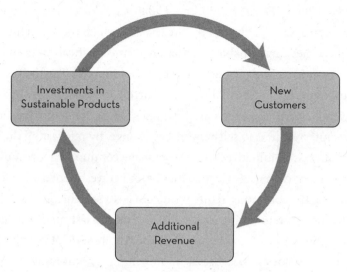

FIGURE 14.4 Harnessing the Reinforcing "Snowball Effect" for Sustainable Growth

underlying systemic structure where change feeds on itself to produce more of the same, and soon it snowballs into a pattern of self-reinforcing growth. The initial changes can be small, yet over time they can grow to be substantial. Maybe a company starts selling a truly better, more sustainable product. Word spreads among old customers, then to new customers; a portion of the growing revenues can flow to increase investments that improve or expand the number of innovative products—making for a welcome feedback loop for growing a sustainable business.

Of course, reinforcing loops can create negative snowball effects as well, as Figure 14.5 demonstrates. Responses of NGOs to what they see as irresponsible corporate behavior can lead to a spiral of negative publicity and boycotts, defensive company communications, and still more aggressive NGO attacks. This tends to be especially likely when companies are either unable or unwilling to take external criticisms to heart and, regardless of their own view of the issues, truly take in the external critics' perspective.

For example, when Coke first found itself being criticized for using water in water-depleted areas, it could have defended itself by technical

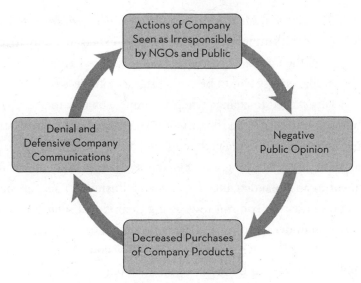

FIGURE 14.5 Negative Reinforcing Loop of Company Actions and Public Perceptions

analysis—arguing, for example in southern India, that it was drawing from deeper water sources than those that were depleted. Instead, it realized that the technical analysis really missed the point. Water was scarce in regions where it operated, and Coke had a social responsibility to step forward and try to contribute positively to the problem. In so doing, it averted a vicious spiral that would have led to a protracted escalation between lawyers and activists.

A positive self-reinforcing effect of just one firm in an industry can change the game for everyone by demonstrating what is possible. And when several organizations, or even business units in one organization, start to shift their choice to innovating and producing more sustainable processes, products, and services that demonstrate "thinking differently" is possible, the effects are often multiplied. Others start to jump on the bandwagon. When you can point to someone who has demonstrated that something is possible, that there's a better way to do things, then others in your own company, industry, and customer base will take notice.

The Alternative Energy division of energy giant BP, for example, had a hard time getting the attention of the corporate board as long as they were losing money. The board tended to view them as an exploratory, research-oriented—even philanthropic—initiative, and expected them to carry the burden of their losses as a requirement for preparing for a future when renewable energy would become a significant piece of BP's overall business. This started to change when Vivienne Cox became head of the solar business and brought a mixture of management savvy and systems-thinking methods that energized people to create a different climate of collaboration and risk taking. In 2006, the board approved an $8 billion investment in an expanded alternative energy business. This new investment allowed them to commit to growing their global solar business by 300 percent in under three years, which they are on track to do. Although in absolute terms, the BP Alternative Energy division and its profits were still small in contrast to the core oil and gas business, once alternative energy was perceived as a viable business, they were able to attract significant capital for further innovation and growth.

Individual companies that take the lead successfully in their industries as part of an integrated strategy can turn their investments into a positive reinforcing cycle, as illustrated in Figure 14.6.

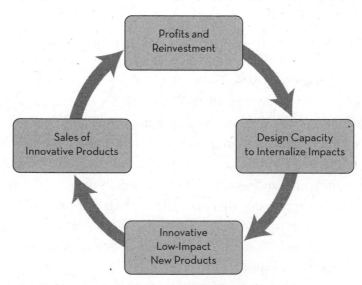

FIGURE 14.6 Regenerative Fundamental Solutions Become a Reinforcing Snowball

The same goes for entire industries. Once Toyota and then Honda proved that it was possible to make money on hybrid cars, other companies began to follow. Some copied or bought the Toyota technology; others committed to developing their own. What was once thought impossible to commit to is now considered necessary. Even the Big Three car companies, seen as laggards at best (Ford had plans to introduce a hybrid by 2002 or 2003 that were delayed by internal management conflicts) and obstructionist at worst, now are making major investments aimed at producing hybrid, all-electric, and alternative fuel vehicles, including those with hydrogen-powered internal combustion engines.

MIT's John Sterman argues that the failure to see this sort of virtuous reinforcing cycle continues to cause people to underestimate the potential of the whole renewable energy industry. "Some people point out that solar power, for example, is currently not competitive with coal and oil, but they are just looking at a snapshot of today's conditions. The costs of new technologies tend to fall sharply through learning and scale economies. These are powerful positive feedbacks: The cost of solar photovoltaics falls 20 percent every time cumulative experience doubles, and the industry is growing faster than 30 percent/year. Total cumulative produc-

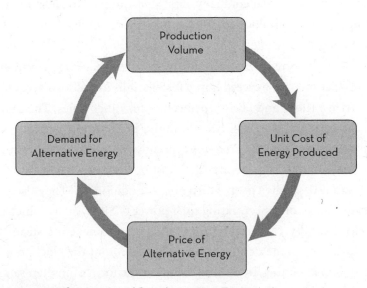

FIGURE 14.7 Reinforcing Spiral for Alternative Energy

tion of solar power in the United States today is only 0.0004 as large as
cumulative fossil fuel production just since 1950. As costs continue to
drop, demand will grow, companies will move down their experience cost
curves, prices will fall further, and the market will grow. We are just at the
start of that process for renewable energy."

Sterman is not alone in this assessment of the industry's growth potential. Photon Consulting, a German research group, projects, "Higher demand for solar energy, triggered by concerns about global warming, will
drive a fourfold increase in the annual revenues of the global solar equipment industry from $20 billion in 2006 to $90 billion in 2010. Profit
growth is expected to accelerate even faster, as costs are contained, pushing margins up to nearly 60 percent."[4]

In the U.S. market, actual growth is in line with these projections. The
year 2007 was a record year for solar energy, with 314 megawatts of new
solar installed in the United States—an increase of 125 percent from 2006.
According to the U.S. Energy Information Administration, solar power
still accounted for less than 1 percent of the total generated electricity in
the United States through the end of 2007. But with the reinforcing spiral
of rising demand and falling costs that is well under way in the United
States and globally, exponential growth will continue. For example, the
revenues of one U.S. solar company, First Solar, jumped to $504 million in
2007, up from $135 million in 2006, while their manufacturing cost per
watt dropped 12 percent.

And the *Wall Street Journal* recently reported that large commercial
solar installations "now exceed home installations in California, reversing
a long-term pattern and likely a bellwether for other states. The bulking
up in the solar industry will become more pronounced as utility-scale
projects get built."[5] As *The Economist* recently reported, "Solar power excites utilities because it generates the most power just when it is needed:
on hot, sunny days when people turn on air conditioners." They also point
to the advantages of concentrating solar power (CSP) systems, which produce electricity by concentrating the sun's rays to generate steam that
drives turbines. "Some designs provide power round the clock, not just
when the sun is shining, by storing energy in the form of molten salt."[6]

Similar snowball effects are also evident in the wind industry. Shattering all its previous records, the U.S. wind energy industry installed 5,244 megawatts (MW) in 2007, expanding the nation's total wind power generating capacity by 45 percent in a single calendar year and injecting an investment of over $9 billion into the economy.[7] Globally, over 20,000 MW of wind power was installed in 2007, bringing worldwide installed capacity to almost 100,000 MW, an increase of 31 percent over 2006.[8] While Europe is currently the most advanced market for wind power, generating over 3 percent of its total power consumption from wind energy, other countries are catching up quickly, including the United States, China, India, and Brazil. The key in all these examples is not the current size but the rates of growth and the underlying virtuous snowball of costs, price, and volume.

Similar self-reinforcing spirals are created when new business imperatives move through supply chains. There is no bigger example of this today than what's been happening at Wal-Mart, the world's largest retailer, which announced a new goal in 2008: to work with suppliers to make many of the products it sells 25 percent more energy-efficient within three years. Noah Horowitz, a senior scientist at the Natural Resources Defense Council, says, "When Wal-Mart asks, suppliers jump. . . . There are positive ripple effects throughout the supply chain." As suppliers work to improve their products, a snowball effect occurs, and innovations will spread to other products, industries, and customers.

These examples show the possibility of many positive tipping points, reversing the negative ones where firms reinforce one another's externalizing of environmental impacts to nature (see Figure 14.1 on page 198). As more companies invest in fundamental regenerative solutions and

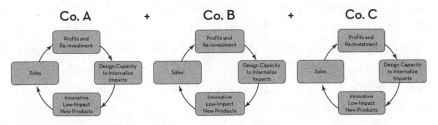

FIGURE 14.8 Reinforcing Collective Impact of Company Investments in Regenerative Solutions

grow the design capacity to deliver those solutions, synergies can create a new tipping point and a powerful snowball effect driving whole industries and even economies to become regenerative.

Organizations willing to innovate and to work with government to raise the bar across their industries are essential for reaching tipping points where snowball effects create exponential positive change. And companies that move first, as Toyota and Honda did by bringing hybrid cars to market, naturally gain significant influence with governments and NGOs when they effectively say, "We agree with you on the vision of creating a regenerative system—let's get to work together on how to achieve this."

When businesses fail in this leadership, governments are left trying to impose regulatory interventions that businesses then resist. Either businesses implement the regulations with little commitment or, worse, they resist even modest steps toward sustainability. This is a tragic waste of resources; money that could be going to innovation goes instead to bolster defensive lobbying, public relations campaigns, or legal actions against proposed regulatory changes. By contrast, when enough businesses truly lead and enough citizens and government officials reach out to work in partnership, self-reinforcing cycles of innovation can potentially draw in all sectors (businesses, civil society, and government) as partners in developing ever-higher business practices *and* regulatory standards. For example, according to a recent report by REN21, "More than 65 countries now have national goals for accelerating the use of renewable energy and are enacting far-reaching policies to meet those goals."[9] The report also noted, "The renewable energy sector now accounts for 2.4 million jobs globally."

Pointing to such a virtuous cycle may sound naive, given the understandable cynicism most of us have acquired from watching governments and businesses consistently fumble their respective leadership mantles. But the imperative of living beyond the Industrial Age Bubble is creating relentless pressures for innovation, new mental models, and better regulation, and it is important to remember that change is rarely led by the current majority.

Indeed, Gladwell's very idea of a tipping point centers on the long-term impact of relatively small groups adopting new ideas and behaviors. In this light, we have found that a helpful tool for assessing different

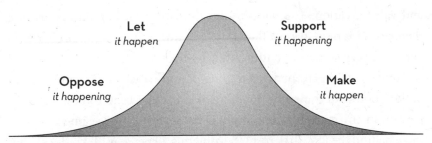

Let
it happen

Support
it happening

Oppose
it happening

Make
it happen

FIGURE 14.9 Leadership Companies Create "Pull" for Change

change prospects takes the form of a curve that characterizes where different groups are on any new issue.

Specifically, for any change, there may be a small number of organizations that are innovative, that think and act as stewards for this change. This kind of "make it happen" leadership functions to prove the viability of new ideas, and, once enough evidence of viability is created, naturally activates a much larger group of players who will support the change. While this second group may not have the creative spark to champion the first stage, they can actively support and fill in the foundation for change.

This way of looking at leadership can help us see what legislative changes are and are not feasible. Political leaders rarely want to enact new regulations without at least a few companies in an industry demonstrating that the rules will work in practice. Politicians recognize that unworkable regulations can be damaging, economically as well as politically. As a result, companies that demonstrate that regulations supporting stewardship of the commons can be successfully implemented can have a hand in shaping regulatory systems (we'll return to this concept in the next part of the book).

The same leadership actions by companies can create powerful tipping points in markets as well. Doug Miller, president of the global market research organization GlobeScan, draws these conclusions: "Our client-specific research repeatedly confirms—whether it's a green product, a green electricity offer, or other sustainability product or service—that at least 10 percent of the market now actually vote with their dollars and will pay a premium for these sustainability attributes. In one U.S. client's case, we've seen the size of their 'active green consumer' segment grow 50 percent over the last two years. That has a big impact in terms of market share and value creation. The reason things can take off like that is because there are a lot more people than one in ten who think along similar lines and have very similar intentions to act—they just don't want to be first! But once that 10 percent act, a tipping point is reached. Very quickly out of the woodwork comes the doubling of that 10 percent. You can get to 20 percent in any market quite quickly because this second segment is right there behind the first 10 percent. Beyond this 20 percent, all kinds of other major market forces can kick in, as happened with the iPod, that drive irreversible changes."

What might it take to get to such a tipping point in your situation? What could you and your organization do to create this kind of critical mass, where an irreversible snowball of benefits rolls across the system as others join? How can you help what initially might seem like a radical idea enter the mainstream?

THE BIG PICTURE: THE "CIRCULAR ECONOMY"

In Chapter 2, we argued that sitting behind the myriad sustainability issues was an industrial system that extracts renewable resources more rapidly than they can be regenerated, and in turn generates waste that undermines nature's regenerative capacity. And throughout the book we have shared stories of how a number of organizations are discovering that expanding the boundaries of their thinking to see underlying limits in resources and waste can also open up strategic opportunities. Putting these two together leads to a simple framework for a new industrial system for life beyond the Bubble.

The figure on page 214 offers a big-picture view of an alternative industrial system where waste is dramatically reduced through conversion into two kinds of usable by-products.

"Natural nutrients" are biodegradable by-products of industrial products and processes that move back into nature's regenerative resources. This category includes composted food wastes, compostable clothing made from organic fibers, and by-products from renewable energy, such as the water that comes from converting hydrogen into electricity in fuel cells.[10]

"Technical nutrients," a term coined by Michael Braungart and

William McDonough in their book *Cradle to Cradle,* are materials that can circulate back into the creation or use of other products.[11] Technical nutrients are soda and detergent bottles that get recycled into new bottles. They are automobile and copying machine components that get remanufactured into new components. They are computers that can be disassembled easily and safely so their parts can be remanufactured. They are superefficient lightbulbs that require less energy (thereby reducing CO_2 emissions) and that also can be taken apart and completely reused after their lifetime. They are also by-products of manufacturing processes that can be used in other processes, such as the waste heat or chemical by-products at Kalundborg or in Per Carstedt's Green Zone that become energy or inputs to other processes.

Figure 14.10 is simple to understand, and we have found that it is a great way for anyone from children to veteran managers to quickly grasp the principles of a truly sustainable economy. In such an economy, we work steadily to reduce all forms of waste (solid, liquid, and gaseous) toward zero and continually find new ways to design products and processes so that former waste streams become valuable inputs to other industrial processes or benign flows back into natural systems.

An economy based on separate circular flows of technical and biological nutrients mimics the living-systems principle of "waste equals food" and has two critical benefits: reduction of waste flows and their collateral damage to communities and natural systems *and* reduction in the amount of natural resources that must be extracted or harvested.

Many companies embarked on developing circular business models long ago and have since reaped substantial rewards. Xerox has been designing copiers to be disassembled, remanufactured, and recycled for years and gains over $400 million in annual direct-to-the-bottom-line savings from utilizing recovered components. BMW and other automakers likewise have found a compelling harvest of economic value in taking back automobiles at the end of their lifetime and designing them so that whole portions, such as dash panels and doors, can be recovered and reused easily, as has Pratt and Whitney in the remanufacturing of aircraft engines. A similar wave of investment and innovation has hit the computer industry in the last two years.

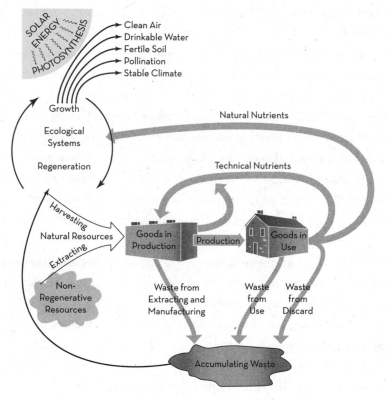

FIGURE 14.10

SUGGESTIONS FOR SEEING
CIRCULAR ECONOMY OPPORTUNITIES

Here's how to start using the circular economy model as a strategic-thinking tool. Take a product or service your company offers and track it from left to right. Go "upstream" to the left. What resources are you extracting? What are the by-products? How have you been dealing with the wastes? If your company provides a service, what key physical products are also involved, such as cell phones and fiber-optic cables? Track these material inputs from left to right and ask yourself where they come from and where they go. If you do not know, find out. Businesses that are thinking about the future, such as Alcoa, do not want to put anything in the "front end" of their value chain that isn't benign or that can't be recaptured and reused.

Life cycle assessment (LCA) can be a powerful tool in tracking all material and energy flows through the entire system. (See Appendix for resources on LCA.) However, be sure that this LCA work is positioned strategically, so that everyone involved can move easily back and forth between the big-picture view of Figure 14.10, and a more detailed analysis of specific products or processes. Use both views to be sure that everyone involved, from senior leaders to front-line employees, has a common overview of the larger system and can navigate together into more detail as needed to understand a particular part more deeply.

In a regenerative circular economy, the goal is zero waste, renewable energy, recyclable materials, and accountability for all materials flowing through the system. So in every place where you can see a waste stream flowing down into the larger pool of waste at the bottom of Figure 14.10—whether in manufacture, use, or discard—stop and think. Alcoa used their zero-waste goal to challenge their thinking about spent pot lining, a hazardous waste generated when the large pots they use to melt aluminum wear out. Their smelters in Italy and Spain now transport this material to be converted into a safe, usable product for the steel and cement industries. Their refinery and smelter in Brazil is now recycling all their solid waste and is also "mining" previously landfilled solid wastes. Other Alcoa locations around the world are replicating these examples.

Every arrow pointing down represents a choice point, where you can choose not to send waste from manufacturing and products into nature. You have two complementary and overlapping ways of doing this: by redesigning the product or process and by recovering and reusing the waste. Remember, there is potential value in that waste stream, value that may have never been considered before. Consider this waste a potential input for your business or for another. How and for whom would this be valuable? Practice comparing its potential value (less the cost of recovering it) to the cost of mining new resources or starting from scratch, in order to see the net potential economic benefit. This is exactly what companies such as Xerox and BMW have been doing for years.

Then consider the risks involved in securing this material in the future from natural resource inputs. Many minerals and other costly inputs are becoming increasingly scarce, and many are extracted today from countries where there is considerable political and economic turmoil. Much as Coke had to do with water, look beyond your immediate supplier and consider the total value chain. Often when you do this, you will start to see significant risks of disruption or price fluctuations. This risk can be quantified by formal risk models; such models will get the attention of boards of directors because they translate risks into financial specifics. These same models can be extended to place financial value on options created to deal with these risks, and take advantage of opportunities on the other side of risks.

Using this big-picture framework will lead to strategic questions that most businesses, operating within narrow boundaries, have long avoided. Why extract more petroleum to make plastic containers when we have huge volumes of the very plastic we need already just waiting to be reused? Dr. Seetha Coleman-Kammula, a former executive in the petrochemical business, says, "Businesses must develop a mind-set like oil companies: there are huge reservoirs of potential value in our waste streams. More than 90 percent of the polypropelene (which is used in dairy packaging and other containers, and is highly recyclable) is discarded. We need to develop the analogue of seismic analysis to find the large pools of potential value and explore how to recover them." In many cases, this will mean redesigning products to increase recovered value, but often the redesign is not costly (like having all polypropelene containers of the same color and adding shrink-wrapped covers for color branding). "Those who learn how to do this will capture immense potential business opportunities."

By taking them back into the recycling and remanufacturing loops, materials can add value rather than do harm. You can identify the choice points where making such investments will provide you with the greatest leverage, either within your company or in your collaboration with other organizations.

In this way, the circular economy diagram becomes a visual heuristic: If you draw an X through a particular waste stream to represent stopping it completely, what would it mean? Some people even like to think of the waste outflows as having a valve or tap controlling the outflow; they want to close it so they don't lose important sources of value. What would it take to do that, and what could the possible benefits be from doing so?

We recommend not doing this sort of analysis alone. It is easy to get overwhelmed by the complexity of it all. Seeing systems is a team sport, and people working together will push each other along as they come up with many new ideas and fresh perspectives. This is important and often gets forgotten: We have seen many well-intentioned managers start down this road and simply give up because they cannot see a way to "move the elephant." We have rarely seen a management team or cross-functional team take this on and not come up with important insights and practical next steps.

CREATING COMMONS TO MANAGE COMMONS

Organizations and leaders around the world are recognizing that either they can expand their thinking to match the real system they belong to or they can artificially shrink the system they are managing to match their thinking. More and more are choosing the former. As André van Heemstra, former Unilever management board member (and co-founder of the Sustainable Food Laboratory, which we discuss in the next chapter) puts it, "The awareness of sustainability has been growing because systems thinking, in different forms, is enabling us to see more interdependencies than we have seen in the past. Those interdependencies make you conclude that it is more than stupid—it is reckless—to think of commercial sustainability in isolation from either social or environmental sustainability."

This growing awareness is leading people to see that we must find ways to manage essential commons such as water and topsoil, healthy ecosystems, rainforests, and stable climate. But we still have a long way to go until we find a number of ways to do this practically. Managing or stewarding these commons starts with a critical mass of stewards—individuals, teams, and organizations who see the risks and who are willing to act. They then must create new systems—formal and informal rules and management practices based on new mental models—that are adequate to the task.

Today, a host of approaches to better managing shared commons can be seen around the world. The most traditional approach is through regulation. But while government regulation is necessary, it is rarely sufficient—especially when it comes to sparking the speed and scale of innovation that is needed today to reinvent products, processes, and business models for life beyond the Industrial Age Bubble.

Moreover, regulations that do not have broad public and business support will be implemented poorly and may even be repealed, as has happened with many regulations proposed during the rapid spread of global business in the past few decades. Another approach that has been growing in recent years is a variety of private-sector certification strategies (such as those for coffee and chocolate) that single out well-managed commons and, by implication, those not being stewarded well.

As we consider the challenges and relative successes of these different approaches, we are starting to believe that ensuring a healthy commons may require developing an effective management commons first. For example, the U.S. Green Building Council's LEED certification system represents, in effect, a new shared body of knowledge, experience, and tools for continued innovation in design, construction, and operation of green buildings and communities. In this case, the total system quality of building—energy use, water use, waste, quality of air, light, and so on—is the commons being managed, and the LEED system is the management commons overseeing it. Why do we call LEED a commons? Because thousands of designers, architects, and builders have a stake in the LEED system working and continually improving. In effect, it is a management commons. This is why diverse professionals and firms collaborate through sharing best practices, design breakthroughs, and discoveries that, in turn, get built into progressively more demanding LEED standards. They all have a stake in making the LEED system work and in continually improving it. This is now snowballing into further development of the market, as building occupants spread the word of significant improvements in energy efficiency, cost of operation, and the health and productivity of people who work in such buildings, which drive demand for more green buildings and new investment in still-stronger standards. This is what we mean: A commons has been created to manage the commons.

This level of collaborative, systemic innovation does not seem to be occurring yet in too many other settings, even though many have recognized key commons and are trying to steward them. For example, many people working in the food business also recognize critical environmental commons (such as fisheries and topsoil and rainforests) and social commons (for example, healthy farming communities). But, so far, this has resulted in different certification schemes, including Fair Trade, the Rainforest Alliance, the Forest Stewardship Council and Sustainable Forestry Initiative (for wood products), the Marine Stewardship Council, and many others. While successful in drawing public attention toward crucial commons, many have struggled with the breadth of implementation needed, and as they have expanded, many are starting to compete with one another. After a while, this confuses consumers ("Whose certification is most valid?") and companies ("Whose certification would be most meaningful for our products?"). In this sense, independent certifiers can end up, paradoxically, embodying the very thing they seek to correct: fragmentation and excessive competition around crucial limits we must all care for. The good news is that, in the past decade, there has been significant progress in starting to protect commons. The second piece of good news is that we all have a lot to learn.

When you contrast independent certification with a system like the USGBC's LEED, several important questions come to mind:

- Is the rating scheme itself transparent?
- Did it arise from a process of collaboration among a meaningful cross section of key players in the respective industry?
- Does it continually lead to more demanding standards, through a process that garners the support of a critical mass of the key private sector interests?
- Is such collaboration ensured as a basis for its continual improvement?

In effect, the basic difference here may be between symptomatic and fundamental solutions. Many certification systems arose as a way to fix an important problem (such as environmental destruction or farmers without livable incomes) rather than in an effort to see the larger system and define commons that need to be collaboratively managed. By focusing on the former, for example, small groups devise systems that embody standards they see as meaningful, but they may end up trying to impose them on others, namely, business interests in the respective industries. Then someone else comes along with a different set of standards or tools and the competition starts.

"Once you reach a point where certifiers and eco-labels are competing to keep their own organizations and brand intact, the whole process may begin to thwart rather than encourage innovation," says Starbucks sustainability director Dennis Macray. Starbucks, in collaboration with Conservation International and Scientific Certification Systems, has developed C.A.F.E. (Coffee and Farmer Equity) practices for assessing healthy social and environmental commons practices for coffee growers. "I think enough of the major players understand the core issues and want to support the basic aims of social and environmental stewardship. But we are struggling now with a better way to do this for producers and consumers."

By contrast, the leverage and opportunity, and the real excitement, comes when individual interests work in concert with others. We have already documented the way that green buildings are taking off, in the United States and the rest of the world. But the movement has also expanded beyond the building industry per se. The number of U.S. cities that have committed to reducing greenhouse gas emissions has grown exponentially from a small start in 2005 to over 715 cities by early 2008. These cities are finding ways to engage their employees, their entire business supply chain, as well as all businesses in their cities, to reduce energy use, scale up use of renewable energy, and cut their greenhouse gas footprint. Similar collaborative efforts are developing among states and regional clusters of states, such as the nine northeastern states of the Regional Greenhouse Gas Initiative (RGGI), which are working to design a regional cap-and-trade program covering carbon dioxide emissions from power plants in the region. And individual states have set their own targets for reducing emissions. New York, for example, plans to reduce emissions to 10 percent below 1990 levels by 2010. Collaboration is building among cities in the United States and around the world to reduce energy use and greenhouse gas emissions, such as through the Clinton Climate Change Initiative and ICLEI—Local Governments for Sustainability, an international association of more than 700 local governments and national and regional organizations that have made a commitment to sustainable development.

All these collaborative efforts are in their infancy. As more people realize that the core challenges of the Big Three global systems—energy and transportation, food and water, and material waste and toxicity—cannot be solved in isolation, these collaborations will spread and become more sophisticated, as people and groups combine systems thinking and skills in collaborating across boundaries. We are just starting to appreciate the level of collaborative systems-thinking skills that will be needed, but there is no doubt this is where real leverage for the future lies.

part V

COLLABORATING ACROSS BOUNDARIES

N ever doubt that a small group of thoughtful, concerned citizens can change the world. Indeed, it is the only thing that ever has," said Margaret Mead. To which we would add, "Depending on their ability to build larger networks." Building a critical mass for change within organizations always starts small, and oftentimes it remains small. Yet some change leaders prove to be masters at building larger networks of collaborators because they know that without this they will accomplish little. Bringing about significant changes in larger systems requires building similar networks connecting many different organizations, and even different types of organizations.

This is difficult work. It takes great courage and even greater patience. It takes facing difficult problems many would like to assume either do not exist or are somebody else's job to fix. Among the many reasons we do not look at problems systemically is that implementing the insights that result would force us out of our intellectual and institutional comfort zones. Unfortunately, we then also define away some of our greatest opportunities to address core sustainability challenges. Fortunately, more people are discovering that collaboration is the human face of systems thinking.

Collaborating successfully requires more than good intentions. It also requires improving your "convening" skills so that you can get the right people together and have more open and productive meetings. It requires seeing reality through others' eyes so that you can better understand what might be holding them and you back from building more open and truly productive partnerships. And it requires forging genuinely shared aspirations to which everyone is committed. In Part V, we will share tools and insights to help you build these collaboration skills—capabilities that are absolutely essential for creating life beyond the Bubble.

[15]

The Imperative to Collaborate

f you sell a new automobile in Europe today, you, the producer, are responsible for taking the car back at the end of its lifetime. Similar regulations have been implemented for most consumer electrical and electronic equipment, such as TVs, video and music players, computers, and appliances. Thanks to the European Union's landmark 2004 extended producer responsibility (EPR) legislation, directives have been established that also include phase-out schedules for a variety of toxic materials and further identification and banning of other dangerous chemicals from various products and production processes. The EPR directives represent the world's first comprehensive government regulations of waste and toxicity—but they will not be the last.

These kinds of regulations change the rules of the game for manufacturers. EPR implies, "If you make it, you own it forever," and can lead companies to design products in very different ways, knowing that they are responsible for them throughout their use and will eventually get them back. Moreover, in the world of global products, many large companies will find that it is less costly to meet the most demanding sustainability regulations for their products rather than, for example, remove lead or mercury only in products sold in the EU and leave them in the same products sold in other regions. This is why more and more global companies like GE are starting to design every product to meet the highest global standard for environmental performance; usually the European market sets the bar their products have to meet.

Traditionally, industries, either knowingly or unknowingly, have been able to pass along waste management costs to society at large, just as they have passed along public health costs resulting from toxins embedded in their products or processes. Initiatives such as EPR internalize these formally externalized costs back to the companies responsible for creating the products in the first place. Gone, for example, are the days when municipalities and regional governments must dispose of these products; this responsibility now sits firmly on the shoulders of manufacturers.

Perhaps even more surprising than the regulations themselves was that they were not met by an army of corporate lawyers and lobbyists focused on repealing them or watering them down. Why? As you will soon see, it was because of an unusual story of European automakers and government regulators who began collaborating across boundaries a decade before the EU mandate was approved.

This is one illustration of a profound shift that has been unfolding for years, as countless collaborative networks have been established around a number of issues pertaining to sustainability and the health of the environment. For example, the World Business Council for Sustainable Development (WBCSD), a CEO-led coalition of 200 companies working together on sustainability issues, claims that its corporate members represent over one-third of the world's GDP. Similar business councils for sustainable development have been set up in other countries, including the United States, China, and Australia.

Other coalitions, such as Ceres and Business for Social Responsibility, provide support for companies who understand and wish to address sustainability issues. The Business Alliance for Local Living Economies (BALLE) is a rapidly expanding network of 15,000 small businesses supporting the growth of locally owned, sustainable companies in the United States and Canada. The Green Power Market Development Group promotes renewable energy sources by guaranteeing large customers for green electricity—and has members such as GM, FedEx, IBM, Pitney Bowes, and Staples.

The U.S. Climate Action Partnership (USCAP) is a group of more than thirty large companies and environmental organizations that have come together to call on the federal government to enact strong national legislation requiring significant reductions of greenhouse gas emissions. Member companies include Caterpillar, Dow, Duke Energy, GE, Johnson & Johnson, Shell, Rio Tinto, and Siemens. USCAP has issued a set of principles and recommendations that underscore the urgent need for a policy framework on climate change. The logic behind CO_2 regulation, for this coalition, is that it will stimulate wider investment in innovation. The founders believe that by championing a broad-based playing field that promotes sustainability, they will not only help achieve a global aspiration but also make it easier for their own companies to take the lead in building a regenerative economy.

The Society for Organizational Learning (SoL) and the SoL Sustainability Consortium, from which a number of the stories and examples in this book arise, involve business and non-business organizations all over the world collaborating for systemic change around core challenges such as food and water, energy, and material waste and toxicity. Worldwide, there are hundreds of such boundary-crossing collaborations in existence, and more alliances of different sizes and in different sectors are being created every day.

When all is said and done, more organizations are collaborating across boundaries because as the complexity of issues grows, people are beginning to understand that any one organization can only do so much. As Randy Overbey, president of Alcoa Primary Metals Development, says, "Collaboration is key for achieving scale."

Behind Overbey's comment lie two specific imperatives that we've seen again and again: the need to build a critical mass for change within an organization and the importance of connecting different organizations so that they can do together what none can accomplish by itself.

While much attention gets focused on highly visible efforts such as the WBCSD, without first patiently building internal leadership networks within organizations to carry forward bold new ideas (as Coke did *before* undertaking its major partnership with the WWF), large-scale collaborations can result in lots of reports and declarations but little real organizational change. Ultimately, however, the scale that Overbey refers to requires reaching beyond individual organizations and building cross-organizational and often cross-sector collaboration.

EXTENDED PRODUCER RESPONSIBILITY

The story behind the EU's extended producer responsibility regulations begins with one company expanding its management boundaries and transforming a limit—the need to recycle more old cars—into a strategic opportunity (two concepts that, you'll recall, we discussed at length in Part IV). But in doing so they had no idea initially that innovating in car recycling and remanufacture would eventually lead to a historic public-private sector collaboration.

BMW had been advancing its knowledge of design for recycling for many years when, in the early 1990s, it wanted to significantly expand its recycling efforts by building a major new recycling center. Management had convinced itself that recovering used components and materials from almost all their vehicles in Germany was both economically sound and in line with society's expectations for the future. In addition, the opportunity to build a large facility that would employ 1,500 workers in the company's Bavarian homeland was politically attractive.

But Horst-Henning Wolf, the man placed in charge of building the new facility, soon concluded that the management plan was not systemic enough. When his team looked closely at the details, they discovered that the financial analysis had omitted a key factor: the total cost of getting all those old BMWs back to one centralized facility. Although he found himself uncomfortably at odds with the company's esteemed engineers, including the board member who championed the project, he was convinced that a single centralized recycling facility would prove uneconomical.

"It makes no sense to transport scrap long distances," he says. "You should only transport value, the recovered materials after disassembly." The original proposal, he argued, used "too narrow a boundary—they only looked at the costs and returns on running the recycling plant by itself."

But there was one big drawback. Wolf's alternative, a network of smaller disassembly facilities, cost more than BMW could invest. "My plan required that we do this collaboratively with other German automakers, which made the plan very risky." Eventually, his bosses were convinced by his analysis—which made the overall costs and benefits much more clear—and canceled plans to build the large recycling center. But they also put him in charge of getting other automakers on board with his plan for a network of smaller disassembly facilities.

Embarking on an odyssey that would eventually last far longer than he imagined, Wolf visited his fellow German automakers, such as Daimler-Benz, Volkswagen, and Audi, to share his vision of a cooperative recycling effort. Because of growing public pressures, recycling was on the minds of many. The concept of EPR had been debated in Europe since the green political parties started to gain power in the 1980s. With 400 million people living in a landmass roughly a third the size of the United States, there's not a lot of "away" in Europe in which to throw things like old cars. Within each of these companies, Wolf found himself pitted against technical experts who had also convinced their respective management teams to invest in advanced recycling for their own cars. But none was considering the implications of a larger system that incorporated multiple players.

"In one meeting," he reports, "an eminent engineering professor made a very elaborate hour-long presentation of a very sophisticated recycling technology he had pioneered. It had many technical benefits, many of which I had trouble following. When he had finished, I apologized for having only one or two slides, and showed them. They summarized our group's analysis of the total costs. When I asked if his cost analysis included the costs of recovering all the old vehicles, he said it did not. The meeting ended in a few minutes."

By the time Wolf was starting to convince his fellow automakers of the plausibility of his cooperative plan, it became clear that some form of government regulation around recycling would come from the newly forming EU. The automakers realized that their best chance of establishing workable regulations was to get all the EU car companies working together with the bureaucrats. If they didn't lead the way, they'd undoubtedly have regulations forced upon them.

Not surprisingly, they asked Wolf and BMW to help make this happen. What had started as an appeal to fellow Germans had evolved into a complex collaborating challenge among all the European automakers and the new EU bureaucrats.

Eventually the businesses rallied around a shared goal for regulations that "encouraged innovation and created broad incentives for businesses to get much more serious about waste and toxicity." Though a few companies might have worked on their own with the government to achieve this, working together gave them a unified voice as well as the opportunity to vet ideas with the many manufacturers who would have to implement them. It also created the broad support needed to sustain the time-consuming process of building shared understanding among very different stakeholders.

Attempts to collaborate across boundaries often fail because the people who need to be engaged—those with both the technical and managerial know-how needed—are unprepared and unwilling to commit the time required. It took almost ten years before a team of negotiators from BMW and their counterpart EU regulators finished crafting the end-of-vehicle-lifetime directive, in 2004. In the three years he was directly involved, Wolf estimates that he spent "about one-third of my time with bureaucrats." The process was slow and a far cry from the disciplined management system at BMW.

"Most of the people had good intentions," he says. "What was time-consuming was the continual education around the practical realities of car design, production, and recovery. Having millions of old cars pile up on dealers' lots was hardly an attractive alternative," but few at the EU had much of a clue about those kinds of real-world problems. "We had to continually stress that regulations that are impossible to implement economically will lead to everyone losing."

In the end, the EU mandates offered workable compromises between government goals and business realities. "Those companies who had been looking at this all along as a systemic challenge stayed in the lead. They had years to redesign their vehicles for easy disassembly and recycling, for example. Many other manufacturers, especially outside Europe, did not have the benefits of this preparation for a future that was coming," says Wolf.

———

For every example of collaborating across boundaries successfully there are many failures. Embedded in successes such as those of Coke and WWF and the European automakers are strong intentions and remarkable patience and perseverance. Less obvious, especially to traditional managers who see such situations strictly as a rational assessment of benefits and costs, are the particular collaborating skills that made these partnerships possible.

Collaborating is ultimately about relationships, and relationships do not thrive based on a rational calculus of costs and benefits but rather because of genuine caring and mutual vulnerability. Building the capacity to collaborate is hard work and demands the best of people, particularly when it involves people from different organizations (or even different departments within a larger organization) with different goals and with little history of working together—maybe even with histories of distrust and antagonism. In particular, we have found that building this capacity rests on three capabilities: convening, listening, and nurturing shared commitment.

[16]

Convening: "Get the System in the Room"

The kinds of large-scale changes that are taking place at Coke or that resulted from the collaboration between the EU and automakers will only occur once you get enough people engaged who have the power to take action. This does not necessarily mean that you should only seek out people in senior management positions. While executive leadership matters, it is but one facet of a far more complex leadership puzzle. We have seen countless meetings of CEOs and senior executives lead nowhere, just as often happens with meetings of senior political leaders. Often, those at the top of institutional hierarchies have far too much invested in preserving the status quo of their own organizations to undertake bold experiments outside their boundaries. And they are often far too removed from the day-to-day realities to appreciate the diverse forces that must be understood to enable real change.

Convening a critical mass of people willing and able to lead, or as the USGBC's Jim Hartzfeld put it, "getting the system in the room," is crucial, but what does this mean practically and how do you do it?

IDENTIFYING STRATEGIC MICROCOSMS

It is usually not possible to get thousands or tens of thousands of people into face-to-face conversations. But conversely, small meetings among people who mostly share the same role in the larger system—just builders, or just architects, or just community activists—generally result in reinforcing entrenched views. Extraordinary change requires building extraordinary relationships, and at some level this requires gathering together diverse people representing diverse views so they can speak and listen to one another in new ways.

As you consider how to do this, keep in mind that there is no simple answer to the question "What is enough diversity?" But there is a guiding principle. Consider all the different parties you know of with a key stake in the health of your organization or community. Then ask yourself a question that Frances Hesselbein, legendary president of the Girl Scouts of America, once posed: "Would each of them see themselves in the room?"

Like all journeys, "getting the system in the room" is a step-by-step process. In addition to requiring great patience and perseverance, it takes insight into who needs to be engaged and when. For example, problems such as the amount of toxins embedded in products reflect deeply entrenched ideas about product design, manufacturing, and business models. Absent external pressures such as the EU's EPR directives, such problems can seem overwhelming—as they did for a handful of people within Nike, who in the late 1990s started asking difficult questions following an eye-opening toxicity report on one of the company's new shoes. Darcy Winslow, then head of a small advanced R&D group, wondered, "Do we really understand the products we—and our whole industry—are creating?" As important, she started to think imaginatively about the "we."

Although she found a sympathetic ear among some senior management, Nike's sustainability efforts at that time were limited to compliance with government regulations (in part, the heritage from the beating it took for the poor labor practices of its contract manufacturers in the mid-1990s), and she was aware that something more was needed. "I knew this had to be about our products because customers experience Nike through our products. We had to find ways to eliminate waste and toxicity in our products."

Fortunately, Winslow had just read Malcolm Gladwell's *The Tipping Point* and was guided by the idea that, as she says, in many settings "once 20 percent of a population begin moving in the same direction, they act as a tipping point for more change in that direction." Gladwell also talks about "connectors, mavens, and salesmen," different kinds of personalities who all play a crucial role in any change process. "I knew that many of our designers were mavens, people who really had a lot of influence because of their technical knowledge and creativity," says Winslow. "Getting 20 percent of 25,000 Nike employees seemed like a tough goal, but reaching 20 percent of 300 designers was a lot less daunting."

Figuring that they also knew many who were natural salesmen for new ideas within the company, Winslow and a few other department heads and midlevel employees became the initial connectors and organized a two-day meeting for 200 of the company's product managers, designers (many of whom are independent contractors, not employees), business partners, and a few executives. Luminaries of the environmental movement spoke, including energy expert Amory Lovins and green architect William McDonough. But the real aim was to get a meaningful cross section of key players in the Nike product system talking with one another, to start to generate a "buzz" around rethinking products at Nike.

But, though exciting, one-shot gatherings do not constitute engagement. People go back to their jobs, the buzz subsides, and things often go back to the way they were. Plus, it will rarely be clear at these early stages whether you've created the truly effective "strategic microcosm" that you need, and if key players are ready to engage.

So, in practice, convening usually becomes a step-by-step iterative process—considering the system you seek to influence, thinking about the variety of key actors in that system, and remembering to include those who traditionally lack a voice in formal decisions or official policies but who possess important circles of influence nonetheless. It also involves understanding how your organization generates distinct sources of value.

For Nike, this has a lot to do with product innovation, which is why designers and product managers are so important.

Once you start to identify and engage an initial strategic microcosm, the real work begins. As with Vermeer and his colleagues at Coca-Cola and Winslow, convening came down to months and eventually years of one-on-one personal conversations.

TOOLBOX
Guidelines for Growing a Strategic Microcosm

In many ways the idea of a strategic microcosm is intuitive and obvious, yet often change leaders, regardless of their formal position, fail to follow any disciplined approach to identifying and building such working groups and networks.

The purpose of the following practice is to keep pushing your thinking about who is and is not included in your initiative. Whether and how you go about engaging new players is dealt with in later practices (see "Stakeholder Dialogue Interviews," page 245), but this process should help you get the right people in the room.

1. Continually reflect upon the system you're trying to change. At this point, it's important to set goals by defining your visions and aspirations and setting key indicators of performance and improvement. Think about the key challenges you're facing, key actors in the system, and the key forces that preserve the status quo as well as those that might help support innovation toward sustainability. Remember the suggestions for rethinking boundaries from Chapter 13. It may help to return to that practice before beginning this one.

2. What are the key voices in this system that you have yet to include in your group or network? Why is this so? Is it because you don't know them or have access to them? Because you believe they do not care about your aims or might even oppose them? Because you believe they do not have influence? Or because they operate on the other side of institutional walls (whether between organizations or other parts of your organization)? The intent of these questions is to help you reflect on your reasoning, not to judge. You may have good reasons for not including or reaching out to certain people, but it is always useful to make these reasons explicit so you can think about and perhaps challenge them.

3. Are there key voices or actors that you may not see? We all have blind spots. The important point is to be open to discovering them. Seek out different opinions about possible key voices and actors you might overlook.

4. If there are important actors in the larger system who are not part of your current circle of contacts, is it time to reach out to them? If not, when might the time be right?

5. How might you go about engaging those currently excluded?

6. Building a strategic microcosm requires ongoing work in organizing; people's roles may shift throughout the process. Throughout your initiative, the people in your "system" will be moving back and forth between the following four groups:

- Core leadership group: those taking responsibility for the initiative
- Circle of engagement: those actively engaged in projects or other work activities of the initiative (regardless of whether this is part of their "day jobs" or outside their formal responsibilities)
- Circle of the informed: those who know about the initiative
- The uninformed: those who do not know about the initiative

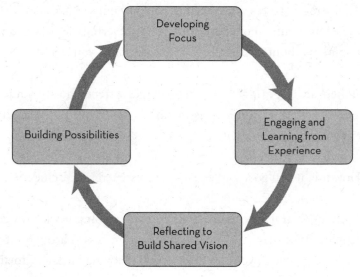

FIGURE 16.1 Building Momentum

BUILDING MOMENTUM AROUND POSSIBILITIES

As people reflect and talk about what matters to them, they start to see exciting new possibilities, which in turn draws others into the conversation—a prime example of the sort of self-reinforcing change we discussed in Part IV.

"It was very organic," says Winslow. "I went knocking on doors. When there was a connection, I just went deeper. The emerging leaders, people who were going to take the idea and run with it, were obvious. They just presented themselves."

While this sounds simple, when examined more closely, engaging people around possibilities differs diametrically from many management-led change efforts, including many sustainability initiatives, as Winslow soon discovered. "We had a mandate from the Corporate Responsibility team to be 'PVC-free,' to get PVCs [polyvinyl chloride, a suspected carcinogen that results in dioxin emissions when incinerated] out of our shoes. But that came across as 'Stop, you can't do that.' To designers, this basically closes a door. We wanted to open doors by saying, 'Think about it this way: There are basically untold opportunities for creating completely new products without compromising performance or aesthetics.' "

Shifting the conversation from the familiar "avoiding something bad" to doing something positive and exciting didn't always happen quickly. Most designers are used to the ever-growing "bad list" of chemicals to avoid, as well as to seeing environmental concerns as "problems." "It took time, and I didn't speak to people just once," explains Winslow. "I had to go back and pursue it again. But it was like finding diamonds in the rough—people who were just waiting to have this conversation."

As Winslow's last comment suggests, the key to building momentum lies in the emotional connection people begin to make to an issue such as eliminating waste and toxicity from products. This takes time and the opportunity to talk openly about what matters. In a corporate setting, where so much gets lost in the quest for profits and market share, difficult sustainability issues touch people in a deep, personal manner—and that can be a powerful catalyst for change. This is the sort of work they will talk proudly about with their kids and spouses. For Winslow, it eventually formed the underpinning of all her efforts at Nike.

"I watched people's reactions to our initial efforts and was so encouraged," she says about her first meeting. "I was getting in touch again with why I love this company. We all have the problems of any big company, but as I rediscovered who Nike is, I realized that we are people who innovate. This company is all about innovation. This is our self-image. Of our eleven corporate maxims, the first is 'It is in our nature to innovate.' That is what really turns people on. We were all seeing that the whole sustainability arena offers untold opportunities for innovation. . . . The more I did this, the more I started to see that the ideas of zero waste and toxicity were natural goals for us."

When Winslow could see how people's passion for sustainability came back to innovation, her whole convening strategy took on a sharper focus. She realized what a lot of people felt. "There must be more to this business than the next cool gadget," as she put it. Designers got excited about design questions such as "How could we design a completely recyclable shoe, or a running singlet that was completely compostable, or find a completely safe alternative to a material or component that was critical to functionality but dangerous to the environment?" Out of such questions problems start to transform into visions, and people naturally begin thinking of ways to create new sources of value throughout the organization.

Shifting conversations from problems to possibilities not only shapes the convening process, it lays a foundation for genuine commitment among those involved and gets them excited about working together, as it has clearly started to do at Nike.

Today, one of Nike's three official management goals is "to deliver sustainable products and innovation." Behind this official goal is a network of hundreds of designers and product managers who share Winslow's passion for the long-range goals of "zero waste, zero toxins, 100 percent closed-loop products," where all manufacturing by-products and materials in products are either reused or biodegradable.

Though the company still has a long way to go before it can realize its zero-waste, zero-toxicity vision, many new products were shaped by these goals—including shoes with no glues or cements, so they can be taken apart at the end of their lives, and products such as clothes that are woven so that no waste is created from cutting the materials used to make them. They have an entire line of organic cotton products (Nike helped create the Organic Cotton Exchange to bring more organic cotton to market worldwide) and an internal sustainable-materials group that informs designers about materials choices, as well as many take-back and recycling initiatives.

But in another sense their convening process—identifying and engaging the key stakeholders for change—is only beginning. They are just now learning how to tap the second major constituency for innovation, by helping customers see how all of this matters to them as well. They recently started a whole new approach to educating customers through their "considered" labeling, which invites customers to consider the social and environmental consequences of their purchasing choices. "It's clear that more and more customers are starting to get the story of how social and environmental issues are intertwined and how all of our purchasing choices have far-reaching influence," Winslow says. "Who knows? This might be our greatest possibility. When you think about it, Nike is one of the few companies that could make this sustainability stuff 'cool.'"

PURPOSEFUL NETWORKING

As the Nike example and others like it show, building leadership networks invariably comes down to investing lots of time in one-on-one or small-group conversations to explore issues and foster engagement. Darcy Winslow spent months and years doing this at Nike, as did Dan Vermeer at Coke, as did the founders of the USGBC and the Cleantech Network. But time does not guarantee effectiveness, and purposeful networking is different from personal networking.

Connections lead to more connections. In addition to going "deeper" with particular individuals, network leaders like Winslow, Hartzfeld, and Carstedt are always asking, "Who else should we be talking with about this?" In this simple way, existing networks of common interest and concern start to identify themselves. "The emerging leaders . . . just presented themselves," as Winslow said. Purposeful networking starts with a perspective on who the key players are in a system, such as the product designers at Nike or the architects, designers, builders, and owners in the construction industry. If you do this well, over time your perspective will evolve and you will see other roles that were less apparent to you at the outset. Yet this happens only as you better understand who the key actors are and how they're shaping the larger system you belong to.

As you engage different people, invariably their responses will differ. While it might be a natural instinct to try to convince those who show little interest in the questions you are pursuing, or to obsess about particular people or roles you feel are crucial, it is usually more effective to look for those who seem to understand the importance of the issue right away—those with whom, as Winslow said, you sense "a connection," and who are willing to "go deeper." "Often," says Per Carstedt, "I found that you can tell in a matter of minutes how genuinely interested a person was."

This does not mean that everyone else is unimportant, but purposeful networking is about shaping, and continually reshaping, a collective sense of key questions and opportunities. The process will lead to surprises. Invariably, you will find that people whom you never expected to be interested or whom you thought had little interest will start to get engaged, in part because of the influence of others whom they respect and in part because no one ever really asked them or listened deeply to their views. This is why it is crucial to learn how to suspend prior judgments and preconceptions. Many who will prove to be important partners will be people you never knew or about whom you had contrary opinions.

Lastly, many who fail to show much interest early on often respond differently later, when they see a critical mass starting to form around issues that concern them. "We found that a lot of people who showed little apparent interest in our ideas at the outset," says Hartzfeld, "we couldn't keep out of the meetings later on, once they saw that some real momentum was building."

TOOLBOX
Stakeholder Dialogue Interviews

One of the foundational practices of convening is purposeful interviews with key stakeholders, such as opinion leaders in areas outside your department. These interviews are usually done one-on-one or with a small group. The key to doing this well starts with the inner state and orientation of the person doing the interview.

Often, people approach meetings with key stakeholders with the aim, either explicit or unstated, of engaging the other or others in their initiative. This often produces disappointing results; stakeholders can feel like they are on the receiving end of a sales pitch and respond with either polite but noncommittal agreement or outright rejection.

At the other extreme, the interviewer enters with an open mind and just asks lots of questions. This often also fails to generate much real energy among stakeholders, as the interviewer offers little of substance with which others can engage, and may even lead interviewees to become suspicious of a hidden agenda.

The alternative is to make your own concerns and aspirations clear and come to learn, rather than to advocate or sell your own ideas. Imagine that the person with whom you are about to talk could really be a teacher for you. If you are willing to sincerely adopt this attitude, you will often find that it is a powerful self-fulfilling prophecy. Here are some useful tips for doing this:

1. **Preparing.** Joseph Jaworski, a pioneer in these kinds of learning interviews, says that the most important time is the hour before an interview, when he enters a quiet state.[1] He makes no effort to focus on particular questions or aims, and does his best to let go of any stereotypes or other prior feelings he might have about the person he will be interviewing. His goal is simple: to relax and clear his mind as much as possible so he can be fully present during the interview. Whether or not you have an

hour free beforehand, taking a few moments to relax and let go of worries or preconceptions is always useful.

2. **Opening.** Tell the interviewee why you are there, what is important to you, and what you are interested in learning. Be honest and concise. If there is something specific you feel is appropriate to say about why you wanted to speak with this person, say it simply and without hyperbole (for example, "Your views are widely respected in the organization" is a much more effective approach than something like "You are one of the most brilliant people who have ever worked here and everyone respects you so much").

3. **Engaging.** It is usually best to ask one or two simple and open-ended questions that give people a chance to reflect on their experience and feelings. Obviously, the nature of the question will depend on the setting and your overall aims.[2] In her interviews with designers and product managers at Nike, Winslow would relate what she and her colleagues had learned about waste and toxicity problems and explain why she thought this was important for Nike, and then ask something like "What is most important to you about design and new products at Nike? And how, if we were at our best, would you see us facing these challenges?"

4. **Following the flow.** Follow the conversation as it emerges. Keep in mind that the word *converse* derives from the Latin *convertere*, which means "turning together." This is a wonderful image for moving with your partner and beginning a true dialogue (a word that has a similarly interesting derivation; it stems from the Greek *dialogos* ("flow of meaning").[3]

5. **"Jumping off the bridge."** This metaphor for letting go of whatever it is that's holding you back from connecting with the interviewee comes from Ursula Versteegen, who noticed, after more than a decade of these sorts of interviews, that she would sometimes get to a point where she became unwilling to leave her "safe ground" and move with the emotional state of the other person or people.[4] How this wall arises is different for each of us, but it is usually associated with feelings that cause us to dis-

tance ourselves from others, such as anger, apathy, or sadness. Many of us respond internally to such emotions by ignoring them and going "back to task." "My feelings have nothing to do with waste reduction or alternative energy," we tell ourselves. But they have everything to do with building a relationship in the here and now, with "total presence," as Versteegen puts it.

6. **Expanding the network.** If there is a real connection and you can tell the other person is genuinely engaged (if, for example, she or he says something like "This has been a great conversation" or seems eager to schedule a follow-up), you can ask, "Is there anyone else I [we] should talk with who shares your concerns or who could contribute in this overall effort?" In this way, networks of like-minded people start to "present themselves," as Winslow put it. (In general, it is usually not a good idea to ask this question if the other person is not clearly engaged in the conversation, as he or she may consider such a request intrusive and is unlikely to respond usefully.)

7. **Closing.** So often, workplace conversations end with a feeling of incompleteness; it is a real luxury to have even a few moments to pause and ask, "How was this time useful for you?" or "What do you think needs to happen next?" or "If we really made progress in this area, what do you imagine we might accomplish?"

Ultimately, no set of tips can encapsulate the capabilities of a master in stakeholder interviews. Every situation is unique, as is every interviewee. Your ability will flow from your willingness to embrace that uniqueness and be yourself—and be genuinely curious.

RESPONSIBILITY FOR THE WHOLE

People naturally invest time and energy in convening when it's a way to express their own passions and visions. But, paradoxically, their willingness to let go of cherished beliefs and views is also crucial to allowing something bigger than themselves to emerge.

By definition, convening strategic microcosms means bringing together people with very different views of problems, causes, and solutions. As a result, you will encounter competing explanations for why certain problems exist and different ideas on who should bear responsibility for particular problems and actions. You will naturally agree with some more than others, and find yourself drawn into taking sides. It is pointless to try to suppress your own views. But it is equally counterproductive to be governed by them. As a convener, your fundamental task is to create safety and openness so people can take in multiple views and build the capacity over time to actually "hold" or consider these differing views seriously, as we will explore further in the next chapter. This all starts with conveners with a larger sense of responsibility who can avoid getting too attached to any one specific vision or idea.

Looking back on the remarkable patience and goodwill required on all sides to persevere through years of negotiations for the EU's end-of-vehicle-lifetime directive, Horst-Henning Wolf states, "The key was that we said from the beginning, 'We will take responsibility for the car.' This was always our view at BMW, but we had to get agreement with all the auto companies. Then we could speak with one voice to government. This made the EU regulator group much more willing to work together with us. They did not have to try to force us to be responsible."

When conveners take responsibility for the health of the larger system that lies beyond their specific vision, new visions can emerge. Recall that when the organizers of the USGBC started off, they did not have the idea of a LEED-type rating system. They knew only that they needed to "get the system in the room" and to "see the building as a system." Beyond that, they had a bias toward voluntary free-market mechanisms to encourage innovation, and they knew they would need to build momentum one small step at a time—in other words, to "seek agreement and go." The galvanizing vision of a comprehensive rating system that incorporated all the primary dimensions of a healthy building and that could guide a market-based process of innovation and continually rising standards emerged only over time. Whether or not they realized it, their success as conveners came from not having "the answer." After all, it is much harder to engage people in "your program" than it is if you invite them to help shape the program.

The willingness to make the health of the larger whole more important than personal agendas becomes all the more critical as the group becomes more diverse. As Oxfam GB President Barbara Stocking, a co-founder of the Global Sustainable Food Laboratory (a cross-sector alliance we discuss in the next chapter), says, "We simply have to face the fact that these large systemic problems are going to continue to get worse if we don't start working together. This will not be easy. For example, many in the NGO world do not much like big business. But we must decide what is more important: our past politics or the future we hope to influence."

[17]

Seeing Reality Through Others' Eyes

ew systems are more daunting than the global production and distribution of food. Agriculture is the world's largest industry; it is
also among the most problematic of our global systems. Even the
largest food corporations, such as Unilever, can do little by themselves to
influence the forces driving overproduction and eventual loss of key agricultural resources (including topsoil), falling prices and farm incomes
over the past fifty years, and deteriorating farming communities.[1] That
said, the Global Sustainable Food Lab, an effort to bring together diverse
actors from business, civil society, and government to better understand
the ways food is grown, harvested, bought, and distributed around the
world, is an unusual initiative that may well hold valuable clues for collaborating across boundaries in the twenty-first century.

The Food Lab's mission is to bring sustainable food systems to the
mainstream by designing, implementing, and sharing innovations in policy and practice.[2] Among its diverse membership are Unilever, HJ Heinz,
General Mills, Starbucks, Sysco, Costco, Green Mountain Coffee, Carre-
four, Oxfam, the Rainforest Alliance, the World Wildlife Fund, the Kellogg
Foundation, and the Bill and Melinda Gates Foundation. After almost two
years of convening informally, the Food Lab began in 2004 with an initial

forty-person core leadership group.[3] This team came from multinational corporations, small organic farming businesses, global and local NGOs, worker unions and cooperatives, and governmental ministries. Though most were at the vice president or director levels in their organizations, they each committed forty days of their time (in addition to their other responsibilities) over the first two years of the project to better understand global food systems and how to work together to change them.[4]

In a speech given a couple of years earlier, Chris Pomfret, VP of Marketing for Unilever Europe, expressed the urgency that compelled such commitment: "'Can sustainability sell?' is the wrong question. The real question is: 'Can a business like ours survive in the long term without sustainability?'"[5]

In our experience the Food Lab is unique in its attempt to build deep and ongoing collaboration among such a large and diverse group of organizations. Before we examine some of its particular activities, it will be helpful to reflect on some of the capabilities and ideas that helped it come into being and that guide its mission.

BUILDING RELATIONSHIPS

The more daunting the change necessary, the more sophisticated the collaboration skills must be of those leading the change. This sounds almost self-evident, yet it is easy for people seeking to create new products, processes, and business models for life beyond the Industrial Age Bubble to become so absorbed in advocating for what they think needs to change that they pay little attention to how they will build and sustain the relationships needed to achieve the change.

We often find that most sustainability advocates fall into one of two camps: Either they think that the reasons to change are so clear and compelling that anyone awake must be on board, or they look at the enormous gap between what is and what is needed and become cynical, arguing that the changes needed will never occur or demonizing those who preserve the status quo. In between are a smaller number who have both a passion for the vision and an understanding of the need to build the collaborative networks the vision requires.

Over time, those who develop the skills necessary for life beyond the Bubble become masters not only at focusing on getting the right players involved but also at fostering deeper conversations and relationships among previously distrusting parties. As the founders of the USGBC put it, "Once you've got the system in the room, you've got to get them to stop throwing chairs at each other."

CONVERSATIONS THAT SHAPE THE FUTURE

But, in fact, throwing chairs can be a step above the "terminal politeness" that dominates and ultimately stifles many such groups. Harvard researcher Chris Argyris calls this "smoothing over," and like its counterpart "speaking out," it represents a natural reaction in working groups of all sorts and especially those trying to collaborate across boundaries. Like the instinctive fight-or-flight reactions to physical threat, people in groups dealing with others who see the world very differently often feel trapped, with only these two possible options: extreme politeness or debate.

Though the surface behaviors differ, in fact the outcomes from smoothing over and speaking out are similar. The reason is that at a deeper level, both work in ways to preserve the status quo. Groups who smooth over do so by simply avoiding threatening issues. In groups characterized by speaking out, as one manager put it, "We all speak our minds here, but no one's mind is ever changed."

But there are other options, ways of interacting where the past no longer dominates, as shown in Figure 17.1. You'll recall that focusing on the future is essential to moving toward the above-the-line strategies in the Sustainable Value Framework we introduced in Chapter 9. Similarly, in our experience, we have found that above-the-line conversational states are necessary for collaborative efforts that can lead to such strategic innovations. Otherwise, posturing and the pursuit of individual agendas ultimately will thwart significant innovation.

Above-the-line conversations start to develop as enough people begin to genuinely appreciate one another's ways of looking at reality. The first stage in such conversations, empathetic listening, is easy to espouse but not so easy to do; because we all get so caught up in our views of reality,

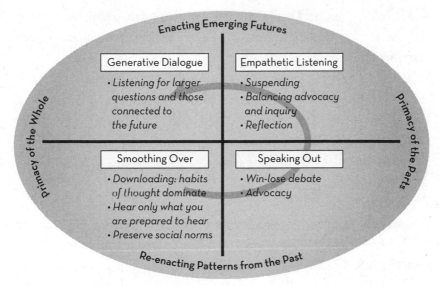

FIGURE 17.1 Four Types of Conversation
Source: Developed by C. Otto Scharmer.

we often find it hard even to pay attention to what other people are really saying. The second stage of deeper conversation, generative dialogue, can be quite different from normal business conversations. People speak about what is true for them, without attempting to imply that this truth is universal. They likewise take in other people's truths. There is little pressure to agree. Indeed, a certain trust develops that in speaking and listening honestly, a deeper understanding of the world or a particular issue is possible. This is where real "thinking together" begins.

Both empathetic listening and generative dialogue ultimately involve people becoming more open and more vulnerable, opening both their minds and their hearts. For pragmatic managers, opening the heart may seem "soft" and a long way from what is needed for tackling difficult problems, but just as there is a "thinking of the head," we believe there is also a "thinking of the heart." The former has to do with reason and logic, while the latter has to do with meaning and becoming fully engaged, two qualities that are essential for tackling systemic problems. This understanding sits behind Darcy Winslow's focus on conversations where there was "a connection," or Dan Vermeer's comment on following the "creative energy" at Coke and cultivating a "bias toward engagement and under-standing one another."

Ultimately, above-the-line conversations depend on three skills: learn-ing how to suspend immediate assumptions, reflecting on mental models we had previously taken for granted, and balancing advocacy for our ideas with inquiry into other opinions.

SUSPENDING ASSUMPTIONS

It is natural to take our perceptions as objective, yet nothing could be further from the truth. Women see situations differently from men. Sales-people see a different reality than do engineers. Chinese see a different world from Americans. This is not good or bad. It is human. We are not machines passively recording a separate external reality. We are living be-ings continually interacting with that reality and, through that interac-tion, constructing our awareness.

With a bit of thought most people can appreciate that none of us really sees reality as it is. Most people can also see how, over time, our personal perceptions can become self-reinforcing and gradually build up mental models, untested assumptions, and habitual ways of seeing—such as when we develop stereotypes of certain types of people.

The problem is not these habitual mental models in the abstract but their pervasive influence in our daily lives. As the old saying goes, "The eye cannot see the eye." To do so, you need a mirror; you need to reflect.

This is what we refer to as "suspending assumptions"—in effect, hold-ing them out in front of you. Rather than asserting that what you believe is the truth, people who practice suspending their assumptions recognize that their views of situations are, in fact, *their* views. This subtle shift brings with it greater humility and ability to listen to others. In working teams, suspending assumptions breaks down the rigidities in thinking that otherwise thwart dialogue; as a result, people become more willing to inquire into their own and one another's views. As one very "nuts-and-bolts" CEO commented when asked about the differences he saw in his organization after several years of work in organizational learning, "It used to be that people said, 'This is the way things are'; now they say, 'This is the way I am seeing things.'"

Teams that develop the practice of suspending assumptions often use a tool called the Ladder of Inference.[6] The ladder is a metaphor for how our minds work, as we move quickly from observable data (what a video recorder would record) to many levels of inferences about that data: immediate meanings, assumptions based on those meanings, conclusions, and more general beliefs reinforced by those conclusions.

When teams or working groups get stuck in unproductive conversations, you can be sure that it is because members have moved up their ladders of inference and cannot get back down. For example, recall the stuck management team wrestling with differing views about alternative sustainability investments we introduced on page 141. When Ted, the VP

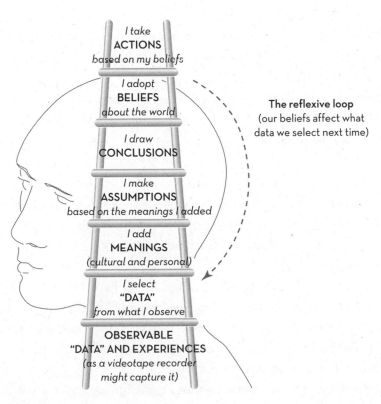

FIGURE 17.2 The Ladder of Inference

of EHS, says that he believes the company should "completely rethink our approach to capital budgets" and "swing at least 30 percent of our future capital allocations to renewables," you can easily imagine Joanne, the VP of Operations, thinking, "That's way too big a bet." Based on the immediate "meaning" that's formed in her mind, she may very well also assume that "Ted is way too emotional about these issues; he seems to be ignoring the huge uncertainties" or simply that "Ted always runs with the pack," based on her view that he's advocating sustainability because it is politically correct to do so.

Based on her conclusions, she counters Ted's enthusiasm for renewables by pointing out, "Oil was half its current price only two years ago. . . . Price fluctuations are inevitable in this business."

These statements reflect Joanne's assumptions about fossil fuel prices and renewables—views that are perfectly understandable. What is problematic is not Joanne's views but that they emerge as reactions to her inferences about what Ted said and that she does nothing to *test* her inferences. This is so common in teams that few would even notice it. But it is a primary reason why differences of view become sources of embedded conflict rather than opportunities for learning.

For example, Joanne could have said she was worried about the uncertainties in Ted's proposal and asked Ted what he thought about this. This could have led to the team exploring the major elements of uncertainty and risk and even agreeing to have someone prepare a more complete risk analysis of different options. Instead, she reasserted her core belief, "The world will be living off fossil fuels for a long time," and the conversation went nowhere, merely reinforcing old divides among the team members. This is an example of how speaking out reinforces patterns of thinking from the past.

The tragedy is not the speaking out in and of itself, but rather that no one on the team noticed that it happened—that is, no one recognized the opportunity for learning that flickered in front of them and was immediately extinguished. Both the learning opportunity and the potential strategic investment opportunity were missed.

By suspending assumptions, we recognize inferences we are making and then seek more data to confirm or refute them. It is not that assumptions about complex sustainability issues such as those being debated by the team can be decisively proven or disproven. But the discipline of testing our assumptions forces us to make them explicit, opens the possibility that they might not be 100 percent correct, and lays the foundation for learning over time. Conversely, failure to suspend and test assumptions is the most surefire way to guarantee patterns of interaction that simply reinforce positions from the past. In this way, untested assumptions come to govern organizational actions, just as they undermine genuine attempts at collaboration.

BALANCING ADVOCACY AND INQUIRY

Conversely, productive conversations are marked by high levels of inquiry and high levels of advocacy. People are simultaneously passionate and curious. They are comfortable sharing their views, but they are also prepared to look closely at those views and the assumptions that lie behind them. They expect others to see things differently, and they are good at learning how to appreciate what leads others to see things as they do.

Ironically, inquiry is often mistakenly taken as a sign of weakness, an indicator of uncertainty. Most successful people have gotten to where they are, in management and other professional fields, because of their capabilities to formulate their ideas and express them in ways that compel others' attention and even assent. Their success as advocates may even have been reinforced by investments and support for their causes, or articles written about their style and work. But rigid advocacy becomes counterproductive when people face truly complex problems that require tapping into collective intelligence.

For example, Jim Hartzfeld of the USGBC said that it was clear that the expertise needed to devise an integrative rating system for green buildings resided not "in any one expert's head, but in bringing the expertise distributed across the industry into the conversation."

When leaders of collaborative initiatives truly believe that their success or failure hinges on fostering collective intelligence, knowing how to help people suspend assumptions and balance advocacy and inquiry can make all the difference. Hartzfeld, Bob Berkebile, and the other founders of the

USGBC knew not only that they had to get the different vested interests into the same room, but that they had to transform the way these people typically interacted.

They developed a strategy of continually exposing one another to their different areas of expertise. "People would advocate strongly where their energy and experience lay," says Hartzfeld. But each expert saw only "one part of the elephant" and had to learn how to suspend their respective passions for ventilation, or energy efficiency, or recycled materials in order to pay attention to the other parts. "People continually had their perspective expanded by everyone else's," says Hartzfeld. Gradually, this evoked curiosity about subjects outside their expertise. "Invariably people would say, 'There's more to this than I thought.'"

Similarly, they deflected the tendency to "leap up the ladder" and make strong negative inferences about one another (or worse, to invoke old stereotypes that reinforce divisive feelings) by structuring meetings so there was "time for people to talk about what was important to us personally, why we were volunteering our time and energy to work on this together," says Berkebile. The result was that "when various people's views came into conflict, there was also some understanding of one another as individuals who cared deeply about real change."

(Another tool for helping groups diagnose particular patterns of smoothing over or speaking out is the Four-Player Model—see the Toolbox on page 276.)

When your group gets stuck, in either smoothing over or speaking out, getting "above the line" to more generative interactions can seem daunting, but here is where the overall context of collaborating for sustainability innovations can make a big difference. Because issues such as water, green buildings, and eliminating waste and toxicity really matter to people, even small steps in the direction of truly listening to one another and harnessing collective intelligence can multiply. Just as meaningful issues can cause people to hold on to entrenched views, once people get a sense that letting go might lead to real change, the willingness to do so can surprise even the most entrenched cynic.

Perhaps this is the real message of the experiment in "seeing reality through others' eyes" that produced the LEED system. Neither Hartzfeld (a manager from Interface, where he was first exposed to organizational learning tools such as the Ladder of Inference and systems thinking) nor Berkebile (an architect) would call himself an expert group process facilitator. But both understood the basics of how to improve the quality of conversations and, as a result, tapped into a deep current of potential change. This became even more evident once the LEED system really took off, creating a self-reinforcing cycle of learning and innovation that continues today as new standards are created to guide new waves of green building. Looking back, Hartzfeld says, "It is clear there was widespread pent-up desire to act—to design and build greener buildings—waiting for some common vehicle to direct it into collective action."

In our experience, this is not unique to the LEED system and green buildings, but characterizes the whole sustainability field. When individuals within systems are open to change, those systems—which may have seemed impossible to shift—can also open up and change.

OPENING HEARTS AND MINDS:
LEARNING JOURNEYS

With an understanding about mental models and generative conversation, the Sustainable Food Lab initiative (introduced in the beginning of this chapter) moved quickly from an audacious idea to a working reality.

From the outset, Hal Hamilton, co-director of the initiative, and his colleagues faced the challenge of getting a number of busy, committed, and very different people to slow down and think together about how each actually saw these complex and emotionally charged problems. "Most food companies think the answer to improving their business is to use technology to increase productivity," says Hamilton. "On the other side of the street, many activists are dedicated to fighting big corporations, which they see as destroying local farming communities and ecologies through falling incomes and overproduction. Governments get caught in the middle between corporate pressures to boost production and drive prices down and the political instability of farmers displaced from their lands. I've been working in agriculture for over thirty years and the idea of everyone working together often seems like a romantic fantasy."

The journey to a deeper dialogue started with in-depth interviews with each of the initial forty lab team members, followed by a week-long capacity-building workshop, where they all were introduced to core tools and principles of systems thinking, reflection, and thinking about the future together, many of which we've shared in this book. These initial steps served to help people grasp the basics of collaborative learning. But for most of the participants, the Food Lab really started with week-long "learning journeys" to rural Brazil.

Learning journeys are expeditions taken in search of a new understanding of an issue or a set of issues. Learning journeys mean leaving the familiar behind and going to see unfamiliar aspects of a system firsthand. Depending on what you are trying to understand, that may mean simply traveling to another part of your company and "shadowing" or following a colleague whose work you have never done. Complex issues often require travel by groups (sometimes to other regions or even other countries) who are seeking to build a collective understanding of a system or a part of a system. But often the system we need to see firsthand is just around the corner, so to speak. The key is moving outside of the familiar, not necessarily moving great distances physically. It all depends on your aims.

We all know some parts of the system we belong to firsthand, but we know many other facets only through books and articles, or through reports and figures. When done well, such as the Coke-WWF trip to the Quiangy preserve in China, learning journeys not only take people physically to places they have not been, but open awareness beyond the intellect. "Going there" means seeing a different place firsthand, talking with people we usually do not talk with, seeing how people live, work, play, raise their children, and help those who are sick: Only then do we start to sense, rather than just understand intellectually, a larger system. Especially important is to use the direct experience to consider views very different from our own, views held by people whose historical experiences of the system we belong to may differ.

The Food Lab's learning journeys to Brazil revealed aspects of the industry both robust and fragile. The trip included visits to huge sugarcane and soy farms, large processing plants for food and ethanol, cooperatives that served small farmers, coffee and sisal producers eking out a living on tiny parcels of land, innovative specialty producers of grapes for European markets, and marginal plots reclaimed for the settlement of landless farmworkers. Many of the community and environmental activists within the initial Food Lab team were meeting with multinational companies for the first time. Of the corporate team members, many saw the plight of rural farmers in ways they never had before.[7]

The group traveled everywhere together, so they had lots of time to talk about what they were seeing and notice how differently they interpreted and reacted. For example, visiting a farmer cooperative elicited hope for an NGO team member: "This is a real way that small farmers can achieve a critical mass of economic and political power." But it elicited skepticism from a corporate team member: "They seem too disorganized to accomplish much." Another corporate lab team member later commented, "I am still amazed that people can look at the same thing and see such different things. . . . I find it confusing. There is so much I don't understand about others' perspectives."

Surprisingly for many, people discovered that wrestling with one another's very different experiences and views was as important as "solving the food problems themselves" because, as one NGO participant put it, "We are not likely to do one without the other. We have gotten to know one another as people—not just businesspeople or civil society people—to see that we do not have to agree with one another, and that is a good thing."

The experience, as one participant said, "began to penetrate the superficial façade of polite agreement" (smoothing over). As discussed above, prior to the trip, many saw open debate (speaking out) as the only alternative to this politeness. With enough time for reflection and conversation, learning journeys can start to reveal a third possibility: above-the-line conversations that open hearts as well as minds. Gradually, relationships based in genuine respect and empathetic listening can start to grow.

C. Otto Scharmer, who developed the "Four Types of Conversation" figure shown earlier in this chapter, characterizes the states "above the line" as "a generative field"—one where our aspirations for futures we truly desire become more dominant than the anchors tying us to the past. While many collaborative efforts strive for these kinds of conversations, few are successful because they are unable to overcome what Scharmer calls "the voice of judgment," which keeps people attached to their views, and "the voice of cynicism," which hardens their hearts through the belief that genuine change is not possible.

You don't need to travel as far as the Food Lab team did to understand how the following five elements of all learning journeys can help open your eyes to a larger reality beyond the one you usually see:

1. Bring together a diverse group of people that, to the highest degree possible, represents the larger system you belong to.
2. Identify the different facets of the system that you will explore.
3. "Go there together"; travel with the entire team.[8]
4. Set aside ample time to reflect and talk together about what you experience.
5. Pay careful attention to the intentions and commitments that arise from your reflection and take time for these as well.

The last element is an essential aspect of all learning journeys, whether they involve traveling to a different country, to the offices of one of your suppliers, or even down the hall to a different department. Learning journeys, at their essence, are about "sensing" (or opening awareness to the present moment), but the goal is not simply awareness for its own sake, or to only deepen relationships between key players, but doing this in the context of compelling issues about which people care deeply. The team members must ultimately be prepared to reexamine their own beliefs and tried-and-true approaches in the service of genuine change.

TOOLBOX
Protocols for Balancing Advocacy and Inquiry

When you feel passionate about something as politically charged as sustainability issues are today, it is essential to learn how to balance your advocacy for the issue with a humble questioning approach. Learning this skill is perhaps the best way for individuals, even those working by themselves, to begin changing a large organization from within. You don't need any mandate, budget, or approval to begin improving these conversational skills. And you will almost always be rewarded with stronger relationships and an improved reputation.

Use these conversational "recipes" whenever a discussion offers you an opportunity to learn—for example, when a team is considering a difficult point that requires information and participation from everyone on the team. For additional tools and suggestions, see *The Fifth Discipline Fieldbook*, pp. 255–58.

1. PROTOCOLS FOR IMPROVING YOUR ADVOCACY SKILLS

Make your thinking process transparent by walking up the Ladder of Inference slowly.

What to do	What to say
State your assumptions and describe how you arrived at them.	*"Here's what I think and here's how I got there."*
Explain your assumptions.	*"I assume that . . ."*
Make your reasoning explicit.	*"I came to this conclusion because . . ."*
Explain the content of your point of view: Who will be affected by what you propose? How will they be affected? Why?	

Give examples of what you're proposing, even if they are hypothetical or metaphorical.	*"To get a clear picture of what I'm talking about, imagine that you're the customer who will be affected...."*
As you speak, try to picture other people's perspectives on what you are saying.	
Publicly test your conclusions and assumptions.	
Encourage others to explore your model, your assumptions, or your data more deeply.	*"What do you think about what I just said?" or "Do you see any flaws in my reasoning?" or "What can you add?"*
Refrain from defensiveness when your ideas are questioned. If you are advocating something worthwhile, then testing any potential flaws in your plan will only make it stronger.	
Reveal where your thinking lacks clarity. Rather than making you vulnerable, it defuses the force of advocates who are opposed to you, and invites improvement.	*"One area in which I could particularly use some feedback..."*
Even when advocating: listen, stay open, and encourage others to provide different views.	*"Do you see it differently?"*

2. PROTOCOLS FOR IMPROVING YOUR INQUIRY SKILLS

Ask others to make their thinking process more transparent.

What to do	What to say
Gently walk others down the Ladder of Inference (see page 255 for a refresher on the different steps of the ladder) and find out what their assumptions might be.	*"What leads you to conclude that?"* *"What data do you have for that?"* *"What causes you to say that?"*
Use nonaggressive language, particularly with people who are not familiar with these skills. Ask questions in a way that does not provoke defensiveness or "lead the witness."	*Instead of "What do you mean?" or "What's your proof?" say, "Can you help me understand your thinking here?"*
Draw out people's reasoning. Find out as much as you can about why they are saying what they are saying.	*"What is the significance of that?" "How does this relate to your other concerns?"*
Explain your reasons for inquiring, and make it clear how your inquiry relates to your own concerns, hopes, and needs.	*"I am asking you about your assumptions here because . . ."*
Test what others say by asking for broader contexts or for examples.	*"How would your proposal affect . . . ?" "Is this similar to . . . ?" "Can you describe a typical example?"*
Make sure you understand what others have said.	*"Am I correct that you're saying . . . ?"*
Listen for the new understanding that may emerge. Don't concentrate on preparing to destroy the other person's argument or promote your own agenda.	

3. PROTOCOLS FOR FACING A POINT OF VIEW
WITH WHICH YOU DISAGREE

What to do	What to say
Again, inquire about what has led the person to this view.	*"How did you arrive at this view?"* *"Are you taking into account data that I have not considered?"*
Make sure you truly understand the view.	*"If I understand you correctly, you are saying that . . ."*
Explore, listen, and offer your own views in an open way.	*"Have you considered . . . ?"*
Listen for the larger meaning that may come out of honest, open sharing of alternatives to your own assumptions.	
Raise any concerns and state what is leading you to have them.	*"I have a hard time seeing things that way because of my experience. . . ."*

Building Shared Commitment

Trying to get people committed to a sustainability initiative is a bit like trying to be happy: The harder you try, the less successful you're likely to be.

The challenges are all the greater in would-be collaborations where diversity is high, organizational affiliations are complex, and entrenched worldviews are strong. Conventional management approaches to building commitment—such as performance management or reward systems—are of little help. First, when people are working together across boundaries within or among different organizations, there is usually no clear authority structure to administer such rewards. Second, because the aims of such collaborative initiatives often take time to evolve, it can be difficult to gauge success. Third, the depth of commitment required usually far exceeds what can be fostered by normal carrot-or-stick approaches.

Instead, you will find that shared commitment arises through focusing first on engagement—connecting to what matters to you and the larger organizations involved—and then on creating the opportunity for both focus and commitment to deepen naturally over time.

FOSTER ENGAGEMENT, AND
LET COMMITMENT DEVELOP

Recall the mantra of the U.S. Green Building Council founders in their early days: "Seek agreement and go." Rather than allow themselves to be overwhelmed by the enormous challenges before them, they focused instead on building momentum by starting with small, tangible tasks. As Jim Hartzfeld explains, "We looked for particular questions or tasks that groups had energy to work on and said, 'Let's go. We'll learn more from getting to work on these than from just debating the big issues where we all disagree.'"

Such strategies could be seen as ways to avoid deeper issues, but that's only true if they lead to a pattern of ignoring the big issues indefinitely. Rather, what we have seen is that engagement builds relationships. People start to get to know one another through common tasks. It builds shared understanding, however limited. And, if coupled with time for reflection and deeper conversation, getting people engaged can make it easier for diverse players to gradually talk together about their larger aims and deeper concerns. It is always easier to turn a canoe once it is moving in the water. It takes a lot more energy to turn it when it is sitting still.

CONNECT WITH WHAT MATTERS TO YOU
AND YOUR ORGANIZATION

Your ability to foster commitment will never be greater than your own commitment. The key in fostering shared commitment lies in connecting to what you care about and what the organization cares about, and gradually knitting the two together.

All organizations, especially those that live for a decade or longer, have within them the capacity to create and innovate. Otherwise, they would never have survived as the world around them changed. The problem is that often this capacity atrophies, and even very successful organizations fail, despite having resources, talent, market position, and plenty of motivation to survive. Pursuing the profound innovations needed for life beyond the Industrial Age Bubble offers an extraordinary opportunity to tap and even grow that generative capacity—if for no other reason than the depth and breadth of the changes that are required.

Costco, one of the largest retailers of food in the United States (it is the largest wholesale club), has become a leader in prototyping healthy food supply chains through their work with the Sustainable Food Laboratory. Joining the Food Lab was not the result of a CEO request or a means to fulfill a food sustainability strategy. Instead, the story started with one woman who was not directly involved in the food side of the business.

Sheri Flies had worked for the company for twelve years as corporate counsel when she became interested in sustainability. "I knew a bit about food systems and the plight of farmers driven into poverty around the world by falling prices, but I was not a professional. I personally bought Fair Trade coffee. But I kept thinking, 'There must be more I can do.'"

But to find a viable path, she had to find how to connect her concerns and her company's, and doing this required learning things she knew but didn't know that she knew.

Sustainability champions who fail to understand what their companies stand for frequently end up trying to push their ideas into the organization. They achieve marginal impact at best and risk alienating a great many people who might otherwise be open to becoming engaged themselves. When Flies started to meet representatives of other Food Lab companies, such as Unilever and Green Mountain Coffee, at member meetings and learn about the various projects, she could see the potential relevance for Costco, but she had no idea how to get other managers at the company on board: "Costco is a company that has its own way of doing things, and talking about transforming relationships across the supply chain would have seemed too 'far out' at that time."

She began talking to others in the company and, to her surprise, discovered some who were already working seriously on creating more sustainable food supply chains. They just didn't label them as such. Eventually she found ways to position what she had in mind so that it resonated within the company's management.

"It took me a while, but I gradually started to discover how to connect with our corporate DNA," she says. "We have a tradition of long-term relationships with loyal suppliers. We are a 'handshake' company at our roots. We value key suppliers and see it as part of our business that they do well, so that we all can do well. All of this stems from our core commitment to quality for our customers. We are the only company in our business, as far as I know, that has a corporate policy limiting how much we can mark up any product, because to mark it up further would be unfair to our members. To achieve this, we must have reliable, high-quality supply. So we have a predisposition to truly care about our suppliers.

"I could see that what was needed now was to just expand the boundary of that caring. I just needed to help managers see that reliable food supply chains today required looking beyond our immediate suppliers to who supplies them. This would lead naturally to a different degree of proactiveness to assure healthy conditions for farmers and farming communities."

Tapping the generative DNA of an organization creates the spark needed for commitment and innovation. There is no magic formula for doing this, and it always involves idiosyncratic features that make each organization, like each person, distinctive. Nonetheless, we have seen again and again in companies with a strong underlying identity that people who have an open mind and who are committed to the health of the larger whole, and who also possess ample doses of patience and humility, will eventually find their way to this connection.

When they do, leaders such as Flies and Darcy Winslow of Nike also help many others in the organization to rediscover what they stand for. In the pressures of the day-to-day delivery of "results," it is easy to forget that organizations are human communities. As a community, the organization came into being because there were enough people who cared about something to pursue it together. At Nike, it was passionate runners trained by a legendary coach who had a major breakthrough in creating running shoes for world-class athletes.[1] At Starbucks, it was coffee lovers. At Google, it was technology visionaries who wanted to shape the Internet. Costco was created by a group of people with extensive retailing experience who were genuinely dedicated to high quality and low cost for "member" customers. As time passes, businesses evolve and new circumstances and visions shape new ways of operating. But, as in any human community, roots matter, and connecting with them leads to change processes that have much greater potential to elicit widespread engagement and success.

CREATE SPACE FOR INTENTION AND ASPIRATION TO GROW

Fostering genuine commitment is difficult territory to talk about in the abstract, because invariably it is intensely personal. Yet, paradoxically, it is not about us at all.

As one CEO once put it, "All genuine commitment is to something larger than ourselves."

From watching gifted leaders of all sorts, our conclusion is that they approach the matter of shared commitment with patience and profound respect for personal autonomy. But this does not mean they stand by passively. They work tirelessly at convening diverse players who represent key stakeholder interests and helping people see one another's realities and deeper aspirations. They honor history and physical place. And they become very good at "holding a space," creating an atmosphere where people feel safe to reflect and be open and honest with one another. Put another way, they have a sense for the sacred.

In the two years after Sheri Flies had gotten involved with the Sustainable Food Laboratory, she quit her job as corporate counsel and switched to the food side of the business. After intense operations training, she took responsibility for several pilot projects—opportunities to prototype new management practices for healthy value chains. Each involved fostering new scales of collaboration beyond what anyone had attempted previously.

One of these concerned premium French green beans that Costco sourced from Guatemala. After a year of convening and immersing herself in the on-the-ground realities of this food chain, she found herself in a very unusual business meeting.

On a cold January morning in 2007, Flies sat in a solemn ceremony in a reconstructed chapel of a 400-year-old convent in Antigua, Guatemala. Beside her was the project team she had assembled: Costco's assistant vice president for procurement and general merchandise manager, Frank Padilla; Dale Hollingsworth, one of Costco's buyers; two local Costco buyers; the director of CIAT (the International Center for Tropical Agriculture, a regional NGO specializing in tropical agricultural communities); Tulio Garcia, co-founder and director of the Cuatro Pinos Cooperative; several local farmers and employees from the co-op; and the president of a food wholesaler, co-op customer, and Costco supplier, the Los Angeles Salad Company. The occasion was a mass dedicated to Garcia's son, Juan Francisco, who had died in a tragic car crash earlier in the year. The pilot project itself had been, at Flies' suggestion, named in his honor.

As she sat in the service, Flies thought about what had brought her to this point. Knowing that a healthy green bean chain meant healthy farming communities that could protect their local environment, she had already taken several extended trips to Guatemala and worked with Mark Lundy of CIAT (whom she met through the Food Lab), and together they all agreed to participate in an independent audit of the entire supply chain in the country, to try to track all dollar flows in order to determine who added value at each step, as well as to assess the social and environmental impacts.

The audit started to assemble a picture of what was working and what was problematic in the system, but it also raised a difficult question: "Who was this audit for?" It would be typical in a situation like this for the corporation to take action unilaterally based on such a study without concerning themselves with the actions of the cooperative or others in the supply chain. In this case, they decided to include all the key players in a review of the audit, including local farmers (who had never seen people from the corporate office getting so involved in the field) and representatives from the farmers' co-op.

"It would have violated the sense of relationship we were building to not all do this together," says Flies. Furthermore, they decided to have the meeting not in the United States, where Costco was headquartered, but in rural Guatemala, near the highlands where the Mayan farmers lived. They wanted to foster a different experience for meeting attendees, and when Garcia suggested that they start by attending the mass that had been scheduled for his son, Flies agreed, following the instinct of a partner she had come to know and trust.

During the service, many of Juan Francisco's family spoke about his life. "It was very moving," said Flies, "and a little bit of a shock to the

Costco people. This was not your typical "buyers' meeting." But as the service went on, it was clear that they, too, were caught up in the feelings of the moment. "One of my areas of learning through the past two years since I started this work," says Flies, "was the importance of the sacred when we come together for serious conversation—a simple prayer for guidance, blessings from an elder, or just giving each person a chance to express their deepest intention when opening a meeting.[2]

"When Tulio mentioned the mass for their family, we both felt that it would be a perfect setting for all of us to recognize the families and communities we were part of. What I didn't know was the impact it would have on the others. It turned out that Frank Padilla hadn't heard a full Catholic Mass in Spanish since he was a child. He told me later how it brought him back to his own roots of family and place. I believe it was also a healing experience for Juan Francisco's family, and I never expected we might help them in this way."

After the mass and a large family meal, the project team met, sitting in a circle, and reviewed the audit report, which everyone had read in advance. It documented the vulnerability of the farmers, environmental and social problems, and the forces continuing to drive the business "into greater and greater stress." Flies and Lundy posed three questions: "What are the main things you hope to achieve through our project? What surprised you about the report? What are the main barriers you feel exist to realizing your highest aspirations for the project?" In the conversation that ensued, people spoke candidly, and many heard perspectives that they had never heard directly before.

The next morning, the group drove four hours to a remote village for two days of conversation with the farmers and their families. "It was very cold in the highlands when we arrived, but there were the farmers waiting for us," said Flies. "They had a presentation planned. Each family sat down together with us, one family at a time. Everyone talked—kids, parents, grandparents. For some people, everything had to be translated twice, from their native language, Quiché, into Spanish and then into English. They took us to their fields and into their homes. They told us their children have shoes and more clothes, are now able to go to school, and that they have more money to buy food. All of this was because they have a good market for their crops and have learned better agricultural practices from the co-op. Despite the stresses and risks documented in the report, much had been achieved, especially in the partnership between Costco, LA Salad, and Cuatro Pinos."

Near the end of the visit, one farmer said, "This is the first time we have ever had an equal voice." Another added, "Everyone listened."

"It was interesting," said Flies, "that when we asked the initial questions that first day, everyone's goals for the project were different. I think this was very important. It showed that we could really be honest with one another, and it sort of symbolized the whole idea behind the project: really seeing our different circumstances and needs and yet still being committed to a system that can work for everyone."

After three days, the Costco people left, committed to working more closely with Cuatro Pinos by offering business advice, helping to improve sustainable yields, and developing general procurement procedures that more specifically recognized the health of the farming communities. Since then, they have also helped the cooperative to establish additional crops. All of these initiatives are part of the larger Juan Francisco project.

Looking back at the meeting in which the study was reviewed, and Costco's continued work since, Flies describes the biggest shift as follows: "Our buyers know who grows the product; they no longer make decisions in a vacuum. This is not just the case for the Cuatro Pinos farmers but for many others elsewhere. People see now that this is where teaching sustainability starts—not just with ideas and metrics but with knowing the farmers and knowing that they get a fair return."

For example, they learned that LA Salad and Cuatro Pinos have set up a reserve fund (into which they put 10 percent of all sales) so that farmers are always paid on time despite losses due to weather or transport problems. "This is a huge deal for them," says Flies. "This is a business where there always are things you cannot control, and traditionally the people who suffer most are the farmers." It also showed the Costco people how committed "middlemen" such as LA Salad (a link in the value chain that large retailers often want to eliminate in order to lower costs) could actually contribute to the security of the system in ways that Costco could not.

In turn, the project has informed several other similar supply-chain projects in the company and seems to be leading to self-reinforcing growth in innovation. "When I started, this was really fringe stuff," says Flies. "Sustainability is no longer fringe in our company; it is mainstream. Our shareholders ask about it. People throughout the company are asking what they can do, and many people in different areas are now working on projects." Beyond individual value chains, new projects are being explored that will help entire industries, such as the rapidly growing U.S. organic milk business: "It is so important that people learn how to see the entire system, what questions to ask, and how to see the typical unintended consequences of management policies," says Flies.

In one sense, the work of innovators such as Flies comes down to helping people recognize that seeing systems ultimately means seeing one another. Time will tell how widely this subtle lesson spreads. At the end of the day, Costco is a business, and a business mentality inevitably pervades the interactions of people within the company. "While this [mentality] is practical for making sound business decisions, people get so used to it that they often cannot set it aside and truly look more deeply, into themselves and into the larger system," says Flies. "We may end up making the right decisions for the wrong system. If we can't change how we are with one another, how will things ever really change?"

Opening minds and hearts starts the process of moving beyond our own views and agendas so that we can start to connect with one another and truly work together to create new systems. But there is a third opening that we've seen time and again among people who have embraced systems thinking and collaborating across boundaries—an opening of the will. This is what happens when people, individually and collectively, truly become open to their sense of purpose or destiny. These, again, are unusual words to use in conjunction with developing practical approaches to very real problems such as healthy food systems and robust farming communities. Yet they are, as Flies says, often exactly what is missing.

TOOLBOX
The Four-Player Model: Identifying Current Patterns in Your Working Team

Over our years of working with teams, we have noticed that there are observable and powerful patterns of behavior that significantly impact a team's ability to produce results. David Kantor, a pioneer in applying systems thinking to groups, has observed that there are four types of individual conversational behaviors that continually recur in human interactions. These four "conversational actions," or types of statements, occur regardless of the content of a conversation—but we find they are particularly relevant for the intense conversations that often occur around subjects such as sustainability.

The four types of action and their purposes are shown in Figure 18.1 below:

In a well-functioning team, each one of the actions is present and effective, and there is balance among the different types of actions. In effect, the "diamond" in Figure 18.2 should be full and symmetrical, with no particular weak sides or distortions. Conversely, when one or two of the behaviors is absent or much weaker, the diamond collapses.

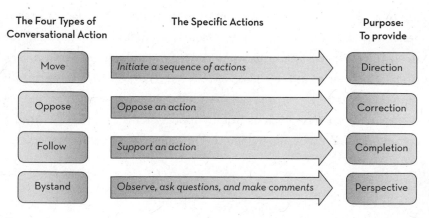

The Four Types of Conversational Action	The Specific Actions	Purpose: To provide
Move	Initiate a sequence of actions	Direction
Oppose	Oppose an action	Correction
Follow	Support an action	Completion
Bystand	Observe, ask questions, and make comments	Perspective

FIGURE 18.1

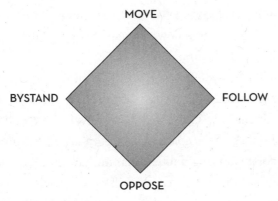

FIGURE 18.2 Four-Player Model

In a productive conversation there's a balance between advocacy and inquiry, and each speaker comes "down the ladder" to share his or her reasoning or feelings in an open way that invites responses and further exploration.

For example, an **effective mover** might advocate a position or action for the group, but would do so in ways that invite others' opinions. A poor mover, on the other hand, often takes a bull-in-a-china-shop approach by attempting to force her or his view on the group.

Similarly, an **effective opposer** is firm but respectful, often advocating a different direction than one initially proposed: for example, "I disagree with Bill, and this is why . . . but Bill, what do you see that I'm missing?"

An **effective follower** is clear and often takes a proposition one step further or offers sincere emotional support: "I agree with this position and here's how I would move to action . . ." Poor following is weak and ambiguous: "I guess that's okay with me" (or even silent assent).

Lastly, an **effective bystander** can observe and offer comments that bring another perspective without proposing a particular solution. A bystander can also ask questions that cause people to look at a complex issue with fresh eyes or offer a personal reflection, such as "I have noticed that in the last few minutes the energy in the group has dropped—are we missing something?" An example of ineffective bystanding is disengaged silence; people don't speak up because they are afraid of sticking their necks out or getting caught in power dynamics (we call this type of silence the "disabled bystander"), or just don't care.

How do you know if you have a well-functioning team? First, assess the presence or absence of each type of behavior. Then assess how effective it is. Overall, what characterizes a healthy team is balance and fluidity. All four actions should be common and seen as valuable, and individuals are fluid in their ability to take on different roles.

Here are some of the specific characteristics of a well-functioning team that David Kantor and Stephen Ober's research has identified. As you review this list, think about your own team. How many of these characteristics do you consistently demonstrate?

A Well-Functioning Team

1. The team has the capability to engage in all four behaviors in observable, balanced sequences.
2. Individuals in the team have the flexibility to engage in more than one of the behaviors.
3. The team, and individuals within it, do not tend to get caught frequently in repetitive, almost ritualized patterns of interaction.
4. Members of the team are adept at playing the enabled bystander role in order to help them stay unstuck.
5. People on the team are able to make clear, rather than mixed and ambiguous, statements.
6. When no resolution is possible, the team is clear about this and identifies the important questions or next steps toward whatever degree of resolution is appropriate.

Stuck Teams

The four-player model is especially useful in helping teams diagnose when they are stuck and see what is needed to get unstuck.

There are certain recurring patterns that arise when a team gets stuck. While even healthy learning teams will get stuck at times, recognizing when one or more of the four roles is missing, or noticing if any of the following patterns arise, can help get you back on the right track.

1. **Yes-men.** One or two powerful figures emerge, and the rest follow their lead without questioning.
2. **Death by meeting.** A few people do all the talking, transforming the rest of the group into disabled bystanders.
3. **What are we doing here?** No one takes a stand on an issue (makes an effective move), so there is no clear path forward.
4. **The debating society.** People get stuck in "move-oppose" dynamics—in other words, people get stuck in arguments in which they rarely suspend or shift predetermined positions.

WHAT TO DO WHEN A TEAM GETS STUCK

Let's return once again to the story about the stuck management team in Chapter 10 to see how the "debating society" pattern develops. Specifically, Ted, the vice president of Environment, Health and Safety, and Joanne, Operations vice president, quickly get stuck in a "move-oppose" interaction, in which neither makes any effort to shift. The result is that everyone else ends up taking sides. Stan, the vice president of Public Affairs, chimes in on Ted's side, and then the CEO, Robert, sides with Joanne by concluding that no new actions are warranted at this time.

When someone makes a move, and the next person opposes that move, and so on, teamwork deteriorates into a behavioral tennis match. Following and bystanding are either absent or ineffective at bringing perspective or closure. Note that Anthony, the vice president of Strategy, makes a bystanding comment at the end, when he asks, "What are the implications for the future of our company if you [Robert] are wrong on one or both of these issues?"—but the comment comes so late in the meeting that it's unclear if it has any effect.

What happens when your team falls into a recurring pattern such as the move-oppose pattern? Does it get stuck? Do other behaviors disappear? How can you support each other in bringing forth effective bystanding when you get stuck?

Here are some basic steps and developmental practices for your team to get unstuck and become more effective:

1. Have each person identify their favorite action. A good way to do this is to have each person in the team go to a corner of the room that represents their preferred action or the one they think they are most skillful at.

2. Look at how the group naturally distributes itself. Is it all movers, all opposers, et cetera? Rarely are teams perfectly balanced.

3. Ask yourselves, "What are the consequences of our present preferences in terms of how we work, resolve particular issues, or make people feel their ideas are taken seriously?"

4. Ask everyone to reflect on what skills they want to develop. A useful step is to have people move to the corner of the room that represents their aspirations.

5. Talk about what it would take for each member of the team to progress in their learning and how the team could support them (everyone can also work on building their skills for balancing advocacy and inquiry in order to support the entire process).

6. Finally, as a team, commit to regularly reflect on your patterns of interaction, to recognize stuck patterns, to acknowledge progress, and to continue to improve.

part VI
FROM PROBLEM
SOLVING TO CREATING

As we said at the outset, problem solving differs from creating and, though both matter, the vast changes required for creating a regenerative society will not be achieved just by reacting to crises after they arise. They will require inspiration, aspiration, imagination, patience, perseverance, and no small amount of humility. They will require networks of committed people and organizations who not only learn how to see the systems shaping how things work now, but also create alternatives.

People creating together work in different ways. They are anchored in the future rather than in the past, drawn forward by images of what they truly want to see exist in the world. They learn how to work with a distinctive source of energy that animates the creative process, the creative tension that exists whenever a genuine vision exists in concert with people telling the truth about what exists now. They learn how to let go of having to have everything worked out in advance and to step forth with boldness into immense uncertainty. And they learn that tapping these capacities cannot be achieved without people being who they truly are and learning how to integrate their own lives. As one woman put it, in frustration, in a team meeting, "I hate all this crap about 'hats,' the manager hat, the spouse hat, the mommy hat. I am just me and this is my life; I don't go around switching from one person to another based on circumstances."

The organizations that truly lead in the profound changes starting now to unfold around the world, who do not get stranded in just being "less bad," will be those who convert sustainability challenges into compelling strategic opportunities. They will be the ones that create the truly new products, the new businesses, the new energy infrastructures, and the new management practices and organizational structures. Operating consistently in a creative orientation is neither magical nor mystical. It is simply people working at their best, passionate and personally committed yet selflessly being stewards for a future, many aspects of which they will never see.

[19]

Innovation Inspired by Living Systems

Businesses innovate or they fail to survive. What will differ for life beyond the Industrial Age Bubble will be what *inspires* that innovation.

Ultimately, the shift from a reactive problem-solving mind-set to a creative one is all about inspiration. More specifically, it's about taking nature as our primary source of inspiration. "What we kept coming back to again and again," says Jim Hartzfeld of the U.S. Green Building Council, "was the simple idea of doing things like nature does them. Seeing the building and the larger human community within and beyond it as if this was a living system. By continually reminding people of this, it became a beacon to cut through the difficult conflicts and the huge areas of uncertainty we had to navigate."

Similarly, Nike's Darcy Winslow hired Janine Benyus, who introduced "biomimicry" principles in her 1997 book of the same name, and her colleague Dayna Baumeister as consultants in her efforts to build excitement among the company's product designers about natural systems. The first of several multiday workshops brought together representatives from twenty different functional areas within Nike, such as design, logistics/

transportation, human resources, organizational development, and engineering. "Janine's work has become a continual reminder to all of us," says Winslow, "that no matter how difficult the design challenge, we have 3.5 billion years of experimentation we can draw on."

Another inspiration for Nike and many other companies and groups, including Steelcase, USGBC, Seventh Generation, Interface, Herman Miller, and Ford, has been the cradle-to-cradle design ideas of architect William McDonough and chemist Michael Braungart.

Of course, before there were modern sciences such as chemistry and petrochemistry, the study of nature was the common foundation for societies that endured millennia. In fact, returning to nature as a teacher and a cornerstone for strategy and innovation is not even a recent development in the world of business. Almost twenty years ago, for example, a team of Xerox engineers made its own startling and cathartic discovery of this teacher while rethinking product design.

ZERO TO LANDFILL

Before the world had ever heard of biomimicry or cradle-to-cradle design, a remarkable new green product line was built by a team of engineers at Xerox. The ambitious Lakes concept was transformed into a whole new generation of copiers, first released in the late 1990s. Sales from this Document Center family, by many accounts, were pivotal in maintaining the company's solvency amid extreme financial stresses in the late 1990s and early 2000s. Moreover, design innovations embedded in the product have yielded over 200 patents, inspired countless imitators both within the copying industry and beyond, and eventually won the product the National Design Quarterly Award and team leader John Elter a nomination for the National Medal of Technology.

When a group from the SoL Sustainability Consortium visited the DC 260 manufacturing site in 1999, they walked into a state-of-the-art "lean" facility that was full of sunlight and buzzing with energy. The first thing people noticed was how clean and quiet this assembly facility was. Everything seemed to have a tag on it—for example, every shipping container was tagged with the name of the supplier to whom it would be returned.

Suspended overhead was an enormous sign: "Zero to Landfill, for the Sake of Our Children." Only later did they learn the story behind the sign.[1]

In the early 1990s CEO Paul Allaire charged Elter with leading Xerox into the digital age by developing a new generation of digital copiers that could print, copy, scan, send and receive documents, and communicate directly with PCs—all thanks to reliable networks, the emergent World Wide Web, and digital architecture that could integrate all these functions.

"It was a 'clean sheet design,' where we could start from scratch, develop the specifications that made the most sense, and invent the processes needed to deliver a different product," said Elter. "It was a bet-your-company type of situation."

Given a blank canvas on which to re-create copying for the digital age, Elter and his colleagues took the liberty of breaking rules all along the way, starting with the way they formed their team. In particular, Elter wanted his team to have a deep appreciation for ecosystems, and how the product would need to be designed for the environment from the beginning. The design objective was to be able to reuse and/or remanufacture all parts.

"We knew it would take new thinking to do what we were setting out to do," he recalled, "so we wanted to form the team from the outset in a way that would get people connected to their purpose, the company's purpose, and to one another more deeply than normally occurs."

Elter hired a small New Mexican company named Terma, now called Living Systems, that had developed an innovative process for helping people to connect in a deep way to the relationship between themselves and nature. It was decided to take team members, in groups of a dozen or so, through this process, which included a two-day wilderness "solo." Initially these were held in New Mexico; later they continued in the mountains of upstate New York, closer to Xerox's Rochester headquarters.

"The solo was crucial because we knew people had to get to a deep place, where they could let go of a lot of history and what they thought they knew," Elter explains. "I don't think we appreciated just how deep it would be for some. There were many who had never been by themselves like that in nature, and although it was completely safe physically and we had lots of support from the Terma staff, it took some to new places in themselves. Alone in the high desert, watching the sun set and moon rise, with the incredible New Mexican night sky, and then watching a day dawn, from complete darkness to the first twinges of light until the sun starts to radiate and fill the sky, can be a profound opening for people."

At the end of their solo time, the groups would gather for their walk back to the retreat center. During this time, one group was intentionally guided past a large landfill. Someone suggested they go down into it and see what was there. When they did, they discovered part of an old Xerox copier.

"It is hard to fully explain what happened then," says Elter. "But after two days in the pristine wilderness, the waste of it all really became clear. We were standing in the midst of something that simply never happens in nature. The fact that these people knew all about the copier, how it was designed and built, what was in it, how long many of the components would take to decay—it really hit people. The collection of metal, plastics, rubber, and hundreds of different chemicals that go into making a copier would be sitting there a lot longer—several hundred times longer—than it ever sat in a customer's office. Were we designing products for customers or just organizing the assembly of lots of materials, almost all of which had been extracted from nature, for a brief visit to a customer on their way to a landfill?

"Engineers naturally calculate. I think in that moment a lot of engineers were multiplying the thousands of copier machines that companies make and customers ship to landfills around the world every year, and multiplying that by the number of different companies and the number of different industries all doing the same thing. That's a big number. That's a lot of junk in a lot of landfills.

"At that point, someone said, 'Let's stop.' Then someone else added, 'What if nothing we make ever ends up in a landfill again?' People didn't need to say anything in response. They knew she was right. That's when our vision, 'Zero to Landfill,' was born."

The inspiration of building machines where everything could be used and reused led to an extraordinary wave of creativity. Design engineers know that great creative work comes from understanding constraints. No artist paints on an infinite easel. No sculptor sculpts with materials that are infinitely malleable. Music gets performed with instruments that have limitations. Constraint is crucial to creativity. But something was different now. As Elter later said, "For the first time in their lives, the engineers felt like they were not working on just typical constraints from management, like unit manufacturing cost; Zero to Landfill was nature's constraint."

Over eight hundred managers, engineers, and technicians were involved in the creation of the new Document Center DC 260. At the outset of the project, a Xerox veteran commented, "What is needed is certainly a green machine, but even more necessary is the 'greening' of the company itself, the creation of an ecology of the human mind, heart, body, and spirit." As a result, the team's "Bill of Rights" included "managing from the heart," and "people, process, product, planet" became a guiding mantra.

After almost six years of development, Xerox introduced a line of copiers that transformed the industry and then the company itself. As for the new machine, it was (and still is, in later models) more than 93 percent remanufacturable and 97 percent recyclable. For more than ten years it was manufactured in waste-free plants. Nothing—not material scrap, not packaging, not one piece of plastic, not even the drinking cups used during the creation of the machine—is simply disposed of and sent to a landfill. The Lakes team even managed to convince its primary suppliers of the importance of their Zero to Landfill vision, and many adopted similar measures.

Equally remarkable about the Lakes Project was its net effect over time. Current Xerox CEO Anne Mulcahy points out that due to the reuse and remanufacture of parts and components, "We estimate that we have given life to the equivalent of more than 2.8 million products. Last year alone [2006], we diverted more than 122 million pounds of waste from landfills." Since 1991, in fact, Xerox has diverted 1.9 billion pounds of waste from landfills. Elter estimates that this saves the company more than $400 million per year in manufacturing and component costs.

We will return to the principles and understanding that characterize projects such as Lakes and explain how you can embrace them too. For now, it is enough to recognize that it is not about copiers, but about what is possible when talented people breathe life into products for a regenerative economy.

LIVING SYSTEM BUSINESS MODELS

The business model that drives virtually all Industrial Age companies can basically be reduced to "selling stuff." After customers have gotten the value they seek from their car, computer, or iPod, they discard the product at the end of its service lifetime and replace it with more stuff. In effect, people buy a thing for its temporary value; when there is no more value, no one wants it any longer. Disposal falls on the shoulders of the customer—and ultimately upon society as a whole. But in a circular economy, designing products for "life after life" means also designing business models with the same aim. While this might be aided by government regulation, as with the EU's end-of-vehicle-lifetime directive, it can also be accomplished through innovative business models inspired by nature.

Shortly after John Elter retired from Xerox in 2001, he joined Plug Power, a leader in innovative fuel cell technology and natural gas "re-forming" (the converting of natural gas into hydrogen), as its chief technology officer. He brought with him the Zero to Landfill vision; in fact, the U.S. Fuel Cell Council has since adopted the goal for the entire industry.

But, beyond technological innovation, Elter also brought important questions about business models. "Designing products to be remanufacturable is of little use if they are not actually remanufactured, and this depends on having easy and cost-effective ways to get the products back when customers are done with them," said Elter.

Elter and his new colleagues at Plug Power set out never to sell products, but rather to lease them and thereby retain ownership, as well as the responsibility for taking them back at the end of their service life. The aim is not only product recapture but also the alignment of producers' and customers' interests in ways that "selling stuff" alone never could achieve.

Elter says, "Businesses that once thought about themselves as designers of stuff, and who more or less ignored what happened to the stuff once they sold it, will now be designers of not only the products but also the flows of continual use and reuse, which will mean that the 'stuff' never leaves their attention." This will focus companies *completely* on the value-in-use of the products, the value to the customer, because the product is guaranteed to come back. Elter says, "It will be more like loaning something you value to a friend, rather than selling something to someone you don't really care about."[1]

For example, short service lifetime is a major limitation of present fuel cells. When Plug Power leases rather than sells the fuel cells, Elter says, "Service life and reliability become *our* problem, not the customer's, because we have to take the product back and replace it if it is no longer serving—or else we lose the customer's business. This both builds better customer relationships and motivates us to keep improving."

It also means that customers can align their own concerns about reducing waste with their desire for improved service from improved fuel cells. Much like the aspirations of new mission-based companies such as Seventh Generation, this means moving beyond "transactional" relationships between customers and producers and toward working together to reduce waste and improve an important alternative energy product.

Most traditional business models make selling something more important than creating genuine value for customers. The side effects, however, are unsatisfied customers and overflowing landfills. In effect, this traditional model represents a fundamental disconnect between business and their customers, on the one hand, and the larger community, on the other, perpetuating a system that creates enormous flows of wasted materials and energy.

The disconnect suggests significant possibilities for companies to rethink how to create more value for customers, the community, and the environment, all at once.

[20]

Unleashing Everyday Magic

The Xerox story is one of hope and inspiration, not fear, a fitting reminder that the verb *to inspire* originally meant "to breathe life into." Stories like these, beyond the specific lessons and ideas they convey, breathe life into our sense of possibility and our own potential.

"At some logical level, there is really no way to explain what the Lakes team was able to accomplish," says John Elter. "We went from a prior product with over 2,000 parts to a totally new platform with less than 200, which all went together with screws and snaps for disassembly. You don't get those kinds of changes from just solving a lot of technical problems."

But in another sense, while magical, what Xerox was able to accomplish is not mysterious. We have no idea of our capacity to create the world anew. But first we must understand the profound shift in orientation that comes when reacting to problems is transcended by creating, and the commitment, skill, and vulnerability that this demands.

POSITIVE VISION VERSUS NEGATIVE VISION

"As the saying goes, at some point we had to put up or shut up," muses Jeffrey Hollender, founder of the highly successful consumer goods company

Seventh Generation. "So we decided that rather than campaigning and try-ing to stop things we didn't like, we would just create a company that tries to change the nature of consumption by working directly with consumers to help all of us see our potential impact in creating a healthier world."

Hollender, whose background included social justice concerns and marketing, wanted to "develop a business where the more products we sold, the more positive an impact we would have on the planet. Many of us are cynical about how much of a difference we can make. We designed the company with the simple idea that buying everyday products could give people hope by showing that their actions—as small as it might seem to choose which roll of bathroom tissue to buy—actually make a difference."

Tragically, this spirit of "creating" is virtually the opposite of the attitude that has characterized much of the history of the environmental and social justice movements. Consider the many worthwhile movements with *anti-* in their label: anti-smoking, anti-drugs, anti–nuclear arms. Now many around the world are mobilizing to fight climate change. People invest enormous amounts of time and energy trying to make a better world by fighting against the world they don't want. The same type of negative vi-sion stategies frequently play out within companies: Bosses motivate peo-ple to change by stressing what will happen if they fail to do so, consequences that range from losing market share to losing their jobs.

Fighting threats you seek to avoid can be a powerful motivator, but only to a certain extent. Once the threat goes away, so too does the moti-vation to change. Negative visions can also lead to demonizing others as the source of the threat, rather than developing an attitude of shared re-sponsibility for the problems and for the solutions. Ultimately, change strategies based on reacting to threats limit the commitment, imagina-tion, and collective intelligence needed for ongoing innovation. In short, fear cramps imagination. And the commitment generated by fighting something or someone differs fundamentally from the commitment gen-erated by working to bring something you truly care about into reality.

But, people ask, "Aren't the sustainability problems we face today truly desperate? Isn't it vital that our societies wake up and see the urgency of change?" Yes, they are. And yes, it is. But while we all need wake-up calls to remind us that change is needed, it is how we respond to these signals that makes all the difference. The difference between a creative mind-set and a problem-solving mind-set is like the difference between a person who, after a heart attack or stroke, chooses to start living differently and one who lives in constant fear of another catastrophic health event. It all comes down to choice and the capacity, regardless of circumstances, to focus on a vision of what we truly desire instead of what we seek to avoid.

The view, shared by many within organizations and throughout society, that change will never occur without desperation and fear carries with it a subtle and profoundly limiting message—that we are incapable of changing simply because we have a vision of what we truly want. If the desperation theory were truly correct, we never would have learned how to walk, talk, ride bicycles, or become a violinist or engineer. These profound learning processes were driven by aspiration, not desperation, and learning to create a regenerative society and economy will be no different.

CREATIVE TENSION VERSUS EMOTIONAL TENSION

But vision alone, no matter how positive, is not enough.

In our work over the past three decades with leaders in all sorts of positions and all sorts of settings, we have found that a defining feature of those who accomplish remarkable results is their intuitive understanding of these differences between problem solving and creating. It shows up in the types of energy and commitment they tap, in their patience and ability to build momentum, and ultimately in their ability to help people manage and make use of the inevitable tension between powerful visions for the future and an honest reckoning of what exists today.

"Just as Socrates felt it was necessary to create a tension in the mind, so that individuals could rise from the bondage of myths and half-truths," wrote Martin Luther King Jr., "so must we . . . create the kind of tension in society that will help men rise from the dark depths of prejudice and racism."[1] In this statement, King identifies the core principle underlying the creative process, what we have come to call creative tension.[2] King is famous for his dream of racial equality, but he did not just sit back and wait for his vision to come to fruition. Many of his leadership strategies involved "dramatizing the present situation"—in other words, showing the reality of race relations in American society at the time through marches, sit-ins, and other acts of civil disobedience. King's vision had power precisely because he effectively showed how it differed from the current reality.

King chose his words carefully, knowing that the word *tension* suggests anxiety or stress. But creative tension does not by itself produce either anxiety or stress. It is simply the gap between the image of what we truly want to see exist and the world as it is today. Imagine a rubber band stretched between your vision and current reality, as it is between the two hands in Figure 20.1. When stretched, the rubber band creates tension, representing the tension between the upper hand, the vision, and current reality. What does tension seek? Resolution. There are only two possible ways for the tension to resolve itself: pulling the vision down toward reality, or—if the vision remains steady—pulling reality toward the vision.

In this way, the tension between vision and current reality naturally creates energy for change. Neither holding a vision nor seeing current reality, by itself, creates this energy.

The real artistry of leadership comes not from creative tension alone but from understanding and working with its inevitable companion, emotional tension. Dealing with fear, anxiety, stress, anger, sadness, resignation, and even despair is an inescapable aspect of leadership because

VISION

CURRENT REALITY

FIGURE 20.1

such emotions naturally arise when we face the gap between our visions and reality. When you consider the enormous size of the challenges related to food and water, energy and climate change, waste and toxicity, and the growing gaps between rich and poor, you would not be human if you did not experience emotional tension.

By distinguishing emotional tension from creative tension, masterful leaders keep from undermining their own efforts. For example, if we feel deeply discouraged about our lack of progress on developing an innovative sustainable product, we may feel a strong desire to get rid of that feeling of discouragement. There is one immediate remedy: lower the vision. We may say to ourselves, "There's probably not a market for that product anyway—it's time to abandon the project." Our emotional tension can be relieved by adjusting the one pole of the creative dynamic that is always under our control—the vision. By lowering our goals to be closer to our current reality, we reduce emotional tension. But the price we pay is that we also abandon what we truly want. Similarly, another way to get rid of negative feelings temporarily is to pretend everything is fine when it's not. This is the strategy of denial, a common practice for individuals, and in teams, in organizations, and in society. But it purchases emotional relief at the expense of also reducing the creative tension, and the likelihood of actually changing reality.

By contrast, the strategy that effective leaders and teams come to rely upon for dealing with emotional tension is to tell the truth. In doing so, they simply acknowledge negative emotions as one more facet of current reality. In effect, they allow their inner reality to be every bit as "real" as the outer reality of climate change or water shortages, and continually work to tell the truth about both. When emotional tension is viewed in this way, focus returns naturally to the question "What do we want to create?" Just like other aspects of current reality, emotional tension may not change immediately, but it will change over time.

Transforming emotional tension into creative tension is especially challenging when dealing with sustainability issues that naturally evoke strong emotions, and it takes time and practice to learn how to do it, as well as a good deal of personal maturity. Few capacities are more important for individuals and teams seeking to contribute in areas where fear, anger, and distrust are rampant. These situations are difficult enough on their own. They do not need our own fears and anxieties added in as a persistent background state.

SEEING OPPORTUNITIES FOR INNOVATION VERSUS BEING LESS BAD

A history of negative visions and simmering emotional tension around social and environmental problems has, as Hollender says, left many people cynical. It often seems that the best we can do is cope with seemingly unsolvable problems. But doing less harm (emitting less CO_2, polluting less, using resources less rapidly, giving more aid to help poor people), while laudable, still differs from working to create what we truly seek.

Green designers William McDonough and Michael Braungart have a great analogy for this distinction: If a car is heading south, slowing down does not cause it to head north. Sooner or later, you need to turn the car around 180 degrees. While slowing down may be an important first step, it does not guarantee the real change that is needed. No matter how "less bad" you are, it will not make you good.

It is not surprising that so many of the sustainability innovators we have talked about emphasize opportunity, not just remediation. "Once people grasp this reality" of climate change, Carstedt says, "you must help them focus on . . . how to pinpoint an opportunity, some action they can take. You don't unleash that energy either in individuals or in organizations if you don't help them to see the opportunities."

Such a shift occurred when Alcoa's managers convinced themselves that they could pursue aggressive waste reduction targets and not only stay in business but be better off. So, too, did it happen when DuPont started to see the large opportunities in bio-based feedstocks and began shifting away from petrochemicals in the 1990s—well before this decision was justified by short-term costs. Horst-Henning Wolf and his EU automotive industry cohorts showed how to work with creative tension even in challenging business-government negotiations.

Historically, the private sector has responded to government regulations in one of three ways: grudging compliance, which requires enforcement to keep up the pressure; genuine compliance, in which regulations are adhered to and accepted; or commitment, going beyond their mandates to encourage innovation.

Wolf and the European automakers could well have opted for viewing the looming EU recycling regulations as a problem, something to which they would need to react, in which case they would have seen the EU bureaucrats as opponents and battled against them with lobbyists and lawyers. Instead, they developed a shared vision that recovering and reusing automobiles was the right thing to do and that, with smart regulations, it could create an opportunity to accelerate innovation. They adopted the stance of voluntarily assuming responsibility for cars at the end of their lifetimes, worked together to create regulations that recognized the realities of car recovery and take-back, and helped their government counterparts appreciate that society would benefit from a workable system wherein companies that were more innovative prospered. Similarly, coalitions such as the Regional Greenhouse Gas Initiative and the U.S. Climate Action Partnership are assuming leadership positions in addressing climate change, proposing cap-and-trade systems in the absence of federal action.

Giving up all negative visions will not prove easy, and it may not even be necessary to do so. Many successful advocacy organizations are based on the villification of harmful processes or products; their survival depends on instilling fear and even demonization of the things they're fighting. The people in these organizations are not crazy or shortsighted. Such groups often have come into existence because there were real problems to be tackled and powerful actors wedded to maintaining a destructive status quo. In shaping life beyond the Bubble, many visions will be needed.

The main point is to understand that strategies based on negative visions, emotional tension, and being less bad differ fundamentally from ones guided by positive visions and creative tension. The danger is not negative visions. The danger is being guided only by negative visions.

Our point is that negative visions can take us only so far—and that strategies based on negative visions and emotional tension differ fundamentally from ones guided by positive visions and creative tension.

ALIGNING THE PERSONAL AND PROFESSIONAL

When we first visited the Lakes Project at Xerox, we saw more than a state-of-the-art, zero-waste, lean manufacturing facility; we also met many members of the team. It was clear from our conversations with them how deeply these hardheaded, pragmatic engineers had become committed to and passionate about their Zero to Landfill vision. Many talked of what the project meant to them. But it wasn't until late in the afternoon that we all felt the depth of these statements.

We were packed into a noisy, stuffy meeting room adjacent to the assembly area. Our hosts had offered a more comfortable venue, but we had decided in favor of this room because it was where the team had held its regular 7:00 A.M. "sunrise meetings." A young woman, one of the lead designers on the Lakes team, had just completed a technical briefing on the overall system design of the new product and was commenting about how meaningful the whole process had been for her when she was interrupted with an unusual question.

One SoL consortium member from Ford, a veteran of many organizational learning projects, said, "I understand what a great opportunity this was for you, and how exciting it was. I work with engineers and I know the intellectual excitement of pushing the technological envelope. But what I really want to know is why you did this. What I mean is, what was the stand you took? And who were you, taking that stand?"

The woman looked at him in silence and then, in front of many peers and a few bosses, said, "I am a mom."

It is a tragedy of the modern workplace that many come to believe that they cannot bring their whole selves to work, or that they must be someone else in order to succeed—someone smarter, someone tougher, someone more articulate, someone more focused on the customer. We manage appearances. We commit ourselves to the company's agenda. We act professionally. After a while, we have lived so long in the house of mirrors that we can easily mistake the image we are projecting for who we really are. The poet David Whyte quotes an AT&T manager who wrote, "Ten years ago, I turned my face . . . and it became my life."[3]

Here is one way to understand where some of the music comes from. When people truly discover some aspect of their vision and have the opportunity to dedicate themselves to working on it, when they can tell the truth and focus on aspirations instead of on "being less bad," when they can be themselves, then something changes. An inner alignment starts to develop that can release extraordinary energy and creativity, qualities previously dissipated by denial, inner contradictions, and unawareness of the situation and oneself. People can start to bring all of themselves—individually and collectively—to their endeavor. They learn that we are good enough as we are, and that we all have a long way to go. When our inner and outer work align, creating regenerative businesses becomes inseparable from, as Plug Power's Roger Saillant puts it, "struggling each day to become a human being."

NOTHING NEW UNDER THE SUN

As King's reference to Socrates suggests, there is nothing new about this way of understanding the creative process. While cultures around the world appreciate the importance of genuine vision, so too do they value truth-telling and helping people see what really is. In the West, we have, for example, the New Testament admonition "And the truth shall set you free." The same wisdom exists in other cultures. King acknowledged that his civil disobedience strategies were patterned after the non-violent methods of Gandhi, who brilliantly distilled ancient India's spiritual principles into practical change strategies.[4] Gandhi, in turn, was influenced by a still earlier civil disobedience practitioner, Thoreau—himself inspired by wisdom traditions from the East and Native American cultures.

This universality of the creative process will prove essential in confronting today's global sustainability challenges. The term *global* has two meanings. The one we all know points to the scope of climate change, deteriorating ecosystems, and embedded poverty. The definition we often forget is "everywhere." In this sense, the global subsumes the local. Global problems are everywhere. They are here, now. They do not exist only in some far-off place. They touch each of us and are part of each of our lives and communities. As we take this in, we realize that there is an intimacy to climate change and deteriorating ecosystems are intimate challenges that have the power to bring us together, and that each of our visions matters if we are to create something different in the future.

The creative process is part of our common heritage as human beings, and accessing this perennial wisdom will be key to liberating our individual and collective potential in the months and years ahead.

[21]

You Don't Have to Have All the Answers

The creative process is a learning process. No matter how clear your vision at any point in time, this doesn't mean that it will produce results that happen tomorrow. It won't.

It is only in the process of working to bring a vision into reality, and seeing what is effective and what isn't, that you will gain key insights. While many people grasp this basic idea in principle, a distinguishing feature of successful creators, like successful entrepreneurs, is their mastery of it in practice. More often, most of us find ways to ignore much of the feedback we are getting, because we have not mastered what Robert Fritz—an accomplished musician, composer, writer, and filmmaker, and the person who first made the distinction between creative tension and emotional tension—calls "create and adjust."

Alan Webber, co-founder of *Fast Company* magazine, talks of this process as "a constant dialogue with your environment over whether a new idea is pregnant or not . . . whether and how the idea . . . as you've conceived it needs to be further evolved." This does not mean continually changing and adopting every suggestion you get. It does mean, as Webber says, being vigilant regarding ways in which we close our minds and, in effect, say, "No, this idea came from my mind fully hatched, and if we can't do it the way I've conceived it, I'm not going to do it at all."

This understanding of "create and adjust," of course, is what the founders of the USGBC expressed in their "seek agreement and go" approach to building momentum in the early stages of getting the diverse and conflicting interests in the building industry working together. It is also embodied in what Per Carstedt learned about the value of tangible prototypes.

MAKE IT REAL: LEARNING THROUGH PROTOTYPES

Speeches, essays and statistics, and stories of urgency and opportunity only go so far. They are no substitute for tangible prototypes.

Prototypes such as Carstedt's Green Zone allow people to learn through doing, as happened when Carstedt discovered how "industrial ecology" concepts, developed for large industrial complexes such as Kalundborg in Denmark, had to be adjusted to a cluster of small businesses—a car dealership, a Statoil energy (gasoline and biofuel) filling station, and a McDonald's restaurant. For example, in addition to using waste heat, they discovered that waste cooking oil from McDonald's could be converted to biofuel to sell at the service station next door.

And when GE was running pilot projects on how to distribute small solar generation systems for rural villages in India, they learned that they would need local partners. Not only would they need local workers who could install and service the systems, but the electrification projects would not be sustainable unless they also promoted local employment. Once the villages had electricity, they invested in refrigeration, which increased the amount of agricultural produce they could store and sell. That added real value, reinforcing a positive economic cycle, and gave people a tangible way to improve their well-being.

Practical know-how, in turn, fosters a sense of possibility about "what we can *do*." This is why, by contrast, so much academic knowledge tends to be pessimistic. Academics, even brilliant ones, frequently spend a lot of energy talking about problems instead of what can be done differently. Even when they've conceived solutions, there can be a large gap between the concept and the implementation, and little focus on what it would take to get people working effectively together to achieve success. For example, for years academics have been studying the problems of increasingly scarce water and topsoil, but prior to initiatives such as the Coke-WWF partnership and the Sustainable Food Lab few had any sense that NGOs and corporations could actually work together toward solving these problems.

Tangible prototypes also can bring together diverse interests and areas of expertise to form a community of learners. The three different businesses that made up the Green Zone had different business models, attracted different types of customers, and required different management skills. Yet they found they could learn a lot from each other about waste and energy. The USGBC founders similarly encouraged collaborative learning by getting competing interests to work together to develop countless prototypes of what eventually became the LEED rating system.

Perhaps most important, concrete embodiments of big ideas spark imagination in ways that abstract arguments cannot. This was Carstedt's biggest lesson from his work on the Green Zone. Initially he didn't really think the project was that exciting because it involved only existing, proven technologies. But people started to come from all around the world to see it. "I missed the whole point . . . the importance of something that people could touch." All of a sudden, people could imagine what a "circular economy" would really look like—"it became real for them." Once he understood this, he and a growing number of colleagues started to move to the larger vision of prototyping an entire "bioregion." This happens for customers in established markets as well. For instance, when people see a Toyota Prius, they naturally start asking why there aren't more automobiles like this.

In many ways, sustainability will be as much about seeing latent needs in the market as it is about implementing new technologies, and for this tangible prototypes are crucial. Such latent needs—desires that customers have never expressed because there was no way to express them or they had not given them much thought—are difficult or impossible to discern with standard market research methods, such as focus groups or surveys, but they come to the surface when people see tangible embodiments of new ideas. When people are asked questions like "How much of a premium would you be willing to pay in the purchase price of a car that gets 35 percent better fuel economy?" it puts them into a rational, analytic mind-set, and they tend to respond conservatively (after all, no one wants to give the "wrong answer" and look foolish). But when they see a car that grabs their attention, they respond emotionally. They start to believe that, as Jeffrey Hollender said, there are many small steps we can take toward sustainability, and many want to be part of that journey.

Toyota, which has sold more than 1 million of its Prius hybrids since going to market in 1998, is now very focused on these latent needs and, along with a few other companies, including Honda, is making major investments in further drawing forth what may be *the* major auto market of the future. In 2007, the company initiated a pilot program for a plug-in version of the Prius with higher-capacity batteries. It can be charged overnight, a low-demand period. Electric vehicles may soon store enough excess power to feed electricity back into many customers' workplaces and homes during peak-demand periods, when power is most expensive. At the Detroit auto show in January 2008, Toyota president Katsuaki Watanabe promised a predominantly electric vehicle in test fleet markets by 2010. Such fleets offer yet another way for corporations and governments to take the lead on sustainability issues, pilot-testing new products through highly visible initiatives meaningful to both employees and outside stakeholders. The vehicle has also been approved for similar testing on public roads in Japan.

Lastly, seeing new ideas becoming real naturally builds enthusiasm for still larger visions. (See the Creating a Balanced Portfolio of Visions Toolbox on page 343.) People say, "If we can do *this*, why couldn't we do *that*, too?" Companies see success and either emulate it or, better yet, want to show that they can go further. This is competition at its best, reminding us that the word *compete* comes from the Latin *competere*, meaning "striving together." As Carstedt said, if one Swedish auto company succeeded with a flexi-fuel car, "the others would have to follow." And they did. Which is why GM is now attempting to catch up with Toyota in the electric vehicle market—another example of the principle "innovate or be left behind."

ASKING FOR HELP

Often people in important leadership positions think they have to have all the answers, and those "below" them hold the same view. Ironically, this fails to tap the collective intelligence that can arise when those in visible positions openly ask for help.

At Alcoa, the group of managers that assembled in 1997 to transform the company's approach to environmental problems realized the need to shift the locus of responsibility from environmental managers (environment, health, and safety, or EHS, managers in most companies) to plant managers and their line leaders, and through them to people at all levels in the hierarchy.

"When we set our zero-water-discharge goal, we didn't know how to do that," says Pat Atkins. "If a plant in New York called me and said, 'How in the hell am I going to get to zero water discharge?' I couldn't send them a list of twenty-two things they could do to get there. I couldn't even give them a process for convincing their management to give them the money to do whatever they wanted to do. But I felt that if it was possible to do it, and if they really were motivated to stop using water, they're the people who had the most knowledge about why and how we use water and how to do it differently. They would come up with the tools and the procedures and the processes to do something different."

Looking back now, Atkins sees the power of getting everyone thinking about waste reduction, not just the relative handful of professional plant environmental experts: "When you've got 130,000 Alcoa employees, each of them thinking about this for ten minutes a day, it's amazing what happens."

Nineteen ninety-seven was an important year in the oil industry as well. John Browne, then chairman and CEO of BP, gave a historic speech at Stanford University in which he publicly broke rank with all the other major oil companies, declaring that the threat of climate change was sufficiently credible that it could no longer be ignored and that "there comes a time when prudent precautionary actions must be taken." In effect, he continued, if our societies wait for complete unanimity among scientists about the threat posed by continued increases in greenhouse gases in the atmosphere, by the time that unanimity is achieved it may be too late to do anything about the problem. While such words seem much less radical today, a public statement of this sort by an oil company president was unheard of at that time—most would not even attend public meetings on the subject then.

What was less public was that Browne really did not know how BP would achieve the commitment he made in the speech to cut the company's emissions in line with the Kyoto Protocol within five years (leveling emissions at 1990 levels). It is not that unusual for CEOs to make such public commitments for their companies. What was unusual was that shortly thereafter Browne wrote to the top 350 people in the company, saying in effect, according to Bernie Bulkin, then BP's chief scientist, "Now that I have made this commitment, I want to hear from you. If we are going to do this, your business units are going to do this. I need your ideas."

This request for help sparked meetings and conversations around the company about how to reduce CO_2 emissions. Bulkin illustrated how these conversations unfolded. "Exploration people said, 'When we drill test wells, we have nothing to do with the gas, so we flare it [burn it off], which produces lots of CO_2 for nothing.' Then someone else said, 'We hate drilling these test wells. They are very, very expensive. Why don't we see if we can use seismic data better so we don't have to actually drill test wells?' Everyone had an idea. BP has saved hundreds of millions of dollars as a result."

Asking for help has two benefits, one obvious and one more subtle. First, it generates a remarkable diversity and depth of ideas and energy for change. Second, it engages people in changes that really matter to them.

After BP merged with Amoco in 1998, they polled employees from the two companies about what was important to them. The Amoco company employees frequently named job security and other traditional concerns. Overwhelmingly, the primary concern of most BP employees was, according to Bulkin, "'Are we going to maintain our leadership position on environmental issues?' This was a complete surprise. Nobody had any idea that the BP employees felt this was so important."

SUGGESTIONS FOR PILOT PROJECTS

Prototyping is all about building momentum. Without a clear way to focus energy on tangible steps, the "stretch" of achieving long-term solutions to profound sustainability challenges can generate more emotional tension than people or organizations can tolerate. Initial tangible accomplishments are often the low-hanging fruit of waste reduction—decreases in water or energy use, or perhaps the creation of a single new product. But in one sense, the fact that these are relatively easy steps to accomplish is secondary. Like any learning process, creating life beyond the Industrial Age Bubble can only be done one step at a time.

If you're trying to build up momentum for sustainability within your organization, one of the crucial determinants of success is choosing the right pilot program at the right time. To that end, you and your team can use the Sustainable Value Framework from Part III (page 122).

The Framework can be a very useful tool in determining your team's focus by first giving you an understanding of which quadrant you are currently working in. For example, pilots focused on waste reduction belong to the lower left quadrant (internal present). As we have said, such efforts can be useful to gain further leverage in that they demonstrate tangible economic benefits. Also common are external-present pilots (lower right quadrant) that can help to open dialogue with key external stakeholders and lay the foundation for potential collaboration. Like many global companies, Coke participated in a variety of groups to better understand water issues around the world before undertaking its major partnership with WWF.

The Framework will also help you to sharpen the focus of your pilot by clarifying whom it intends to serve and over what time horizon. It can help you anticipate which kinds of pilots and prototypes will be necessary for your innovations to spread throughout the organization and beyond. For example, if you want to build a bridge to another quadrant as your work progresses, consider whom you would you need to engage early on to do this.

Many innovative companies pilot new sustainable products by using them internally with interested business units or regions (lower left quadrant). For example, GE has piloted high-efficiency electric motors, light-ing, solar power, and water purification systems at its own locations around the world. This has given them practical feedback on product per-formance as well as crucial market feedback about the needs of regions such as India and China. If you deliberately involve sales and marketing people in internal pilots, their firsthand experience can help in under-standing how new products can create value for existing customers and entirely new market segments (top left and right quadrants, respectively).

Directly engaging new departments in your existing or potential cus-tomer base at the piloting and prototype stages can in turn become im-portant learning opportunities for you and your customers. As a senior sales manager in the GE lighting business said, "Before we began working on innovative, high-efficiency lighting systems, I was always relegated to dealing with the purchasing person, who only had one objective—to get me to cut our prices year after year. Now we often talk with engineering or marketing teams, and we have completely different conversations. They are keenly interested in our experience, and we help them rethink from the very beginning how their new stores will be designed and lit."

It can be useful to involve members of NGOs at the piloting and pro-totyping stages. They often have knowledge and experience with issues and areas that are important for businesses to be effective with more sus-tainable products. If a business is committed to reducing the negative im-pacts of current products or processes today (lower right quadrant) and creating more regenerative ones, these partnerships can be a rich source of feedback, innovative ideas, and access to new markets (top right quad-rant). DuPont, GE, BP, Unilever, SC Johnson, Nike, Procter & Gamble, and a host of other companies large and small have recognized the impor-tance of engaging NGOs in their initiatives. The Base of the Pyramid Learning Laboratory at Cornell University is one forum where many of these companies are collaborating on pilots and prototypes in developing countries and accelerating their collective learning.

[22]

From Low-Hanging Fruit to
New Strategic Possibilities

M any companies start the sustainability journey with waste reduction or energy efficiency improvements because there is
an immediate "business case": These are costs they are already
paying and so improvement translates directly to the bottom line. But
many never move beyond this low-hanging fruit because they fail to sum-
mon the imagination and courage to face the fact that they are selling the
wrong products (such as gas-guzzling automobiles) to the wrong customers (rich consumers who should consider reducing their consumption,
not increasing it) based on the wrong business model (maximizing sales
of physical products and hence waste, not sustainable value). By contrast,
a relatively smaller number are continually elevating the vision, and rees-
tablishing the creative tension, by reaching out to new markets and engaging new stakeholders, including possible investors and different sources of
capital. Inevitably, though, this starts with engaging people, inside and
out, in a new conversation.

THE ELEPHANT AND THE (GROWING) FLEA

In the seven years after John Browne's Stanford speech, BP went through a major rebranding, jettisoning its former moniker, British Petroleum, in favor of the simpler BP and adopting the green and yellow sunburst icon as a symbol of moving "beyond petroleum." They made a host of cleaner-burning fuels available to consumers and implemented a myriad of energy efficiency and waste reduction initiatives that saved hundreds of millions of dollars and significantly reduced greenhouse gas emissions. In addition to being part of numerous climate-change initiatives, they also broke ranks with the mainstream strategy among U.S. corporations to use political lobbying to maintain the energy status quo by becoming the first major corporation with offices in the United States to ban contributions to U.S. political action committees.

But more than 98 percent of their profits still came from the core oil and gas businesses, and as Vivienne Cox, a senior executive then running the highly profitable trading business, said, "The BP branding was getting a bit stale"—it was mockingly referred to as "beyond pathetic" and "beyond plausible" by those who doubted the company's resolve to truly lead the coming transition to alternative energy in any meaningful way. "We were still investing more in advertising than in developing renewable energy," says Cox. "Our solar business had lost half a billion dollars over the preceding thirty years, and the wind initiative amounted to two projects."

At that time, Cox was asked to take on renewable energy. Her track record of business success in many positions within BP came, in part, thanks to her longtime practice of the kinds of deeper conversations that are essential for fostering innovation.[1] So it was no surprise that she soon convened 150 energy leaders from BP's sites around the world for a dialogue to "appreciate the global context" in which they were operating. The meeting, which was held in early 2005, included a sobering presentation by the new head of Strategy.

The leaders were bluntly informed that the industry was at a crossroads and that the classic capital-intensive, engineering-driven, Big Oil business model that had been successful for fifty years had no chance of remaining successful for another fifty, in large part because of the coming need for radical reductions in CO_2 emissions worldwide. Though the term wasn't used explicitly, they were, in effect, told that the 80-20 Challenge was staring them in the face. After two days of conversation, many left the meeting with a different senses of the types of problems, and opportunities, that an energy company such as BP would be facing.

Seeing the need for a deep and expansive rethinking of the entire business, Cox organized a Strategy Festival several months later. She made a point of inviting skeptics as well as enthusiasts for alternative energy, and immersed everyone in energy facts and trends, with the simple idea hanging in the background that the future would be different from the past. "The walls were covered with pictures, numbers, and graphs of the power industry, the trading industry, and alternative energy," she said. Eventually, all the "strands came together around the notion of low-carbon power."

They proceeded to put together a business model around the core idea of low-carbon power, focused specifically on four areas: solar, wind, hydrogen power (an ongoing collaboration with GE), and gas-fired power. In the ensuing weeks, many in BP began to talk about alternative energy. Yes, many of these alternative energy businesses were long-term, but there was money to be made in the short and intermediate term that could fuel longer-term investment. "People could see that there were 10–14 percent returns in wind." Though the dollar volumes of these businesses were minuscule relative to the core oil business, they were "real businesses," not simply charitable contributions.

Two months later, Cox took the new business model back to Browne, who challenged her to "get other executives within BP talking about this," which is just what she did. By the end of 2005, BP had formed a new business, BP Alternative Energy, and approved $8 to $10 billion in investments over the next ten years.[2] The company was preparing to move beyond the low-hanging fruit.

In two years, BP Alternative Energy has become one of the biggest players worldwide in renewable energy. They are the biggest wind company in the United States in terms of land, with the aim to be the world's largest wind power developer by 2015. They are the only foreign company to sell wind power in India. They have doubled their solar businesses in India, China, the United States, and Spain and have firm plans and commitments in place to grow their global solar business by 300 percent in under three years. Collaborations on two major hydrogen power projects are under way, with more in development.[3] BP is also making investments in biofuels research, including $500 million over ten years in the world's first dedicated biosciences energy research laboratory, at the University of California at Berkeley.

Behind these impressive figures is a brave new world for a traditionally conservative oil company, used to making large financial bets based on highly sophisticated engineering and financial analyses. Despite the exciting possibilities, much more is unknown than known about how to succeed beyond the Bubble, and Cox is experienced enough to know that so far they are only taking small steps and BP could easily lose its resolve if pressures from its core oil business force retrenchment.

If anything, the further they go, the more novel the world of alternative energy becomes relative to the oil business. Cox now believes that the future will require not only different investment criteria and different management skills, but very different business models and partners as well. The oil business is highly capital-intensive and employs relatively few people, generating enormous cash flows, mostly through small networks of well-established large businesses (including a variety of technical service providers, engineering and construction firms, and downstream partners in petrochemicals and plastics).

This new distributed energy business will be more like "a local water catchment" than huge oil field development, says Cox, so success may depend on local networks of businesses and cooperative management, much like the networks Coke and WWF are trying to foster around watersheds. Additionally, current energy use is centralized through established distribution channels (gas and oil) and national grids (electricity), but there is an enormous need to serve those who are underserved by the current energy model. After all, almost a third of the world's population is not connected to centralized electricity grids and is not likely to become connected in the near future.

Combining these two elements—new partners and new markets—gives alternative energy, according to Cox, a necessary "social function." It means growing a business that will be in the hands of more people and not simply under the control of a centralized distribution company located far away.

BP is already selling a non-polluting "biopellet" stove to off-the-grid villagers in India (aimed at replacing unhealthy cooking practices in poor villages). The stove, using technology originally developed at the Indian Institute of Science, burns fuel produced from pellets made from agricultural waste. In addition to the institute, BP has worked with local producers and distributors (of the stoves and the fuel), microfinance institutions, philanthropic capital to help initial funding, and village cooperatives for sales and distribution. The business took shape as the result of a year-long market investigation done not with a typical market research firm but with a local community development organization specializing in women's cooperatives. In effect, BP has done exactly what Costco did: It has expanded its boundaries and reached way beyond its normal business partners to embrace an entire value chain and improve the lives of poor villagers in the process.

Cox sees all of this as the type of experimentation that is needed to develop radically different businesses and business models. "No one knows how these new energy businesses will develop, but we know there is no way we can learn it all ourselves. This will require unusual alliances. We have to get very good at finding new partners and learning together on the ground from concrete business prototypes."

She finds this "relational" model of management more helpful than ever in countries such as India. "The beauty of it is that the relational model is how many of these cultures work naturally," she says. "Operating this way taps into their abilities to innovate, rather than forcing them into our more traditional command-and-control model, which actually undermines the source of value they could bring." She also knows that such changes are not easy to digest in the traditional BP management culture. "In this way of working, you've got to have a lot of humility. You don't have the answers. You're creating space for relationships to form and innovation to emerge, which is the responsibility of senior leadership." But this takes a lot of courage, "especially in a larger system that does not usually work this way."

Those willing to pursue such learning in the service of truly new visions will likely discover that the world is more ready for alternative energy and alternative businesses to provide the energy than many expect. Before announcing the biopellet stove at a meeting in India in 2007, Cox was prepared to encounter the argument that as a developing country, India has the right to grow, so BP should "get off their backs" and stop preaching about alternative energy. Instead, she found many Indians intent on leapfrogging the West and coming up with completely new ideas and new solutions. "This is a business that's real, that's generating profits. But most importantly, we are beginning to shift the nature of the conversation of what's possible, both inside BP and outside," she said.

SUGGESTIONS FOR BUILDING MOMENTUM FOR INNOVATIONS "ABOVE THE LINE"

To keep your organization from getting trapped in only undertaking sustainability initiatives with short-term benefits, you will need, as Vivienne Cox and her colleagues at BP did, to gradually build a business case for investing in the future and to nurture a broader network of leaders who see these same possibilities. Here, too, the logic of prototyping can be very helpful toward creating modest practical steps from which everyone can learn. Often organizations become paralyzed by debates between making major bets and doing nothing (recall the stuck management team on page 141).

The two Toolbox practices that follow focus on internal (upper left quadrant) and external (upper right quadrant) investments in the future. Recall that the former focuses on new products, new technologies, and new management infrastructures and capabilities (such as BP's new internal networks and skills at shaping entrepreneurial business opportunities in the developing world). The latter focuses on new markets, new partners, and new understandings of the external world, such as BP's reaching out to partner with organizations and microcredit providers in reaching new markets.

Start by picking a particular initiative you believe has potential to demonstrate new possibilities and to engage important stakeholders. Depending on the nature of your initiative, you may find it helpful to use the first template (pages 317–18) to focus on whom you can engage *inside* your company or organization. You can then use the second template (page 319–20) to help you expand your focus by engaging others and building momentum *outside* your company. How you blend these areas of focus will become more clear as you build momentum. For now, assume you are starting internally and engaging key people within your organization.

In exploring both internal and external future investments, do not get so caught up in new technologies and reaching out to new markets and partners that you lose sight of how this will become a viable and manageable business.

For example, the first template starts with questioning the potential business value of your idea and encouraging you to seek out skeptics—as Cox did for her Strategy Festival. Then it includes a variety of questions to identify key players in the initiative and determine what sort of help they will need and how each would define success.

The second practice focuses on identifying lead customers and engaging those outside your organization. Throughout both practices, keep in mind economic viability.

Recently, when we asked Cox what she is learning from her many innovative new ventures, she responded, "There is no shortage of opportunity, and happily enough we are finding lots of people with the entrepreneurial savvy to explore and develop these start-up businesses, often in pretty chaotic market environments. But at some point you need to shift gears and also bring in the discipline to manage these well, and there it can be difficult for the entrepreneurial types to also bring in that discipline. If we are to grow small start-up ventures to create benefit on a larger scale, we and our partners need to be able to walk on both sides of this street."

Remember that the spirit of prototypes is that you do not need to have all the answers; you are merely trying to show "proof of concept" now, and you can expand the variety of key players actively involved down the line. As BP's Bernie Bulkin said about the role of pilot projects and prototypes when the company first started down the path of lower-carbon fuels and alternative energy, "We are working on several early initiatives, and when we are successful in the first steps, what now looks impossible will then seem possible."

TOOLBOX
Looking Inside Your Own Organization for Energy and Commitment

The following template takes the view of a new team leader undertaking a prototype investment. If you do not have the explicit authority to start a pilot project within your organization, think through the questions below and ask yourself what you would have to do to engage others or build a team that would have such authority.

- Identify key areas where your innovation concept needs to be proven in practice. In particular, where are skeptics in your company saying, "This is not possible"? What do you need to do to prove it is possible? Engage skeptics and "opposers" by inviting their criticisms of your ideas—an irresistible offer they will surely take up—but don't expect them to move your ideas forward right away.
- Then ask, "Who are the specific individuals or teams within the company who would want to find a way to make the innovation work—to prove it is possible?"
- Who are the visionaries in the organization who hear the word *impossible* and can't wait to get started? These people are at the make-it-happen end of the normal curve in Figure 14.9 on page 211, at the opposite end from the skeptics or "opposers."
- Draw a "network map," starting with your core team and connecting out to others in your company who might be involved, with lines representing chains of personal relationships between your core team and these people. Who might be interested in one of your prototyping tasks? Are there other places where this network naturally extends to people beyond the boundaries of your company? Can you see a line of personal connections to those external players?

For each key person you've identified, draw a box with the person's name at the top and the role you can imagine him or her playing at the bottom. For example, someone's role could be to create a prototype that proves some "impossible" aspect of your project is actually feasible.

Anticipate how you can use your internal network map to find ways to support those people in their prototyping efforts.

- Pick initial team members for prototypes carefully and define your job as their supporter: choose key members who are fully committed to making the prototype work, and constantly check with them on the challenges they are encountering. Ask how you can help them and what resources they need.
- Continually make linkages to key organizational issues and goals so that your initiative is seen as relevant and timely.
- Avoid large-scale bureaucratic "rollouts" and big campaigns in the early phases. Your first goal is to demonstrate what's possible with highly tangible prototypes. Many teams deliberately work quietly until they achieve them.
- Build contingency plans, and always have multiple pathways in mind. Use these contingency plans to learn from setbacks and failures quickly, and to translate lessons into new strategies and tactics.
- Communicate while doing. Actively manage links and communications with all key internal stakeholders to generate curiosity. Ask for help and build commitment and support when necessary.
- Constantly create clear evidence for change and for the benefits of growing your pilot to realize economies of scale and other reinforcing snowball effects.

TOOLBOX
Looking Outside Your Organization for Pilot and Prototype Sites, Markets, and Relevance

You can use this second template to focus beyond the boundaries of your own company or organization as you anticipate and respond to latent needs emerging in the marketplace.

- What key people in your company are most likely to see the latent or emerging market first? (Often those focused on marketing and future business growth will see the opportunities earlier than technical people, who are more likely to see the obstacles.)
- What lead customers are already interested in your idea? Invite them to help you develop and test prototypes and partner with you on pilot projects.
- How can you leverage customer engagement and interest? How can you ensure that at least some of your senior managers and executives are directly engaged with these customers?
- Are there specific places (or communities) where conditions are most favorable for your innovation to flourish? How can you tie your idea to a latent or emerging segment of the market? For example, do more people in a particular market consider greenhouse gas emissions when they are deciding to buy a product? Where is the political climate most favorable to an idea or program like yours? For example, where might politicians be inclined to support clean energy technologies once they understand that doing so will create more jobs and a more viable economy? Do you have the relationships you need in these locales or markets to make a pilot sustainable? If you don't, can you create them, as the U.S. Green Building Council did by launching local chapters to support regional prototypes of the LEED system?
- Look at all regions and markets in the world—regardless of where your team is located—and find the market that is most advanced in

the arena of your innovation. For example, in California and Israel the market for electric cars is far more advanced than elsewhere. Likewise, you'll find more support and prototypes for water conservation products in very dry regions. Where constraints and limits have already been reached (regarding air pollution or fuel or water supply and security, for example), the needs in that market are much more visible and are likely already driving pilots and even the growth of substantial market segments. Such areas can provide great learning opportunities for your team.

- Pay attention to your company's organizational DNA. Every organization and community has its own points of pride, past accomplishments and strengths that you can often build on, allowing you to quietly launch high-leverage prototypes that have much more potential to grow.

- How can you build loyal, flourishing communities around your prototypes? For example, how could you directly connect different customers of your company who are piloting new products so they can interact directly, share their experiences and lessons with you and each other, and build a support community that is self-sustaining?

DEVELOPING MORE COMPREHENSIVE STRATEGIES

Eventually, comprehensive strategies will cover all four quadrants of the Sustainable Value Framework, connecting internal and external efforts, and present and future-oriented investments. A good example is Per Carstedt's current work with developing bioregions. Interestingly, as this pioneering work has become more widely recognized, this strategy is spreading well beyond northern Sweden through a major EU-funded project to help ten regions around the world—including Rotterdam, Madrid, Nanyang (China), and São Paulo—develop beyond fossil fuels.

In Sweden, Per Carstedt and his colleagues began their work by tackling the first two problems at the center of Figure 22.1: resolving the "chicken-and-egg" challenge of increasing the number of vehicles that could run on ethanol while simultaneously increasing the number of ethanol fueling stations, which naturally require a significant number of vehicles on the road in order to be viable. In effect, this represented an internal future investment for automakers (new vehicles, initially from Ford and later from Saab) in conjunction with an external one (new ethanol fueling stations, built by a number of different people).

As Figure 22.1 demonstrates, this balance of "upper left" (new vehicles) and "upper right" initiatives (new fueling stations) is connected to four additional subsystems that also needed to be addressed:

1. Feedstocks (the materials used to create fuel)
2. Fuel production

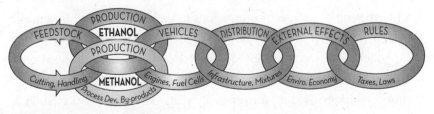

FIGURE 22.1 Developing Bioregions

3. The fuel's effect on the environment/economy
4. Rules and regulations

Each of these subsystems translates into opportunities for innovation, growth, and job creation. In this case, Sweden is addressing the second subsystem, fuel production, by building the world's most advanced second-generation cellulosic ethanol production facilities, which use forestry waste products as feedstocks rather than crops such as corn or sugar beets. They are also addressing the third and fourth subsystems (environment and rules) by forming partnerships that will make clear the tangible benefits the new initiatives will have on the economy and environment, while eventually building up the political might to create laws that will make it possible to scale up their initial efforts.

Many of the initiatives in the biofuels sector, unfortunately, are opportunistic and, as a result, focused only on the present. Many are quick-fix solutions that ignore unintended side effects—for example, taking existing crops such as corn and diverting them to ethanol production. This ignores the side effects not only on food prices but also on net CO_2 production (which in some cases even exceeds that from conventional gasoline) and, especially for sugarcane, on watersheds. With the world hungry for alternatives to fossil fuels, frameworks such as Carstedt's that bridge the present and the future and internal and external perspectives are needed to bring sanity to the biofuel landrush.

For example, one of Carstedt's major projects today is in Tanzania, which he sees as a good example of how patient development of long-term sources of fuel, stewardship-oriented local entrepreneurship, and investment in appropriate infrastructures could lay a foundation for sustainable energy and economic development. "They have lots of sunlight, which can be converted to energy [through solar power and biomass]. They have people with deep connections to their land, their children, and their spiritual roots. But they also have lots of people trying to exploit them—including, recently, biofuel production to make short-term profits." In advising the government, Carstedt is attempting to focus their attention on understanding longer-term sustainable feedstocks (such as crop waste) and production capabilities, and on creating local entrepreneurial leadership and enterprises that also have a larger mission of fostering overall development of the surrounding communities. But there is immense pressure for short-term gain. As he says, "We have only one chance to get this right."

It's Not What the Vision Is,
It's What the Vision Does

As organizations internalize the creative process, their understanding of the real function of vision undergoes a subtle shift. People and groups obsess about "getting the vision right," but often miss the whole point of vision as an active force, not just a set of words. It's not what the vision is, it's what the vision does.

ZERO SEEMS LIKE THE RIGHT NUMBER

When Alcoa set their stretch targets for zero process water discharges and zero waste to landfill, they were actually inspired by a development that occurred several years earlier, when Paul O'Neill first became CEO. He was reviewing the company's accident and fatality statistics. O'Neill, Atkins, and a few others were wrestling with whether these kinds of accident and fatality goals really make sense.

"From the time I first joined the company," recalls Atkins, "arguments had raged about safety in Alcoa. Some would say, 'Yeah, you need to set safety goals, but you can't set goals that are ridiculous. You can't set a goal of cutting your accident rate by 75 percent in two years, because people will just ignore it. They'll say that's a bunch of guys sitting in air-conditioned offices in Pittsburgh coming up with impossible things to do.' Others argued that if you don't set stretch goals, people won't really work hard, and they'll say Alcoa doesn't really care if we injure 300 people a year because that's just the way life is."

Shortly after O'Neill took office, he recast the debate. Atkins recalls him saying, "I am of the opinion that zero is the right number. You cannot plan to kill three people a year because you killed four people last year and you want to get a little better. And you can't plan to have a thousand people going to medical centers in Alcoa's plants. So the goal is zero. Zero fatalities. Zero lost work days. Zero injuries. Zero reportable incidents."

Although the debates continued, as a result of O'Neill's stand, safety goals at Alcoa today are, and for many years have been, zero, zero, zero, and zero. Since the late 1980s, Alcoa's accident rate has gone down by a factor of fifteen. It is now the lowest of any industrial company in the United States, even passing DuPont, widely considered the gold standard in industrial safety among large companies.[1]

Organizations of all shapes and sizes adopt visions that have little real impact. After a while, they usually end up fostering more cynicism than commitment. This is rooted in a profound misunderstanding on the part of managers who think the point of a vision is to come up with eloquent words that somehow inspire or motivate people. Motivate them to do what? To comply with what the managers want them to do? This will hardly unleash creativity and commitment.

Even worse, vision statements are often developed to combat criticism that the company does not have a vision, thereby subtly reinforcing a problem-solving mind-set, as opposed to a creative one. Closely related is the misunderstanding that we should only set visions that we know we can achieve. But this is like driving by looking in the rearview mirror. It is neither inspiring nor particularly useful when the world around you is changing.

There is one and only one way to assess a vision: what is attained relative to what might have been attained without the vision.

This simple principle is beautifully illustrated in a book by the former basketball star Bill Russell, who, when he retired, had been a member of Boston Celtics teams that won more professional basketball championships than any other team in history. Russell explained that he had devised a 100-point rating system whereby he judged his play after every game in ten areas on a 0-to-10 scale. In his entire fourteen-year career, he never rated himself at 100. In his best years, he averaged in the low 90s. Judged by the way most people think about visions, this poor man was an abysmal failure. He played a thousand games in his life and never achieved his vision. Yet he was the most successful player in history, judged by what he and his teammates achieved and the unprecedented eleven championship rings in his collection.

Visions that truly make a difference come from the heart as well as the head. At Alcoa, people came to see that zero was the right goal for both worker fatalities *and* water usage, even though they did not know how to achieve it and even though they may fall short. These targets were right because they express people's genuine longings and desires. They were right because they tapped to the fullest people's capacities to learn, and eventually led to otherwise unachievable accomplishments. The same holds for the future. For example, the company's goal is that by 2025 *any* process, whether heating water or moving air or pumping liquids, should achieve at least 80 percent of theoretical efficiency in terms of energy; although many regard this as virtually impossible, it is the goal nonetheless. This is how people start to operate when they truly understand that "it's not what the vision is, it's what the vision does."

Creating a regenerative society and economy will take leadership from the heart from countless organizations, big and small. There are a growing number of business organizations based on this principle—businesses that exist in order to live out a vision of contributing to the health of larger systems, not simply in order to make a profit.

BUSINESSES WITH A MISSION

Peter Drucker once said, "Profit for a company is like oxygen for a person; if you don't have enough of it, you're out of the game." Unfortunately, most businesses operate as if their purpose is breathing. There is no more basic confusion that pervades the business world than the idea that the purpose of a company *is* to maximize profit. There have always been a small number of businesses that understood this. Today, the extraordinary challenges of creating life beyond the Bubble are bringing forth many more.

In a sense, these are organizations inspired by living systems, firms whose products, processes, business models, *and* management philosophies are based on the idea of a future in which business operates more and more like the other living systems of nature. Such companies are exemplars of stage five of the sustainability integration continuum presented on page 115. And while many are inevitably smaller than more established counterparts, some are already having influence that far exceeds their relative size.

Greyston Bakery, for example, which supplies many of the finest restaurants in New York City, was started in one of the poorest areas of Yonkers by Bernie Glassman in 1982, in order to provide employment. Today, it not only employs over a hundred people but has generated a network of for-profit and non-profit enterprises including shelters for the homeless and apartments for single mothers.

Dean's Beans is not one of the largest coffee roasters, but it certainly has one of the clearest missions: "Our job," says founder Dean Cycon, "is providing great coffee and helping the coffee growers with whom we work around the world to thrive." From the profit on each pound of coffee sold a portion is automatically returned to the supplying coffee-growing cooperative to invest in any way they choose to promote social or economic good for their community. Some of the investments have led to women's programs and reforestation projects in Peru; prosthetics and therapy for 1,600 land mine victims in Nicaragua; a radio program, "Coffee Talk," that reaches 7,000 indigenous growers weekly in Guatemala; well projects bringing clean water to 3,000 people for the first time in Ethiopia; and training in organic certification to gain market access for growers in many countries, including Kenya and Papua New Guinea.

These businesses are not charities. They are successful and growing enterprises. Greyston Bakery has grown from just 5 employees to over 100 and recently moved into a LEED-certified new facility. At Dean's Beans, sales have grown almost 500 percent in the past ten years.

But the way their owners see it, these businesses do not exist in order to make a profit; they make a profit in order to contribute. Cycon says, "I wasn't a businessperson that woke up to the importance of sustainability. I went into business for the specific reason of modeling how business can be and must be a sustainable and proactive player in healing the planet." At Greyston they say it simply: "We don't hire people to make brownies, we make brownies to hire people."[2]

Some of the emerging mission-based businesses are now becoming significant players in influential industries—such as Seventh Generation, whose green household and personal care products (biodegradable household cleaners, recycled non-chlorine-bleached household paper products, diapers, and feminine care products) are so popular that the company (which currently sells to Target, Whole Foods, and a number of other national and local retailers) was recently courted by Wal-Mart, both to stock the products but also to learn about their novel approach to corporate responsibility. Though the company is still small when compared to giants such as Wal-Mart, they have grown to over $100 million in sales, all the while sticking to their mission of educating "this and future generations" about their impact on "our health and the health of the environment."

Buying a Seventh Generation product is like taking a mini-class in sustainability. Packages and containers are covered with information about the toxins embedded in everyday household products, ways to conserve water, or the amount of oil the United States would save if every household used a vegetable-based dishwashing soap rather than an oil-based one (81,000 barrels). The messages are informative and distinctly upbeat, emphasizing the alignment of personal and family health with a healthier environment. The larger message is clear: People can make a positive difference through their everyday choices.

SMALL ACTIONS HELP THE WHOLE SYSTEM

Businesses like these live out visions of promoting the health of larger systems, whether it is the health of their local community (Greyston), their supply chains (Dean's Beans), or the nine "global imperatives" that

Seventh Generation has formulated to summarize the "issues that must be addressed in the world over the next 50 to 100 years," according to Hollender. Seventh Generation's imperatives include changing how business is managed to enhance nature's regenerative capabilities, as well as creating societies that "promote social justice" and "increase capacity for understanding differing perspectives."

Such concerns for the health of larger systems run the risk of sounding detached from day-to-day business realities and even fostering more of the cynicism that concerns Hollender. To avoid this, Seventh Generation tries to use their global imperatives to assess current practices, "to develop the consciousness of watching our actions and watching our thinking . . . to continually check what we are doing against these imperatives," says Hollender.

For example, the company recently set out to more comprehensively assess the environmental impact of their products and soon discovered "how little we understood," Hollender says.

They knew that manufacturing and transportation generated a lot of CO_2, but looking beyond waste from manufacture and shipping to waste from use (see Chapter 2), they discovered that the single greatest impact was that their laundry products were designed to be used in hot or warm water. "When you calculated it, the energy consumed to warm all of that water was by far the biggest single negative impact we had. That was a shock."[3]

Reformulating laundry products so that they would work in cold water went to "the top of the [product research] list." It took almost two years, but in the fall of 2007 they introduced their first line of vegetable-based detergents meant to be used with cold water. They are betting that the new products will give customers concerned with global warming one more way that "their actions, as small as they might seem . . . , can make a difference."

GROWING A BUSINESS THROUGH NETWORKS OF COMMON PURPOSE

The vision of operating like other living systems leads to very different strategies for growth. One of the most surprising facts about Seventh

Generation is its size. Though sales exceed $100 million, the company has fewer than 100 employees, a sales productivity figure that would impress the most callous capitalist.

How have they done it? Through building networks of SEDRs, "self-extending developmental relationships." "If we want to grow the company without just becoming another unwieldy big corporation," says Gregor Barnum, who has been with the company for the past five years, "we have to think differently about how we do it. Our relationships with key business partners are more than a marriage of business convenience."

Barnum and others in the company also know that this is a business model that embodies more of how nature works—growth through building networks of symbiotic relationships. As he says, "There is no one in charge of a forest."

But succeeding in such a strategy takes a particular kind of commitment. "The key is building these relationships slowly, so that people really get to know one another and what really matters to each of us."

Notes Hollender, "You move into a whole different context and possibility when you're talking not about the price on our bathroom tissue but about how we can work together as partners to create some of the changes that we want to see in the world." Barnum adds, "This is pretty counter-cultural for people who think business is all about 'the deal,' but once people know you are serious, it becomes a distinctive feature and advantage for a company."

Growing businesses through networks of common purpose can extend to customers as well as to suppliers. Educating customers around their potential for positive impact is core to Seventh Generation's business model, as it is for Dean's Beans' and Greyston's. But Hollender and his colleagues wondered if they could go further, getting beyond the traditional transactional relationship between companies and customers based solely on selling products.

In partnership with Greenpeace, they initiated an experiment in which they used money that would otherwise have gone into advertising promotions (a key marketing strategy for virtually all consumer goods companies) to finance 100 college-age students in a five-day social and environmental training program titled Change It. "The whole idea," says Hollender, "became about how to get away from interacting with our customers only through the products that people buy. After all, promotions are just a way to incentivize people to buy more. Is that the type of relationship we want?"

They replaced normal promotional materials in the stores that carried their products with signs about making a positive impact on the world and encouraging customers to search out students who had a passion for this. Participating neighborhoods would then track the kids involved and use their experiences as a way of promoting "dialogue with people who are interested in the problems the kids tackle." The core idea was that "connecting with young people as change leaders might help people engage in their community. Additionally, to create systemic change we needed to create change agents who would hopefully influence thousands or hundreds of thousands of people during their lifetimes."

It is too early to assess the broader impacts of the program, but it seems to be hitting a resonant chord in many communities. The students have worked on local projects focused on waste reduction, environmentally friendly product advocacy, energy efficiency, building community understanding of climate change, and reforestation efforts in New Orleans. As important, students are engaging their communities and fostering dialogue; their efforts have been most pronounced on their own college campuses, where a dialogue around the opportunity to express values through purchasing has generated intense debate and significant change.

In the program's second year, over 1,200 young people applied for 200 slots. One of the biggest surprises turned out to be the initial response of retailers: "We've had more retailers want to participate in this program than we did when we were giving away washing machines," said Hollender.

HOW DID WE USE THE VISION TODAY?

As one of our mentors, the late William O'Brien, former CEO of Hanover Insurance, once said, "Over the years, I have found that each person instinctively uses their own 'bullshit meter' to judge visions. At the end of the day, you ask yourself, 'How did our vision influence our actions?' If the answer is 'It didn't,' the vision is just words." The best antidote we know for this is to make creative tension the focus of your day-to-day efforts—that is, continually look at today's realities and problems in the light of your aspirations.

For example, the suspension of advertising promotions sparked some internal fear in Seventh Generation, since promotions were something that a lot of people, including many on the sales team, had a real stake in. "I would say it was scary . . . because we used the question of why we suspended promotions to open things up more broadly," says Hollender.

Conversations were held throughout the company in small groups that naturally led to lots of questions. But as people got into it, Hollender says, "they almost naturally started to reflect on and discover other things that were out of alignment. It becomes incredibly powerful when each person starts to think about their own job, their own work, regardless of what it is, in light of a mission that really matters."

As the process unfolded, a woman in accounts payable became frustrated, saying, "I don't really get how this is going to relate to me. You know, all I do is write checks. I've got a pile of invoices, and I write checks."

"But, as we got into a conversation about social justice," says Hollender, "it dawned on her that she had the authority to pay certain bills before other bills. She didn't have to pay them in alphabetical order. She realized that she could pay an independent contractor earlier than one of our billion-dollar company partners. That would make a big difference to the contractor, but the big company wouldn't notice whether the check came Monday, Tuesday, or Wednesday. When people at all levels make these sorts of connections, you release tremendous energy."

Judging the practical impact of visions takes looking over the long term and the short term. In one sense, what we achieve over years and decades is crucial. But in another sense, either the vision is alive right now or it is not. Visions inspire—*breathe life into*—our work in the here and now, from the most profound to the most mundane. If we want to know what we are really committed to, we just need look at what is around us right now. This is a tough standard, but as people learn to live this way, as Hollender says, they discover reservoirs of creative energy that appear limitless.

NEW IDEAS, OLD ROOTS

Just as understanding the creative process is universal, not surprisingly, the new generation of mission-based businesses builds on some very old ideas, ones that predate the Industrial Age.

They seek, as an essential part of their purpose, to contribute to the health and well-being of living systems. They reject the notion that the sole purpose of business is to make a profit; and they regard the quality of relationships between members, suppliers, and customers as the true indicator of success.[4] In so doing, they are returning business to its origins. The oldest Swedish word for business is *narings liv*, "nourishment for life." In ancient Chinese the concept is expressed by two symbols that translate as "life meaning."

And the root of the English word *company* derives from the Latin *com panis*, "the sharing of bread"—the same root as that for the word *companion*.

In the early 1980s Royal Dutch Shell undertook a study of "long-lived companies," the small number of companies worldwide that had survived for 200 years or longer. When the study was finally published in 1997, former Shell executive Arie de Geus painted a sharp contrast between the vast majority of businesses who think of themselves as a "machine for making money" versus the long-lived ones who see themselves, first and foremost, as a "human community."

Although creating a regenerative society will require leadership and innovation from all sorts of organizations of all sizes, we believe that companies with, in the words of the original Shell study, a "sense of who they are that transcends what they do"[5] will play an especially important role in learning how to rethink not just products and processes but business as an institution for life beyond the Bubble.

[24]

Redesigning for the Future

edesigning an organization is usually considered an activity that only involves senior executives. Though this chapter will appear most relevant to them, team leaders and members at all levels can benefit from a better understanding of the kind of restructuring that organizations will have to undergo if they are to remain viable beyond the Bubble.[1]

As organizations get serious about moving beyond the low-hanging fruit of waste reduction and efficiency improvements, they invariably discover that traditional fragmented organizational structures must be rethought. Skills in seeing larger external systems and working across boundaries must eventually become embedded in organizations by creating formal management structures, roles, and accountabilities that support this work, and by continually deepening these capabilities.

As we have seen throughout this book, companies are adopting new core strategies to align with the profound changes in the larger business and societal context that sustainability imperatives are provoking—changes that are undoubtedly just the beginning. This is leading to fundamental shifts in their short- and long-term goals, expectations of performance, and priorities—and to the integration of these goals and priorities in the

When strategy and design are aligned
with the current business environment,
performance can be exceptional.

But when the external business
environment changes, the strategy
and organization no longer fit.

Often a new strategy is formulated, but the
organization design has not changed, so the
company lacks the core capacity to
implement the new strategy.

The essential question for senior leaders then is:
What new organization design is required, and
how can we change it?

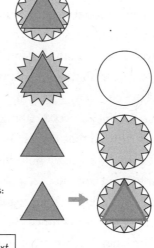

○ *External Business Environment and Context*
✳ *Strategy*
▲ *Organization Design*

FIGURE 24.1 Realigning Strategy and Design Within the Changing Business Environment

heart of the business. It will also require redesigning the organization in a way that aligns with the new strategy. As the figure above illustrates, current organizational structures have evolved in response to the imperatives of the past, not the future, and they will need to change to support new visions, strategies, and goals that fully embrace sustainability.

Like all creative processes, this won't happen all at once, and it can happen at different levels—often work starts in one business unit or division, then later migrates to other business units or the enterprise as a whole.

For example, one multinational energy company came to realize that their central limit to growth was entirely within their own walls, based on their outdated way of thinking. That limit was being set and reinforced by the way they had organized their Environment, Health, and Safety (EHS) department many years earlier.

They'd come to expect that all their long-term strategic thinking and leadership on major environmental issues would come from a group of specialists in the EHS department. But specialists in this department had no authority to engage line managers to actually implement improvements in operational environmental performance, and no accountability, access to capital, or resources to provoke innovation. The company's implicit strategy was to aim for compliance with regulations, but they often fell short. As a result, the regulators withdrew a number of permits that affected the company's growth plans and had a direct initial impact on their bottom line of over $150 million.

Recognizing all this, the CEO initiated an organizational redesign and restructuring by setting a bold vision for environmental leadership that went far beyond compliance, including goals of zero for several emissions that were of concern to their regulators and other external stakeholders.

The chief operating officer became accountable for line implementation of these new environment leadership goals. A senior manager reporting to the COO was given accountability for developing innovative new technologies that would radically reduce the company's environmental footprint. As one executive reporting to the COO put it, "If we had not figured out a way to anchor the notion of environmental leadership in the context of senior operations management and organizational structure, it would've gotten lost very quickly. Consolidating operations management and recasting innovation and technology all happened as an essential part of our response to the strategic drivers of sustainability."

The lesson here is that as you begin to rethink your organization's structure and design, be especially sensitive to the dangers of shifting the burden to specialists. Don't count on a new "sustainability" or corporate social responsibility (CSR) department, a renamed EHS function, or any other add-on department to meet the company's strategic goals. At best, such a group or function can be a temporary catalyst to help develop initial projects and momentum for change, but they cannot be expected to carry the accountability for how business will be conducted as you fully embrace sustainability. That becomes everyone's job in different integrated ways, but especially should be the concern of line managers.

To steer clear of the pitfalls of shifting the burden to an add-on department, approach sustainability the way the best companies have tackled safety. Set lofty goals even if no one knows how to achieve them. Then ensure that the line leaders, not staff, are responsible for meeting these goals. A strong anchor between those in management and staff roles should be an integrated long-term strategy for sustainability, a set of ambitions that you as a group hold together. When managers and staff members are aligned, they aren't working at cross-purposes. They're working toward the same end but with different accountabilities and authorities, designed so all contributions have a tangible positive impact.

START FROM THE TOP DOWN

The CEO, business unit presidents, and senior management of your organization have a crucial responsibility to frame key questions, set the vision for the company, and initiate long-term strategic work over a suitable time horizon—especially when the way forward is not at all clear. They must understand they are accountable for setting a vision and achieving it. Recall that at DuPont, Edgar Woolard's recasting of his title from CEO to "chief environmental officer" was one of many signals that addressing key environmental challenges and opportunities was now a central business imperative across the company. He made it clear that senior business leaders had best assume the same title in each of their business units; units that did not accept the direct charge of creating transformative change risked being sold or shut down. At GE, CEO Jeff Immelt personally initiated long-term strategic scanning work across all business units, with strong support in the early stages from Beth Comstock, a Marketing VP. Before long, however, he engaged the entire top team of business unit leaders and made it clear that their ecomagination initiative (GE's bold new strategic plan for innovation and growth in products that tackle the world's toughest environmental problems) was going to be at the heart of every one of their businesses.

From the top down, the CEO and management team must ask key questions like "What do we need to do to achieve these new goals, and how will we get the work done? How complex is the work? Whom else should we be partnering with to get this work done? Do we have the right talent to do the new work?" So, too, did Vivienne Cox, chief executive of

BP's Alternative Energy business, set the aim for managers at all levels that developing new businesses to bring energy to off-grid customers in developing countries was a business priority.

IT'S OKAY NOT TO KNOW HOW

If you are a senior leader, you and your team don't have to know immediately how you're going to achieve your vision. It is crucial that you don't frame your goal in the context of what you know today. If you do, you will limit the reach of your aspiration.

Technology and competition are going to move fast. Achieving sustainability will mean creating new ways forward with whatever technologies, relationships, partnerships, and processes are required. In the end, everyone will be innovating without anyone having a manual on how to do it.

As one senior manager on a start-up redesign team said, reflecting back on their initial work, "On seeing the ambitious sustainability goals our team were proposing, the CEO swallowed hard and balked on a lot of it to begin with. He got himself anchored into the 'how' a bit too early. We found there was a tendency for most of our executives to fall into that trap."

THE ROLE OF CATALYSTS

It is possible to design deliberately strategic (and often temporary) catalytic roles to help a management team with the organizational redesign work, create enrollment and pull throughout the organization, maintain focus, gather data, give advice, and provoke the line to move forward. Engage credible businesspeople as catalysts, the way the CEO of DuPont engaged Paul Tebo, who had previously been the leader of one of DuPont's largest and most successful businesses. Similarly, the CEO of GE asked Lorraine Bolsinger, a highly respected leader in their aviation business, to be a catalyst for their ecomagination strategy. Both CEOs, and Bolsinger and Tebo, were clear that accountability needed to stay with business unit leaders—only they could be the true leaders. In time, when sufficiently integrated as part of your company's strategy, sustainability should not be in anyone's title.

A STRUCTURE FOR FREEDOM

Spare, lean organizations are best able to promote the creativity needed to achieve any vision, about sustainability or anything else.

As psychologist Erich Fromm said, "Freedom is not the absence of structure . . . but rather a clear structure that enables people to work within established boundaries in an autonomous and creative way."

After all, what is structure? It's how managers design a system of accountability and authority for translating strategy and business plans into roles and formal accountabilities. The goal of effective organizational design is to ensure that the right roles exist, in the right groups and layers, staffed by people with the right capabilities and levels of accountability, performing the right work at the right time, supported by the right resources and authorities. As we have seen throughout this book, sustainability issues cut across all arbitrary boundaries. Therefore, designing mechanisms for horizontal, cross-boundary collaboration is as crucial as getting the vertical accountabilities right.

Rethinking organizational structure is challenging but high-leverage work, as it is an essential part of understanding and influencing the mental models and deep systemic structures and forces at play. These deep structures and forces directly impact the results people can achieve. Organizations get the results they are designed for, and no more. Most are designed for the past and therefore are not set up to reap the benefits of strategic investments in the future.

Start with the Backbone

Start with redesigning the mainstream, backbone functions that represent the core work of your organization. These typically include product design, development, provisioning, production, marketing, and sales. It is in these areas that a focus on sustainability will bring significant rewards and improved performance. Be careful to not make a separation between a clear, long-term strategy for operational excellence in these mainstream areas and meaningful progress on sustainability. For example, your operations management team, who already is accountable for ongoing operations, must also have specific aspects of accountability for sustainability anchored directly in their team roles.

As GE's Lorraine Bolsinger says, "Our ecomagination strategy cannot be seen as the caboose on the train or something that's extra to the business. It has to be 100 percent within the businesses, directed by business leaders. . . . You don't wake up in 2012 and say, 'Did we make the number?' It has to sit in the core of the business, and it has to be true to the culture. Our CEO does quarterly reviews with every business leader across the entire company. Every business has a growth metric, a business metric, an R&D metric, and a greenhouse gas metric that are aligned completely with our four core commitments in ecomagination. And to keep it in front of them, you have to have a high-impact communication plan. We can't put a stand up once a year, run a few commercials, and say, 'This is what we're doing.' We have to be diligent every month on bringing new stories to our colleagues, our customers, and NGOs. That engagement is a huge ongoing issue."

Focus on Innovation Next

Development of new processes, products, and services will also be a key area for rethinking and change. Long-term R&D and innovation work (including the redesign of core processes) is crucial and must be designed into the system. This typically means significantly changing or improving how mainstream business is carried out, and is often project-oriented, but with clear links to mainstream functions.

One senior manager in an energy company describes their experience this way: "We designed the Major Projects Group so they were freed up from dealing with short-term operational issues, and gave them the horsepower they really needed to do these sustainability projects intelligently. They are now enthusiastic supporters of bringing a brand-new way of thinking to the table. For example, they're looking at a life-cycle-analysis type of review as a way to bring more discipline into the front end of how we actually design, engineer, and undertake these very significant projects. The whole idea of full life cycle review is a brand-new idea for us, because it really forces people to reflect clearly in advance before we make major design decisions."

Then Focus on Staff Specialists

Staff specialists can provide timely, high-quality advice and scan externally for challenging global best practices to pass on to business unit heads and other managers. Their roles should focus on sustaining and increasing the value of human and physical resources, plants and equipment, brand, and reputation. Your HR, communications, finance, and legal teams, too, must engage in a strategic manner to support sustainability—it shouldn't simply fall on the shoulders of your line managers.

As managers redesign the organizational chart, it is important to take into account each role's place in the overall design so that everyone's mainstream work is in balance with quality concerns and overall sustainability goals. For example, if a separate environment department exists, it must be clearly structured so that its members can provide advice, leading-edge ideas, and feedback to those working "in the line." That is, the EHS department should help the whole system increase sustainability performance and results but should not be held accountable for actually achieving these results. That ownership stays with the core business units.

Once accountabilities are firmly grounded in mainstream departments, specialist and sustaining groups can engage in an entirely new interplay with line operations and make significant contributions. For example, the operations team of a major mining company recently formed an engineering task force to help them reclaim tailings ponds (holding ponds for the toxic wastes generated in most mining operations). Once that focused team of specialists had demonstrated initial success in reclamation, they leveraged this practical experience and credibility to raise fundamental system-wide questions about why operations continued to create tailings in the first place, and how tailings could be eliminated completely from their process. These questions naturally turned the focus back to operations management and gave their design engineering groups a new challenge to tackle.

This example illustrates how crucial it is to think of the parts of the organization as a whole. That, after all, is how important external stake-holders see you, and how they want to interact with a company. Don't be surprised when they say, "We don't want to talk to your environmental specialist. We want to meet with the CEO, chief operating officer, or the division president." So the company must be designed accordingly—no division or department can be exempt from integrating sustainability into the key results they produce. If design efforts are not approached systemically, the company can easily be attacked for "not having its act together" in terms of sustainability, and will have trouble attracting investment capital, building social capital and trust with external stake-holders, and achieving its full potential. But proceed with confidence, knowing that the hard work of redesigning is well worth the effort and, even though all designs need to evolve over time, significant improvements are possible and will give every person in your company the robust organization they need for inspired performance toward life beyond the Bubble.[2]

TOOLBOX
Creating a Balanced Portfolio of Visions

A valuable tool to use in fleshing out your future investments is the "balanced portfolio of visions" framework illustrated in Figure 24.2. You can use it to map out a set of visions that span a time horizon from within a year (V1) to fifteen to twenty-five years into the future (V15 to V25) or longer.

Such long-term views will be difficult for many people to visualize. This is the crucial work of senior leaders and can't be delegated, although talented people in groups such as R&D, marketing, strategy, and new-product development can definitely help.

Creating a portfolio of visions can be indispensable in generating and managing the creative tension between current reality and short- and long-term goals. For example, starting with a vision twenty-five years in the future in which your company is producing truly sustainable regenerative products, using only renewable energy, and creating zero waste can be a crucial first step. But to balance this long-term view, engage

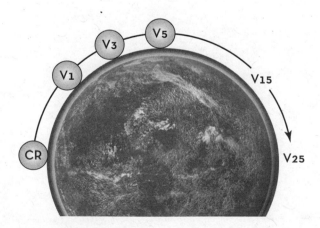

FIGURE 24.2 A Portfolio of Visions

others, and help them direct their energy, you will also need to fill in your one-, three-, and five-year visions. Your investments in tangible options and prototypes make the long-term vision come alive, and as you make progress, what initially appeared to be impossible will seem possible. It is the one- to five-year visions that directly activate the innovation and learning cycle. But you can also use your balanced portfolio to ensure that your short-term decisions are aligned with your long-term destination.

Create one of these portfolios for each of the upper two quadrants in the Sustainable Value matrix—"future internal" to guide your investments in R&D and new technologies, and "future external" to set your aspirations for reaching new markets and building new partnerships.

part VII
THE FUTURE

t is easy to get so caught up in responding to the extraordinary challenges arising from the end of the Industrial Age Bubble that little time is left to imagine what, when all is said and done, this whole business might be all about. Yet each and every one of us committed to this work has a part of her- or himself firmly anchored in this unknowable future.

Of one thing we can be sure: The emerging changes now taking shape around the world are very small compared to what is coming. The 80–20 Challenge ensures this: The infant global society we have birthed has entered its first life-or-death crisis. No one knows how an 80 percent reduction in global carbon emissions can be achieved in two decades, but it won't happen through minor adjustments in business as usual.

None of us authors has a crystal ball. But we have seen many things in the past few years that have moved, surprised, and inspired us. These short chapters share a few of these stories and the possibilities they portend.

The Future of the Corporation

ew buildings in America hold more history than Boston's Faneuil
Hall, witness to many of the great debates that led to the founding
of the United States. That history was very much alive as the sunlight poured down through ceiling-high windows onto the 200 delegates
gathered one cold November morning in 2007 to explore the future of the
corporation. Like those who preceded us two centuries before, we had
gathered to challenge taken-for-granted arrangements concerning institutional power and privilege—arrangements assumed by many today to
be as immutable as the divine right of kings was assumed to be in earlier
times.

We came from many professions and persuasions: Among us were legal
scholars, experts on capital markets and corporate governance, academic
experts in corporate strategy, environmental and social rights activists,
current business leaders, and business "elders" such as Charles Handy and
Arie de Geus.

We came neither to bury nor to praise the modern corporation but to
better understand its evolution and fitness. How is it that business, once
one of several institutional cornerstones of society, became ascendant?

How is it that investors, who once needed protection, now dominate to the extent that thirty-year-old analysts can cause fifty-year-old CEOs to quake at their displeasure? How is it that societies that trumpet democratic values seem to be blind to the fact that their most powerful institutions operate much as totalitarian states? How did we lose sight of the historical perspective that the privatization of wealth was a privilege granted by corporate charter rather than a right gained merely by personal ambition?

The aim of the gathering was to engage these questions and, in so doing, show that a diverse cross section of citizens, including many from within the business world, thought these questions sufficiently important that they should command the attention of the public at large—on a par with climate change and the growing gap between rich and poor, neither of which many of those in attendance suspected would be solved in isolation from rethinking the modern corporation.

The Irish commentator Handy, former chairman of the Royal Society of the Arts and well known in the United Kingdom for his long-running series of radio commentaries, opened the meeting by pointing out that the British monarchy had lasted nearly 1,000 years because successive monarchs adapted, however unwillingly, to the changing society around them. The one monarch who refused to change, King Charles I, was beheaded for his intransigence.

Handy then traced the evolution of the modern corporation to a series of "important ideas with unintended consequences": the private stock corporation, pioneered by the British East Indies Company in the sixteenth century; the limited liability corporation, established in the later part of the nineteenth century in the United States and England; and his "least favorite," the executive stock option of the post–World War II era. All "aided the corporation in its growth in power and influence; all benefited society through material development; and all, in the end, created abuses that have proved impossible to control."

De Geus, like Handy a former Shell executive, followed by elaborating further the history of the second of these ideas, the limited liability corporation, which has come to define modern corporate governance. The LLC came into existence in Europe and the United States in the latter half of the nineteenth century in response to an acute problem: the shortage of financial capital for a rapidly growing business sector. At the same time, a growing middle class was accumulating savings that might, potentially, be invested more readily in businesses. Legislators sought to better connect growing demand for capital and the growing potential supply by creating better protections for the millions of potential small private investors (through mechanisms such as bankruptcy courts and the legal fiduciary responsibilities of corporate directors to investors) and by enticing business owners with the idea of limited liability, so they would not be personally liable to investors should their business fail. The resulting changes gradually paved the way for the historic growth in equity capital, the development of modern stock markets, and the unprecedented growth of business in the twentieth century.

But today, de Geus continued, the financial circumstances surrounding business differ dramatically from those that existed when the modern corporation took shape. The vast majority of equity capital comes not from small investors but from giant capital funds that hardly need the same protections. Unlike the capital shortage of the late nineteenth century, there exists now an unprecedented abundance of financial capital, a result of the rapid development of global financial markets and the pace of innovation in financial instruments.

As evidence of the latter, de Geus cited the historic run-up in the market capitalization of businesses. Whereas as little as a quarter century ago, stock market values of companies were, on average, only slightly higher than the tangible assets of companies (the "book value" in terms of the financial balance sheet), today the average market value of publicly traded companies is more than three times the asset value.[1] While many business analysts attribute this historic rise in market capitalization to investors' valuing intangibles such as a company's knowledge, de Geus argued that no such increase would have been possible without a parallel historic growth in financial capital far in excess of growth in physical and productive capital. Global markets, a twenty-four-hour business clock, electronic stock trading, computer programs to optimize small windows of opportunities in otherwise random fluctuations in stock prices—all have created "a world awash in financial capital."

In effect, there now exists a vast casino sitting atop the real economy, and the casino players, increasingly, are dictating the course of those involved in real businesses. "How is it," Handy mused, "that those who provide the money carry more clout than those who actually create the wealth?"

In such a world of excess of financial capital, it is bizarre that the one and only indicator of a company's success should be returns on financial capital, arguably its most abundant input. For de Geus, this calls for changes in the "rules of the game" for twenty-first-century business that are equally radical as those that created the LLC in the first place: "In a world of constrained natural capital, social capital, and human capital, optimizing only return on financial capital imprisons business in the shadow of a distant past."

Echoing themes from his writings that first popularized the idea of organizational learning, de Geus sees a new learning imperative now confronting business as a whole.[2] "Business is a living system and, like all others, it must continually adapt to be in harmony with a changing environment. Today, modern corporations, conceived and managed as a 'machine for making money,' are no longer in harmony."

"We need a new Boston Tea Party," said Henry Mintzberg of McGill University. The current wave of corporate social responsibility will not suffice to address the "profound imbalance between the business sector and the social sector." His response to the conference's organizing question, "Is the modern corporation fit for the twenty-first century?" was an unequivocal "Yes." "The only problem," he added, "is that the twenty-first century is not fit for life on earth."

Mintzberg added that the U.S. corporate model, with its emphasis on "virtually unbridled" shareholder rights and "executive pay scales out of all bounds with norms in other countries," epitomizes that imbalance and has increased the risks to societies everywhere as it has spread.

Steve Lydenberg, chief investment officer for Domini Social Investments and a thirty-year veteran of analyzing corporate responsibility and investment risk, represented the rapidly growing voice of investors of all sorts who are realizing the risks inherent in the current obsession with short-term investment returns. "Excessive focus on short-term profits . . . causes corporate managers to misallocate assets. It introduces dangerous volatility into financial markets. [And] it means society must divert productive resources to repairing environmental and social damage done in the headlong pursuit of profits."[3]

Jason Clay of WWF, a world authority on agricultural supply chains in business, pointed out, from the perspective of ecosystems, "At present we use one and a third earths. This will grow in the coming decades, to the point that the subsequent adjustments will be increasingly difficult."

It would be easy to reject such opinions as those of extremists or radical anti-corporatists aimed at stopping globalization. But, in fact, Mintzberg is one of the world's most respected experts on corporate strategy. Handy and de Geus are highly regarded among business executives around the world. Clay works with leading corporations in helping shape agricultural industry standards and business practices; he is a key advisor for the Sustainable Food Lab, as well as for the Coke-WWF partnership. Domini is a leading investment firm, with almost $2 billion in assets. Others who spoke included numerous corporate executives, including Bob Monks, former chairman of the Boston Company and an expert on corporate governance, and Jay Hooley, vice chair of State Street Corporation; John Elkington, originator of the "triple bottom line" concept; Rosabeth Moss Kanter, noted Harvard Business School professor; Kent Greenfield, Boston College law professor and a leader in stakeholder corporate law reform; Damon Silvers, associate general counsel of the AFL-CIO; Aron Cramer, CEO of Business for Social Responsibility; and Allen White, former director of the Global Reporting Initiative and vice president of the Tellus Institute, which hosted the meeting along with SoL.

Picking up on Clay's reminder about encountering fundamental limits to material expansion, author David Korten, one of the radicals in the group and a founder of the Business Alliance for Local Living Economies, or BALLE network, said we are entering an "epic institutional transformation," where we must:

- Reduce aggregate consumption
- Invest in the regeneration of living, social, and natural capital, the foundation of all real wealth
- Accelerate social innovations, adaptation, and learning by nurturing cultural diversity
- Redistribute financial power from rich to poor to achieve equitable distribution of the earth's life-sustaining wealth
- Increase economic efficiency by reallocating material resources from harmful to beneficial uses

Korten called the coming era one of "negative returns on financial capital," a phrase that understandably got the attention of the businesspeople and investors in the room. But behind the provocative phrase sits a simple idea: The Industrial Age has been an era marked by the harvesting of natural and social capital to produce physical and financial capital, and the time has come when we have to reverse that process. This will mean reinvesting in these living systems—and developing the societal norms, public policies, and business practices that can make it work. Going back to our simple picture of the industrial system as part of the larger natural and societal systems in Chapter 2, this reversing of investment priorities is an inescapable facet of building a regenerative economy.

The Faneuil Hall gathering proved a powerful forum for listening, for thinking together, and for connecting people with common concerns around important work to be done.

The immediate intent was to give public voice to the need for rethinking the rights and responsibilities of corporations, though no one left the gathering thinking that such changes will be easy. The larger aim was to focus and build critical mass for ongoing work in essential areas, such as legal changes in corporate governance and investment requirements, and redefining fiduciary duty and common indicators for the health of social and environmental systems, both for business and for society as a whole.[4]

The forces in support of the status quo are considerable. But so are the problems arising from the status quo. It is hard to imagine life beyond the Industrial Age Bubble without corporations that operate in very different, and far more systemic, ways.

"Sometimes I think the public forgets that corporate managers and executives are also parents and citizens, people who see the same problems as everyone else," said Nike's Darcy Winslow, another of the speakers. "Charles and Arie are right that the present expectations and pressures often place businesses at odds with the larger world. This can bring out the worst in business rather than the best. Everyone is now trapped in a system that serves very few. And more and more people inside the corporate world see this."

As no doubt happened with earlier gatherings in this historic space, many left the meeting sensing that something important was taking shape. Corporations are artifacts of history. Their design stems from mental models, not the laws of physics. When the time is right, they can and will change, probably far more rapidly than almost anyone expects. Other debates on rethinking the corporation are occurring around the world.[5] As if a sign was needed of the vulnerability of the current system, news that the subprime investment bubble was bursting hit even as the Faneuil Hall meeting was occurring.[6]

Lastly, the gathering also carried an important reminder: that we are still in the beginnings of the democratic era. While the ideal of government by the people is an old one, with roots in Western, Eastern, and native cultures, democracy as the predominant governance system is still in its infancy. Surely, as Charles Handy pointed out, no society can consider itself far down the democratic path when its primary institutions function more or less opposite to its ideals. As Mintzberg said, the temptation for countries such as the United States to consider themselves paragons of democracy and to try to impose their particular model of how it should work distorts the point that we are all learners.

It is fitting that the next step in this learning process should be guided by wrestling with what it will take to evolve businesses and societies to be in greater harmony with the larger living world. Although few of us may think about it, democracy itself is an innovation inspired by living systems, as expressed beautifully by the American poet Walt Whitman over a hundred years ago in his essay *Democratic Vistas*:

We have frequently printed the word democracy. Yet, I cannot too often repeat, that it is a word the real gist of which still sleeps, quite unawakened. . . .

It is a great word whose history, I suppose remains unwritten, because that history has yet to be enacted.

It is, in some sort, younger brother of another great and often used word, Nature, whose history also waits unwritten.

$$\left[\quad 26\quad\right]$$

The Future of Enterprise Variety

The unprecedented growth of the global corporation over the past century can obscure the fact that it is but one of many forms of enterprise crucial to the innovation and change needed for creating a regenerative society. While the rise of the large publicly traded corporation as the dominant type of organization was a defining feature of the Industrial Age Bubble, this is not likely to continue. A more robust organizational ecology is already starting to supplant the corporate monoculture, one that is more in tune with the larger living world and more capable of confronting the host of Industrial Age imbalances threatening our biosphere and our societies. As we said at the outset, nature loves variety, and variety is making a comeback, as evident in an explosion of diverse and influential new forms of enterprise, many of which are easy to overlook given the understandable focus on big business.

Paul Hawken has long been a thought leader regarding business and sustainability. His landmark 1993 book, *The Ecology of Commerce,* became a clarion call for many of the early sustainability innovators within the business community.[1] A successful businessperson himself, Hawken spoke with a credibility few activists had when he said, "There is no polite way to say that business is destroying the world." Documenting the environmental and social side effects of the widespread focus on blind growth and short-term investment return, he argued that business had lost sight of its core purpose, "to increase the general well-being of humankind through service, creative invention and an ethical philosophy."

But, despite his insight and passion, it took years for Hawken to recognize that something very important for the future of commerce, but beyond business per se, was happening all around him. His awakening started simply. After his talks, people would come up to him and hand him their card. He started to save the cards, eventually collecting thousands, and he paid attention to the patterns they presented. The organizations listed on those cards were no random assortment but focused on the recurring core issues defining a regenerative society. They were professionals of all kinds—teachers, lawyers, business entrepreneurs, architects—who "looked after rivers and bays, educated consumers about sustainable agriculture, retrofitted houses with solar panels, lobbied state legislators about pollution, fought against corporate-weighted trade policies, worked to green inner cities, and taught children about the environment."[2]

Moreover, as he continued to investigate, he gradually discovered that while individually most of these organizations were small, together they were becoming a force for large-scale change. The UNDP Human Development Report identifies 44,000 international civil society organizations (often called non-governmental organizations or NGOs) in 1999, up from 700 in 1992 and 40 in 1948. India has between 1 million and 2 million NGOs, Russia 400,000.[3] Today, Hawken has a Web site (naturalcapitalism.org) that lists over 300,000 such organizations representing 195 countries, grouped into broad categories such as sustainable agriculture, terrestrial ecosystems, health, human rights and social justice, sustainable cities, and women. In his latest book, *Blessed Unrest*, he calls the explosion of civil society organizations "the largest movement in all of human history . . . an instinctive, collective response to threat . . . something organic, if not biological."[4]

Together with emerging mission-based businesses such as Seventh Generation and Dean's Beans and networks of all sorts, from business networks such as Cleantech to global youth leadership networks, webs of diverse and interrelated enterprises are emerging that hold immense promise—not only of a far more diverse and interesting world but one where there are more effective checks and balances on the side effects of industrial expansion.

Well before Hawken and others recognized the scope of the civil society movement, global corporations had discovered its political clout. Just ask Royal Dutch Shell, Nestlé, or Nike. All had business-as-usual agendas interrupted by NGOs who, though tiny by comparison in financial resources, wielded a big stick of public opinion.

Shell was forced by Greenpeace and others to abandon its plans to sink an obsolete offshore oil-drilling platform in the North Sea, even though its engineers and the UK and Norwegian governments had approved the plan. Greenpeace claimed it was not environmentally sound to do so, and after pickets formed at Shell gas stations all over Europe and television broadcast images of Greenpeace motorized rafts circling the feet of the massive platform, Shell reversed course, dismantling the Brent Spar platform instead of sinking it.

No less damaging to its brand image was Nike's embarrassment in the early 1990s at facts exposed by several NGOs about child labor at its contract manufacturers in Asia. The same was true for Nestlé, one of the three largest consumer goods companies in the world, when NGOs mounted an effective boycott movement, beginning in the late 1970s, claiming that Nestlé's aggressive marketing of baby formula in developing countries was causing mothers to avoid traditional breastfeeding and contributing to infant mortality.[5] NGOs have been able to skillfully use the Internet to keep Nestlé's boycott in the public eye.

The net of such remarkable developments was that, by the turn of the new millennium, global NGOs such as Greenpeace, Oxfam, and Amnesty International could, in some realms, match the power of global corporations in ways that even governments could not. They had the credibility and media savvy to rally public concern and organize protests against practices that put ecosystems or the disenfranchised at risk, and businesses knew it.

But, as we've noted, stopping something you oppose is different from creating something that is better. Plus today the boundary of management concerns for many companies is expanding, in part because the watchdog role of countless NGOs is now a feature of the business landscape in many places in the world. This is giving way to a second wave of co-creating new systems of commerce based on new and innovative partnerships between businesses and NGOs.

We have already seen many examples of this: Coke and WWF around integrative management of watersheds; Costco, Oxfam, and the Latin American NGO CIAT around healthy food value chains; Seventh Generation and Greenpeace around Change It, the youth change agent leadership development program. The important point in all these examples is that the partnerships are endeavoring to create new systems that did not exist and that businesses, even very large ones such as Coke and Costco, could not bring into existence alone.

Many of these new systems will be local, not global. Creating well-managed watersheds, healthy ecosystems, and vibrant economies that create employment and economic value in balance with stewardship and responsibility are challenges for local communities, not just global corporations. Insofar as value chains continue to be global, they must be managed in ways that better ensure economic, social, and environmental health across the entire chain. But a new symbiosis needs to develop between the two.

Here too enterprise variety is playing a crucial part—especially the emergence of large networks capable of multiplying the impact of many small organizations.

For example, the Business Alliance for Local Living Economies (BALLE) was started around the same time as the Cleantech Network, inspired by *Small Is Beautiful* author E. F. Schumacher and his ideas that sustainable economies must become more locally rooted. Long discounted by pragmatic businesses as romantic and counter to the trends of globalization, Schumacher's ideas, like enterprise variety, are making a comeback as more people understand that sustainability is ultimately both global *and* local.

Today, BALLE has become a network of networks, with more than fifty local and regional business networks in states such as California, Massachusetts, and Pennsylvania and provinces such as Ontario and British Columbia. More than 15,000 small businesses are involved in the United States and Canada.

BALLE was founded by two small-business owners in Boston and Philadelphia, Laury Hammel and Judy Wicks, to promote sustainable local economies in the face of the onslaught of globalization and discount giants such as Wal-Mart and Costco, which can displace and fragment local business communities. "We needed a cooperative attitude in order to transform our economy," Wicks said. Wicks opened her White Dog Café in Philadelphia more than twenty-five years ago and built a loyal clientele by adhering to the idea that quality and social activism are connected. The White Dog was the first business in Pennsylvania to buy 100 percent of its electricity from wind power. It has also been a leader among Philadelphia restaurants in buying most of its products from local, sustainable farms and fisheries. "In this way, I can use my own business as a force for change," Wicks says.

She and the other early members of BALLE have found thousands more who share these ideas, tapping into a burgeoning need within the small-business universe to organize local networks and connect them in order to share values and practical ideas.

For example, Sustainable Connections is a BALLE initiative in Washington state that helps local businesses "reexamine where we buy goods and services, how we consume energy, grow and distribute our food, build homes, and even how we define success in business . . . mentoring a new breed of entrepreneurs that have designed their business with a sustainable vision." In order to leverage local innovations, they emphasize measuring results and "documenting what we do so that others can take advantage of what we are discovering."

The BALLE network points to one additional feature that may become a defining aspect of life beyond the Bubble: how variety and localness orient people toward relationship. Inside the Industrial Age Bubble, bigger was better, and relationships within business tended to be "transactional rather than authentic," as Seventh Generation's Hollender put it. By contrast, smallness forces cooperation and the building of networks where many small actors can gain influence and a sense of connection. "Just as complex organisms are built of cooperating communities of cells, the movement to address environmental and social issues has been built up by small, cooperating groups of people," says Hawken.

Again and again, we have seen the willingness to invest time in relationship building among sustainability innovators: in building new partnerships between businesses and NGOs; in building new leadership networks, such as those in Sweden, at the U.S. Green Building Council, or within large companies such as Nike and Costco; or when large companies such as BP develop partnerships with smaller enterprises in developing countries. This willingness to invest in building relationships even appeared as a key element of the business model of Seventh Generation, a company that is growing yet seeks to remain small through carefully expanding its network of self-extending developmental relationships, or SEDRs.

In all these instances, people are learning how to build extended organizations based on the primacy of relationship—organizations that work more like forests than machines. All of this stands in sharp contrast to prevailing norms in most frenetic large organizations.

This is also evident in the growth of networks of all sorts. "The whole [venture capital] field is about relationships," says Nick Parker, "which may be one reason the Cleantech Network has been so successful." There is no one in charge of the rapidly growing Cleantech community beyond convening meetings and coordinating a basic membership structure; the whole point is to create a set of relationships that can self-generate innovative ideas and initiatives.

Similarly, young people are drawn to networks such as the Pioneers of Change by the simple model of innovation through everyone helping one another. The Pioneers network, started in Europe in the mid-1990s by a small number of college students who wanted, as their Web site describes, "to contribute to a purpose higher than self, yet ... [were] feeling pressured to compromise our personal values and beliefs," has fostered a remarkable network of young social entrepreneurs around the world.[6]

Working primarily through networks rather than authoritarian hierarchies shifts how people think about power and what it takes to get things done. "You see, our power comes from not having and not needing to know all the answers," says Christel Scholten, a member of the Pioneers Network, who also was part of a founding group working on the first sustainable development within the global bank ABN AMRO—her first job in the private sector five years after college. "We don't come in with 'Here's what you have to do.' We join traditional systems and structures and bring a fresh perspective and lots of questions about whether things really need to work as they have. This leads to people opening up who would otherwise defend their ideas if someone was advocating what needed to happen." As Parker sees it, the power is in the network itself, rather than in particular people: "What we really wanted to do, metaphorically speaking, was harness the power of Silicon Valley and put it at service of the planet."

Hawken offers an important insight about this relational view and how it was lost. Sharing a lesson he learned from an indigenous-rights leader, he observes, "The way we harm the earth affects all people, and how we treat one another is reflected in how we treat the earth."[7] In other words, as we have fallen out of relationship with the earth, we have fallen out of relationship with one another.

The primacy of relatedness, with one another and with the earth itself, has, for millennia, sat at the center of diverse long-lived cultures, from native cultures to the ancient Chinese, as beautifully expressed in the opening lines in Confucian sage Zhang Zai's (1020–1077) famous "Western Inscription":

> Heaven is my father and Earth is my mother, and even such a small creature as I finds an intimate place in their midst.
>
> Therefore that which fills the universe I regard as my body and that which directs the universe I consider as my nature.
>
> All people are my brothers and sisters, and all things are my companions.[8]

Cultural historian and evolutionary theorist Thomas Berry says there are three interrelated dimensions of evolution. The first is increasing variety. The second and third are less obvious: interiority and communion.[9] Increasing interiority refers to a richer perceptual universe and awareness of self. For example, recent studies are suggesting that some of the higher mammals can distinguish their own reflection in a mirror from other images, suggesting that they have a level of self-awareness formerly associated primarily with humans.[10] For Berry, this richer interiority creates greater possibilities for relationship. "The universe," he says, "is a communion of subjects rather than a collection of objects." In this sense, variety, self-awareness, and relatedness are bound together in the evolutionary forces of the living world.

Just as the Industrial Age has been an era characterized by the growth and spread of the large hierarchically controlled organizations, life beyond the Bubble may be characterized by a variety of business and non-business organizations based on cultures of relationship rather than cultures of control.

Control is a simple word with very different meanings. Machines are controlled by their operators. Living systems are different. No one is in charge of a forest. Living systems control themselves based on webs of relationships—such as the relationships between the myriad species in an ecosystem or among the diverse individuals in a family. In neither is someone "in control," in the sense that you or I control our cars or managers are assumed to control their Industrial Age organizations. Building enterprises based on cultures of relationship—organizations that not only work like nature but are more harmonious with nature, be it a forest or you and me—may prove a defining feature of a regenerative society.

[27]

The Future of Leadership

t is almost tautological that fundamental innovation rarely comes from
the mainstream. Dominant incumbents in industries rarely pioneer
radical new technologies or products. New social movements do not
come from those in the centers of power. The same will hold true for
much of the leadership required to create a regenerative society. Look to
the periphery, to people and places where commitment to the status quo
is low and where hearts and minds are most open to the new.

The periphery is defined not just by race or economic status, but by the
degree to which different groups have been assimilated into the Industrial
Age mind-set and power structures. Within organizations, this might
mean young people still not socialized into the norms and mental models
of the organization or its market. It might mean women, whose ways of
leading differ innately from men's but, by and large, have had little space
to be expressed fully. Within society, it means leadership from new companies, new social entrepreneurs, new geographic areas, and in all likelihood people and places no one is expecting.

Unleashing the power of organizations and networks of all sorts to create the changes needed in the coming years will require millions of gifted
and dedicated leaders of all sorts, many of whom will not come from

obvious positions of power or have gotten permission for their efforts. This does not imply that leadership from those in positions of authority is unimportant, only that it is insufficient. Where CEO or executive leadership is important, as in the stories of Paul O'Neill and Pat Atkins of Alcoa, or John Browne and Vivienne Cox of BP, or Jeffrey Hollender of Seventh Generation, it invariably plays out in concert with equally important leadership contributions from much less visible leaders within their organizations, both in perceiving emerging issues and in translating new ideas into practical changes.

The idea that leadership can only come from people in positions of power in the mainstream completely misses the basic meaning of the Bubble: We are all deeply socialized to ways of thinking, ways of interacting and working, ways of prioritizing what matters, and ways of producing change that are the product of the Industrial Age. If we think only of leadership as coming from those ensconced within Industrial Age worldviews, paradoxically, we think in ways that will actually make it less likely that the leadership actually needed will come forth.

Plus, there is much to learn from innovators outside the Bubble—people who are showing how core Industrial Age problems can be addressed through seeing existing systems and through building diverse leadership networks capable of co-creating new ones. By challenging heretofore unquestioned Industrial Age mental models, they are showing pathways to a very different future.

There are countless stories we could share about such leadership, but we include two below that have had particular impact on us as authors. One comes from a project in Africa with which we have been involved for some two decades. The other, from China, is more recent but builds on the remarkable popularity of organizational learning that has developed in that country over the past ten years. Both deal with important changes that leaders in positions of power have, by and large, been unable to achieve.

One of the thorniest unresolved problems of the Industrial Age has been the separation of the haves and have-nots and the forces that continue to drive this widening gap. It is impossible to imagine life beyond the Bubble without reversing this trend. In an ever-shrinking global village, growing gaps in opportunity become less and less tenable, if for no other reason than that the problems caused by this inequity quickly spill over borders—witness the pressures Europe and the United States are experiencing in coping with growing migration flows of the displaced and poor from Africa and the Middle East and from Central America, respectively.

The classic Industrial Age response to embedded poverty is various forms of humanitarian aid and governmental assistance. By and large, these have been a tragedy of non-systemic thinking. At best, aid relieves crisis symptoms for short periods of time, but often it only makes matters worse in the long term in a classic shifting-the-burden dynamic. Indeed, the whole aid apparatus set up by the rich to help the poor—the World Bank, the IMF, and related organizations—is itself a set of archetypal Industrial Age institutions governed by Industrial Age management models, funded by Industrial Age power structures, and locked into Industrial Age mental models of development. Not only have these institutions done little to alter prevailing global forces driving poverty (like those embedded in global food systems that relentlessly drive down food prices and farmers' incomes), but they have been largely unable to unlock latent sources of innovation and development within poorer countries.

Fortunately, in the past few decades, there have sprung up countless counterexamples of indigenous development strategies built on tapping the intelligence, resilience, and leadership of the poor to uplift themselves. For example, Muhammad Yunus won the Nobel Peace Prize, showing that local institutions making small loans, often primarily to women, can be catalytic for development. His work has given rise to a global microcredit movement that continues to grow and flourish. Likewise, the Uganda Rural Development and Training Programme (URDT) is seen as one of the most successful rural development organizations in eastern Africa. Today, what was one of the poorest regions in one of the poorest countries is one of the most prosperous.

URDT began working in the mid-1980s with a few villages in the Kibaale district of western Uganda. Rather than follow the standard aid strategies of technical and humanitarian assistance, URDT's founders focused on a core mental model. "The biggest obstacle to development in Uganda," said co-founder Mwalimu Musheshe, "was fatalism, people who believed that they could do nothing to shape their future. All the outside help in the world would not change this; it only reinforced it."

The program depended, from its beginnings, on people's desire to learn. Three-day leadership workshops held in rural villages focused on systems thinking (e.g., understanding the interdependencies of different types of water use and well protection) and personal mastery. Surprisingly, the workshops were attended not only by local villagers but also by others who often traveled several days to the sites. Many came expecting "the usual handout," says Musheshe, but "we gave them no money. We stuck to our vision that we were not there to help people with handouts but to develop their capacities to help themselves."

Soon, local village organizing focused on tangible improvements that people could implement and sustain themselves with only minimal funding: building better grain reserves and water catchments, creating fish ponds, protecting springs, digging better wells, and improving farming practices.[1] Meanwhile, the emphasis on personal growth and community building continued throughout. Many villagers wrote their visions on the outside of their huts.

Over a decade, the plan for the initial small group of villages grew into an integrated development vision for the larger district, which eventually included improved roads, microcredit institutions and a local savings and loan, new schools, a vocational institute to develop entrepreneurial abilities and trade skills, hundreds of new shops and small businesses and prosperous farms, and the first community radio station in eastern Africa, which today has some 4 million regular listeners. As a result of radio broadcasts on civic awareness and political literacy among the population, voter turnout in the area has increased from 45 percent to 80 percent since 2000.

Guided by its original vision of sustainable agriculture, URDT built a thirty-five-acre organic farm to show farmers how to develop their own land and crops in ways that replenish soil nutrients and conserve water. Many local farmers now grow organic crops for export as well as for sale within the region. During this time, population in the Kibaale district more than tripled, from 150,000 in 1980 to 472,000 in 2005.

With their success, URDT gradually developed new systems-change strategies, such as focusing on the high leverage of girls' education. They established the first girls' secondary school in the region in 2000. Traditionally, parents in the Kibaale district "put their sons through school if they could afford any school fees at all and the quality of any girls' schools was very low," says Musheshe. But girls' education, they believed, offered an especially high potential for larger change if young girls could come to see themselves as "change agents," reaching out to family members with little formal education.

For example, students' parents and grandparents come to the school at the end of each term for workshops where they learn about visioning, planning for the future, entrepreneurship, innovation skills, and developing home and farm improvement projects. Many of the workshops are led by the students. As part of the workshops, the girls and their families sit down together and plan projects for the family to do back home, such as starting small commercial organic farm plots and other businesses. In follow-up research, almost 90 percent of the girls' households reported improvements in sanitation, nutrition, and income as a result of the school's "two-generation" approach to education and development.[2]

"The gender inequalities for girls and women are shifting," says Musheshe. "Now girls are seen as people who can create economic value instead of being viewed as a liability due to the cost of having to marry them off someday." In 2006, URDT opened the African Rural University for Women, the first institution of its kind in Africa. The aim is to prepare young women to become entrepreneurs and leaders of rural development projects, and to become the founders of the next generation of URDT-style learning organizations, not only in Uganda but also in other African countries.

It is not easy to explain URDT's success, but perhaps a key lies in their founding premise. The opposite of fatalism is deep conviction in the power of personal choice, expressed eloquently in the first of the organization's founding principles: "The people of Uganda, like people all over the world, are KEY to their own development—no one can develop you until you make the choice."[3] Based on these convictions, URDT has managed to nurture a culture based on a kind of collective entrepreneurialism that is distinctively African. "All people want to live a life guided by their own choices," says Musheshe. "Hundreds of years of exploitation have robbed many Africans of faith in themselves. We have helped people reconnect with this faith and with one another."

The story of URDT shows that, at its essence, leadership often comes down to how people move from fatalism to an awakened faith that they can shape a different future. China, despite its remarkable economic progress over the past two decades, has fallen into the grip of its own form of fatalism, based on an underlying belief in one path of development.

Following the Industrial Age path of consumer-oriented growth driven by cheap energy, the Chinese have largely accepted what they saw as the inescapable side effects of industrialization in terms of resource depletion, concentration of personal wealth, destruction of ecosystems, and pollution. "Pollution is the price you must pay for development," said a young Chinese student in Beijing almost a decade ago. Today, this resignation is being superseded by a sobering awareness that their future, and all of ours, depends on finding a different path.

Between 2000 and 2007, China's CO_2 emissions went from less than one-half those of the United States to exceeding them, making it the largest emitter in the world today. Already, China generates CO_2 emissions on a par with what worldwide emissions would have to be in order to stop atmospheric CO_2 from growing.[4] If this trend continues, within a decade China could be emitting almost half the world's CO_2, almost single-handedly driving the doubling in worldwide emissions that many have forecast for the first half of this century. Conversely, a major shift in China's energy usage would have sweeping global implications for the better. In this sense, China is the pivot for any chance of meeting the 80-20 Challenge.[5]

The good news is that many in China understand this, including many in the most senior positions in government. The question is, what can they do about it?

Recognizing growing internal and international pressures for change, at the Asia-Pacific Economic Cooperation (APEC) Summit of Western heads of state in August 2007, President Hu Jintao declared that China would pursue significant improvements in energy efficiency as its primary

strategy for reducing greenhouse gas emissions, committing the country
to a 20 percent improvement in the "energy intensity" of GDP (the amount
of energy consumed per yuan of GDP) by 2010. This was a bold goal, especially since all of China's state-owned enterprises had been tasked with
energy efficiency improvement targets for the preceding two years, almost
none of which had been met. Even in China, a country known around the
world for its strong central government, systemic change often starts from
the periphery. Today, there are many serious sustainability leadership efforts throughout China, such as the Energy Efficiency and Economic Performance Learning Laboratory.[6] Initiated by Laiwu Steel, one of China's
leading steel companies, and several other Chinese firms (along with BP
and Nike) in January 2008, the project aims to apply systems thinking and
collaborative cross-organizational learning to accelerate significant shifts
in energy use and spread practical know-how.

The project combines organizational learning methods with the "whole
systems" industrial design tools of the Rocky Mountain Institute (RMI),
the highly respected energy consultancy co-founded by Amory Lovins.
There are three interrelated goals: reducing the total energy footprint of
existing manufacturing facilities, designing new ones with radically different energy requirements, and accelerating the shift to renewable sources
of energy for both.

For example, one of RMI's key design techniques is "end use" design.
Designers start by asking what the ultimate aim of any process is and then
explore how to best achieve this aim, as opposed to the more standard
approach of starting with existing energy systems and trying to improve
them. As Lovins says, "People care about warm homes and cold beer, not
how many BTUs they use." As a case in point, Jason Denner of RMI shared
an example of a typical electricity transmission system used to run an
industrial process, starting with a coal-fired power plant that generates
the electricity and going all the way to the end use, running a pump that
transports hot gases in a plant. Typically, this involves a 90 percent or
greater loss in energy throughout the system.[7] This 10:1 ratio of energy
input to end use also means that improvements in end use requirements
magnify benefits throughout the whole system: For every 1-unit savings in
energy needed for the end use, you save 10 units in the power plant. Using

this logic, RMI has shown many companies that by improving end use energy requirements (through, for example, high-efficiency motors, refrigeration, and lighting, as well as large straight pipes that minimize friction), they can create large savings in the total system. Better yet, by rethinking and designing their end use needs, they can minimize requirements from the outset—for example, designing buildings that don't need much energy for heating or industrial processes where waste heat from one process becomes energy for another.

The first step for Laiwu Steel and others in the group is to apply the RMI tools to reduce energy use in existing facilities and to track the benefits. This builds on considerable past progress at Laiwu, for example, which has reduced energy consumption per ton of steel 25 percent over five years and achieved even more impressive improvements in water use, expanding production with virtually no increase in water use, and reaching water usage rates (3.4 tons per ton of steel) that are on par with those of the best steelmakers in the world.[8]

Soon, the companies will start to design entirely new facilities based on RMI's whole-system design, where, from past experience, 70–90 percent savings may be possible. Because China is growing so rapidly and new facilities are being built frequently, there are enormous opportunities for major improvements in energy use through replacing old facilities with new ones that need only a fraction of the energy.

The group also understands that all of this represents only the initial stage of energy innovation; even such large gains in efficiency ultimately serve only to buy time in the race toward alternative sources of energy. Looking at the whole system and its energy use, a 50 percent reduction in energy requirements (per pound of steel, for example) will be offset by the next doubling of steel production. The same is true for the country as a whole, where overall economic activity can double in five years or less. This means that even a 90 percent energy efficiency improvement can be overcome in about fifteen years. In the race between increasing energy efficiency and keeping up with growing economic activity, China's pace of growth will inevitably win out. There is no alternative except major shifts to much less carbon-intensive energy sources.

This is why collaboration and sharing knowledge are vital. The companies forming the initiative set up a formal collaborative organizational structure and a governing body to oversee both the application work and sharing. "We have to do this for the future of our company, but also for the future of our country," said Zhang Seng Seng, the executive vice president of Laiwu and official host of the first meeting. "We all know the time is short and the health of humanity depends on organizations like ours not only meeting world standards in the use of energy but helping to accelerate the transition to alternative energy sources."

Undoubtedly, Zhang is right that the world is watching. While China did not invent the industrial era or forge its ill-fated dependence on cheap energy from fossil fuels, it has inherited its thinking and technologies. Just so, along with India, China is also in the best position to leapfrog into the next era. The Chinese have much of the technical knowledge needed. They have the greatest opportunity to reduce costs by moving up the production experience "learning curves" for alternative technology because most of their industrial infrastructure remains to be built. And they have in many ways the greatest incentive, both for their continued domestic development (900 million Chinese still live in the countryside) and for their opportunities to lead globally in many of the key industries for the future, such as alternative energy.

Ultimately, leadership is about how we shape futures that we truly desire, as opposed to try as best we can to cope with circumstances we believe are beyond our control. It is now fitting that places such as Africa and China, left behind in the advance of the Industrial Age, have the opportunity to play key roles in shaping life beyond the Bubble. In different ways, they are both uniquely suited to do so.

China is one of the oldest cultures in the world and, together with India, holds immense cultural resources, such as in understanding mind-body health and human development. In a world based less on mining natural resources and more on cultivating human resources, tapping this deep knowledge may prove pivotal. In a world that must restore natural and social capital, there is much to be said for the millennia-old Confucian ideology of serving humankind and promoting harmony between humans and nature.

Africa, of course, is older still. It is, after all, our home. Humans as a species arose there. We are all Africans. That our home has been seen around the world as the basket case of modern development should give us all cause to ponder.

In the machine age culture, driven by rapidly advancing technologies, the word *old* gradually became pejorative: New machines and new technology were seen as inherently superior to old machines and old technology. But this is different for the living world, where we naturally appreciate the old tree, the old forest, and, of course, the old stories and the wisdom of the elders.

A society without a way to value its past naturally discounts its future. It seems unlikely that life beyond the Bubble will be possible without leadership from those who can connect past and future and embrace far longer time horizons in both than characterized life within the Bubble.

[28]

The Future of Our Relations

There is one last Industrial Age belief that we have not yet examined. This is an old belief, predating the Industrial Revolution, though reinforced by it. So it is deeply embedded in our worldview and difficult for us to see or to appreciate why it matters. It is the belief that humans are the most important species on earth.

Like other taken-for-granted views that define the Bubble, this belief manifests in contemporary issues, such as the battle to protect and preserve species. But to really appreciate the belief, you must notice the human-centric reasoning that this battle brings to the surface, such as that the reason to protect and preserve species is that we may need them, or that we need to make a good business case for not destroying species, or that the only reason we must heed any of this is because it is in our enlightened self-interest to do so.

All of this misses another reason altogether, one far more important to life beyond the Bubble: to rediscover our capacity for awe at the marvel of the living world and our fellow travelers on Spaceship Earth, without which we are unlikely to rediscover our place in the larger natural order.

Long-lived cultures around the world tell stories in which important lessons for humanity are conveyed by other species. They do this as a reminder that other species have something to teach us. Sadly, given our present disconnection from the larger living world, it is easy for us to treat these stories as little more than Disney fantasies told by cute talking squirrels rather than serious reminders of the intelligence around us.

One who needs no such reminder is Amory Lovins, co-founder of the Rocky Mountain Institute and one of the world's foremost energy experts. Lovins has won countless awards[1] and has established himself as a true leader around energy efficiency, alternative energy, and the redesign of Industrial Age artifacts, from factories and buildings to automobiles.[2] But what few other than his good friends know is that one of Amory's passions in life are his friendships with a good many great apes. As he likes to say, "I have a fondness for higher primates; it just doesn't end with humans."

So one of his most prized projects in recent years was being asked to consult in the design and construction of the new home for bonobos (formerly called pygmy chimps) recently built by the Great Apes Trust in Des Moines, Iowa.[3]

Like any good consultant, the first thing he did on the project was to clarify who his clients were. "The people responsible for the facility are good folks, but they quickly agreed that the place wasn't being built for them."

Fortunately, dealing directly with his clients proved easy because of a unique "lexigram" keyboard that researchers have developed to allow bonobos to communicate with humans. Each of the 500-plus symbolic keys, when pressed, causes an English word to be spoken. Though this limits them to relatively simple English statements, rich communication is possible because many of the bonobos understand thousands of spoken words.[4] As Lovins says, because they can follow what people say, "It's pretty easy for them to know whether or not we understand them and to help us along."

In particular, Lovins quickly discovered that the bonobos knew exactly what they wanted in their new home. For example, when he asked what they like to walk on, they responded, "Logs." They also expressed their preferences about viewlines, colors, and textures, and got to do some of their own interior decoration.

But the meaning of the whole project for the bonobos only became evident near the end of the design work. In a videoconference, one of the architects said to one of the engineers, "So when should we show the drawings to the apes?" Unknown to him, Kanzi, an English-fluent bonobo, was listening on the other end of the call, and promptly typed the lexigrams for "I want to see the drawings right now."

So the team showed the drawings, and videos of the building site, to the bonobos. One of them typed, "Are there turtles in that pond? I want to play with turtles." Another typed, "I want to climb those trees over there." A third was puzzled: She'd been told new buildings would go up, but she saw no building materials in the photos, and all the buildings she knew were made of brick, so she typed, "Need bricks."

All of this went along fine until someone said that when the building was constructed, many more bonobos would arrive. The bonobos became wildly excited. When asked why, the bonobos explained that when they watched videos, their favorite film was *Field of Dreams*. They had suddenly realized that their new home was just like the movie—"If you build it, they will come"—except now it was other bonobos who would be coming.

Most people are stunned when they hear this story. But, in fact, research on human-animal communication has been advancing for many years, and there are many similar stories. Yet, like many bits of evidence from outside the Bubble, relatively few have paid attention. In part this is because the human-centric worldview is so pervasive. But it probably also reflects the fact that appreciating the costs of holding this worldview, like many deep beliefs, takes opening the heart as well as the head.

Roger Fouts's pioneering book *Next of Kin* documents the research over thirty years in communicating with chimpanzees via sign language and the remarkable relationships that developed between humans and chimps in the process, and particularly with Washoe, the elder of the chimp community.[5] Washoe not only mastered the basics of American Sign Language (ASL), but over time she taught it to many members of her extended chimp family. (Today, a basic research protocol followed by Fouts and others is to simply videotape the chimps teaching one another signing, rather than for humans to actively teach it to them.)

Near the end of the book, Fouts tells the story of Kat, a volunteer in their center who became pregnant one summer. Initially "amazed that the chimpanzees could use human language," Kat and Washoe developed a special bond that summer, with Washoe frequently asking about Kat's baby in sign language. Later, when Kat had a miscarriage, she didn't come to work for several days. When she did come in, knowing that Washoe had lost two of her own children, Kat decided to tell her what had happened.

"My baby died," Kat signed to Washoe. Fouts writes: "Washoe looked down to the ground. Then she looked into Kat's eyes and signed CRY, touching her cheek just below the eye."[6]

In her foreword to Fouts's book, Jane Goodall writes: "Of all the facts in my research on the chimpanzees at Gombe [Tanzania], it is their humanlike behaviors that fascinate people most . . . the cooperation, the altruism, and the expressions of emotions like joy and sadness. . . .

"It is our recognition of these intellectual and emotional similarities between chimpanzees and ourselves that has, more than anything else, blurred the line, once thought so sharp, between human beings and other animals. . . .

"Of course humans are unique, but we are not as different as we used to think. We are not standing in isolated splendor on a pinnacle, separated from the rest of the animal kingdom by an unbridgeable chasm. Chimpanzees—especially those who have learned a human language [or the bonobos with their keyboard]—help us intellectually to bridge the imagined chasm. This crossing gives us new respect not only for chimpanzees but for all the other amazing animals with whom we, the human animal, share this planet."

Most species eat members of other species. We are the first species that systematically destroys whole species. In so doing, we violate a basic law of nature, just as fundamental as the principles of zero waste and living off our energy income.[7] If life beyond the Bubble is really about coming home to our humanness, the flourishing it promises is unlikely so long as we hold that humans are somehow separate and superior to the rest of life. That is what Kanzi and Washoe, and many others, are trying to teach us—if we are ready to listen.

A common phrase among Plains Indians such as the Blackfoot and Sioux, used almost as a kind of recurring chant in their speech, is "all my relations." By this they do not mean only the two-legged, but *all* their relations. Let us hope that the rest of us find our versions of that chant as well. A regenerative society is about life flourishing, not just human life.

[29]

The Future of Us

ife beyond the Bubble is not only about our relationships with the earth, with one another, and with other species. It is also about our relationship with ourselves, what it means to be human. It's not only about the kind of world we are trying to create, but about a deeper understanding of our role in it, both in the present and in the future.

We were reminded of this at a recent SoL leadership workshop. It was there that we met Kent Bicknell, the founder of a school thirty years ago dedicated to helping young people prepare for life beyond the Bubble, and a lifelong student of Henry David Thoreau's.[1]

Bicknell told us about a book of Thoreau's that is all but completely unknown. "Thoreau had most of the books that had been printed in his home in Concord when he died. The publisher refused to follow his instruction in laying out certain pages, and the book never sold many copies, perhaps in part due to the errors in the printing, but undoubtedly also due to the book's unusual content."

Exactly why Thoreau retained all the copies became evident the next day when Bicknell came in and laid out on a table a leather-bound book wrapped carefully in layers of protective covering.

"This is one of Thoreau's personal copies of the book in which he had corrected the publisher's error. As far as we know, there are no more than a handful of these."

As Bicknell laid it in front of a group of us, he told us more of the story behind the mysterious book.

A Week on the Concord and Merrimack Rivers tells the story of a river trip that Thoreau took in honor of his brother John, who died in 1842. The book, intended as a kind of protracted eulogy for his brother, is a deeply personal account of rivers, wetlands, birds, and wild game, of harrowing portages and serene vistas as Thoreau's group traveled upriver from his home in Concord, Massachusetts, all the way to the foot of Mount Washington, the highest peak in New England, which they then climbed.

"It took Henry 330 pages to tell of Saturday through Thursday's progress north," said Bicknell, "with many references to the Vedas, the *Puranas,* the Bhagavad-Gita, Confucius, Hafiz, and the Buddha thrown in along the way.

"But his description of the summit, which he calls by its Native American name, Agiocochook—'the place where the Great Spirit dwells'—is unique in American literature." Following the words "We were enabled to reach the summit of Agiocochook," Thoreau wrote . . . nothing.

Instead, he instructed the publisher to leave a large blank space.

"Thoreau loved space in all its forms," explained Bicknell. "It spoke volumes to him." In all his time spent meditating, and in his small cabin at Walden, space and silence represented not the absence of something but rather the presence of everything. "He believed this from his experience in the power of being still and allowing thoughts to withdraw beyond the play of outer senses."

But in the initial page proofs for the book, not all the space Thoreau had requested was there. He demanded that his Boston publisher follow his instructions. When the revised first printing arrived, he saw that some of the space he requested had been added, but in one place, unwilling to reset type for the rest of the book, the publisher had simply cut three lines from the following page—three lines, it turned out, that were essential to what had become clear to Thoreau upon completion of his journey. A few years later, after disappointing sales, the publisher shipped Thoreau over

700 of the 1000 copies that had been printed, into which, occasionally, he would handwrite the missing lines.

Having told this story, Bicknell opened the book he had brought in, and showed us where Thoreau had scrawled in pen the lines of text that otherwise would have been forever lost—but that now showed the meaning of the passage in its entirety. (The handwritten words appear in bold here.)

In summer we live out of doors, and have only impulses and feelings, which are all for action, and must wait commonly for the stillness and longer nights of autumn and **winter before any thought will subside.**
We are sensible that behind the rustling leaves, and the stacks of grain,
and the bare clusters of the grape, there is the field of a
wholly new life, which no man has lived; that even this earth was made for more mysterious and nobler inhabitants than men and women.

Thoreau knew personally of "the field of a wholly new life" of which he wrote. Since his youth, he had found himself "daily intoxicated" by "an indescribable, infinite, all-absorbing, divine, heavenly pleasure, a sense of elevation and expansion" that he had "nought to do with."

He also knew that this joy comes hand in hand with profound humility. All too often, we humans live our lives as if evolution ended with us, as if the human was the last stop on the evolutionary train, as if all life on this planet has conspired to achieve *Homo sapiens sapiens.* Nothing more. Yet this tacit belief also contradicts the very idea of evolution itself, and indeed that of a dynamic universe in which evolution expresses, as the poet Gibran said, "Life's longing for itself."

We are a young species who, uncertain of our niche, has very recently—in a virtual second of life's day on earth—expanded to fill the world. In a sense we are like teenagers, full of enthusiasm and energy, and more than a bit confused. And, like every teenager must, we are about to discover that we are not the center of the universe—not even the center of life on this planet. We are but one of millions, and our merit depends not on our ego, but on our contribution.

"Climate change places us on a much larger stage in time, as our actions are now part of the earth's longer-term climate process itself," says systems philosopher Joanna Macy. "Many people are also taking into themselves the state of the world," she adds, which places us on a much bigger stage in space. Whether we are prepared or not, the teenager is growing into an adult and we must trust that the problems we face, no matter how daunting they appear, are exactly those needed to guide us through the transition.

"This is really about the next level of human development," says Costco's Sheri Flies. "If all of us were able to get to the highest in ourselves, we'd be able to see through these problems."

In these simple words, Flies expresses the spirit that we believe can make the impossible possible and, in fact, already is doing just that.

appendix

PRINCIPLES FOR SUSTAINABILITY

Two of the most widely known sets of principles for sustainability were developed by The Natural Step and Natural Capitalism, respectively.

The Natural Step

The Natural Step (TNS) takes an upstream approach to sustainability and addresses problems at the source. Their definition of sustainability includes four scientific principles. These principles, also known as the "conditions" that must be met in order to have a sustainable society, are as follows:

1. Substances extracted from the earth's crust cannot systematically increase in nature (e.g., fossil-based emissions),
2. Substances produced by society can not systematically increase in nature (e.g., CFCs).
3. The physical basis for the productivity and diversity of nature must not be systematically deteriorated (e.g., deforestation, loss of topsoil).

4. People are not subject to conditions that systematically undermine their capacity to meet their needs (e.g., lack of access to education or clean water).

The principles provide a practical set of design criteria to transform debate into constructive discussion, and they can be used to direct social, environmental, and economic actions. Many groups using The Natural Step have also found it helpful to use the TNS sustainability objectives below, which follow from the systems conditions, to help set specific goals and make progress.

1. Reduce and eventually eliminate our contribution to the buildup of materials taken from the earth's crust. This includes fossil fuels and their associated wastes.
2. Reduce and eventually eliminate our contribution to the buildup of synthetic substances produced by society.
3. Reduce and eventually eliminate our contribution to the ongoing physical degradation of Nature.
4. Reduce and eventually eliminate our contribution to conditions that undermine people's ability to meet their basic needs.

Resources

A global gateway to all eleven TNS country organizations can be found at http://www.naturalstep.org.

Several very engaging and well-designed online e-learning modules, in different lengths and languages, can be found at http://www.naturalstep.ca/elearning/SBNS_Introduction.htm.

The Natural Step for Business by Brian Nattrass and Mary Altomare (New Society Publishers, 1999) is a guidebook of practical advice and case studies on how companies can successfully integrate TNS into the core of their businesses.

Natural Capitalism

Natural capital refers to the resources and ecosystem services provided by nature. They are of enormous economic value—vastly greater than the gross world product. Natural capitalism is a system of four interlinking principles, in which business and environmental interests overlap. The approach assumes that businesses can satisfy their customers' needs, increase profits, and help solve environmental problems all at the same time.

These four principles are:
- Radically increase resource productivity to slow resource depletion, lower pollution, and create meaningful employment.
- Redesign industry on biological lines, with no waste and no toxicity, and constant reuse of materials in continuous closed loop cycles.
- Create a service and flow economy by shifting from the sale of goods (e.g., light bulbs) to the provision of services (illumination) or to a "Why sell when you can lease?" model.
- Take the profits from these kinds of improvements and reinvest them to expand the stocks of natural capital—the basis of abundant future ecosystem services and prosperity.

Resources

Natural Capitalism, by Paul Hawken, Amory Lovins, and L. Hunter Lovins (Back Bay Books, 2000) and "A Roadmap for Natural Capitalism," *Harvard Business Review,* May–June 1999, by the same authors. Or visit http://www.natcap.org.

LIFE CYCLE ASSESSMENT

Life Cycle Assessment (LCA) is a decision-making tool that quantifies the environmental burdens and evaluates the environmental impacts of a product, process, or service over its entire life cycle from cradle to grave, or cradle to cradle (where products are recycled and "reborn" at the end of their life to create new products). LCA has been standardized by the

International Organization for Standardization (ISO) and forms the conceptual basis for a number of other related tools and management approaches (e.g., life cycle management) that are focused on design to reduce the impacts, and optimize the benefits, of product systems—from resource inputs, through to product manufacturing, use, and end-of-life.

Businesses, industries, governments, and research institutes are increasingly using LCA to redesign products, create new product/service/leasing strategies, and select materials and technologies. Specific applications of LCA include the identification of potential process or product improvements and breakthroughs; comparing the environmental performance of products or technologies that perform the same function; or comparing a new technology to an old one. LCA can also be used to support informational labels in either business-to-business markets (e.g., Environmental Product Declarations) or business-to-consumer markets (e.g., supporting identification of best-in-class products for seal-of-approval labels such as Germany's Green Dot program). LCA is also often used to understand the basic environmental profile of materials (metals, energy carriers, plastics, bio-materials) that go into product systems. One of the most important characteristics of LCA is its ability to simultaneously examine multiple stages in the product life cycle and multiple environmental issues. This feature enables decision makers to expose and evaluate environmental trade-offs (e.g., where a change in a production process may reduce air emissions in one part of the system but increase water emissions in another).

The emergence of the life cycle perspective and the type of analysis enabled by LCA studies has had a profound impact on how companies are judged with respect to environmental performance. Until recently a progressive company was seen to be acting responsibly if it managed the environmental aspects of its own operations (e.g., compliance with regulations, having an Environmental Management System, producing and reporting information on environmental performance). Today's marketplaces and regulators are demanding that companies not only control the management of their own operations but also the management, or stewardship, of the upstream and downstream resource and environmental issues associated with their materials, products, or services. A key example of this trend is the increasing market demand for information on the greenhouse gas (carbon) footprint of materials, products, and technologies, and the response of many companies to meet this demand using LCA study results.

Resources

There are a variety of LCA tools, databases, and software available to support organizations interested in understanding the environmental performance of their products and redesigning them. LCA does not have to be unduly expensive or complicated. It can be adapted and introduced in any organization, including very small ones, and expanded over time. The following resources can help in the journey.

Cradle to Cradle: Remaking the Way We Make Things by William McDonough and Michael Braungart, North Point Press, 2002. This book includes provocative and useful design guidelines, based on nature's model that all waste from one system becomes food for another system.

US EPA LCAccess—This site provides educational material for introducing people to the concept of LCA as well as helping practitioners and decision-makers to stay current with the field of LCA. http://www.epa.gov/nrmrl/lcaccess/.

The European Commission Joint Research Council's European Platform on Life Cycle Assessment supports business and policy making in Europe by providing reference data and recommended methods on Life Cycle Assessment (LCA). http://lca.jrc.ec.europa.eu.

International Organization for Standardization (ISO)—Information about the family of ISO standards, including LCA, ISO 14040 series. http://www.iso.org/iso/home.htm

The Eco-Efficiency Learning Module. World Business Council for Sustainable Development and Five Winds International, February 2006. This eco-efficiency learning module includes specific sections on LCA. http://www.fivewinds.com/uploadedfiles_shared/FinalEcoEfficiencyLearningModule.pdf.

UNEP/SETAC Life Cycle Initiative's mission is to develop and disseminate practical tools for evaluating the opportunities, risks, and trade-offs associated with products and services over their entire life cycle. http://www.uneptie.org/pc/sustain/lcinitiative/home.htm.

notes

Chapter 1: A Future Awaiting Our Choices

1 Intergovernmental Panel on Climate Change, *Climate Change 2007: Impacts, Assessments, and Vulnerability* (Cambridge: Cambridge University Press, 2007), is the fourth in a series of such reports. "Nevertheless . . . [the evidence is] sufficient to conclude with high confidence that anthropogenic warming over the last three decades has had a discernible influence on many physical and biological systems."

2 Juliet Eilperin, "More Frequent Heat Waves Linked to Global Warming," *Washington Post*, August 4, 2006; Associated Press, "WHO: Mosquito-Borne Fever Could Spread," *International Herald Tribune*, January 19, 2008.

3 Matt Simmons, "Energy Policy: U.S. Needs to Show World the Way," *Houston Chronicle*, February 25, 2008.

4 "With Globalization, Poverty Is Optional," *The Humanist*, September 1, 2001, and U.S. Census Bureau, 2007, Current Population Survey, Annual Social and Economic Supplement.

5 The net change in emissions (positive or negative) is highly dependent on the source of energy used to run ethanol plants—primarily for large scale boilers to heat the corn mash and for distillation. For example, plants burning coal as their heat source produce about twice the greenhouse gases of those burning natural gas. Alexander E. Farrell, Richard J. Plevin, Brian T. Turner, Andrew D. Jones, Michael O'Hare, Daniel M. Kammen, 2006, "Ethanol Can Contribute to Energy and Environmental Goals," *Science*, Vol. 311. http://rael.berkeley.edu/EBAMM/FarrellEthanolScience012706.pdf.

6 Projected corn ethanol production in 2016 would require using 43% of the U.S. corn land harvested for grain in 2004, requiring big land-use changes to replace that grain. Searchinger et al, 2008 "Use of U.S. Croplands for Biofuels Increases Greenhouse Gases

Through Emissions from Land-Use Changes," *Science*, Vol. 319 ; http://www.sciencemag. org/cgi/content/full/319/5867/1238

7   Report by Group Economics Dept. The Royal Bank of Scotland Group, April 12, 2006.

8   Worldwatch Institute, 2007, http://www.worldwatch.org/node/5461

9   The World Factbook, Industrial Production Growth Rates, CIA, February 2007.

Chapter 2: How We Got into This Predicament

1   David Urbinato, "London's Historic 'Pea-Soupers,'" *EPA Journal*, Summer 1994, www. epa.gov/history/topics/perspect/london.htm.

2   Paul Hawken, Amory Lovins, and E. Hunter Lovins, *Natural Capitalism* (Boston: Little, Brown, 1999), 8. The waste equals 1.5 tons per day if you assume the average American weighs 150 pounds, and twenty times a person's weight per day.

3   Millennium Ecosystem Assessment, *Ecosystems and Human Well-being: General Synthesis* (Washington, DC: Island Press, 2005), www.millenniumassessment.org/en/Synthesis.aspx.

4   UNEP, "The Asian Brown Cloud," Executive Summary, 2002, www.scientificjournals. com/sj/espr/Pdf/aId/5339.

5   Millennium Ecosystem Assessment, *Ecosystems and Human Well-being: General Synthesis.*

6   See carbon bathtub diagram, page 29, Scientists debate how much of the CO_2 emitted from burning fossil fuels can be absorbed in "carbon sinks" such as plants and algae and dissolved into the oceans. Peter N. Spotts, "Nature's Carbon 'Sink' Smaller than Expected," *Christian Science Monitor*, May 3, 2007.

7   U.S. Geological Survey, Mineral Commodity Summaries, January 2004, http://minerals. er.usgs.gov/minerals/pubs/commodity/iron_&_steel_scrap/festscmcs04.pdf.

8   www.epa.gov/epaoswer/non-hw/muncpl/pubs/06data.pdf.

9   W. R. Orr and J. W. Roberts, "Everyday Exposure to Toxic Pollutants," *Scientific American*, February 1998, 90; W. McDonough and M. Braungart, *Cradle to Cradle* (New York: North Point Press, 2002).

10   Jad Mouawad, "Big Rise Seen in Demand for Energy," *New York Times*, July 19, 2007.

11   Energy Information Administration, www.eia.doe.gov, and www.energyliteracy.org/ compare-oil.html.

12   International Energy Outlook, 2007, www.eia.doe.gov/oiaf/ieo/pdf/electricity.pdf; Union of Concerned Scientists, www.ucsusa.org/clean_energy/coalvswind/c01.html.

13   Millennium Ecosystem Assessment, *Ecosystems and Human Well-being: General Synthesis.*

14   Ibid.

15   Ibid.; Jason DeParle, "A Global Trek to Poor Nations, from Poorer Ones," *New York Times*, December 27, 2007.

16   Millennium Ecosystem Assessment, *Ecosystems and Human Well-being: General Synthesis.*

17   For example, Biosphere 2, an experimental man-made closed ecological system built in the 1980s, failed to provide clean air, water, and food for eight people over the first mission's two years. The project cost about $200 million.

18   Millennium Ecosystem Assessment, *Ecosystems and Human Well-being: General Synthesis.*

19   Similar shifts in income and wealth have occurred in developing countries; for example, the poorest 10 percent of Americans have seen their income share fall from 3.5 percent to less than 1 percent in the past twenty years.

20 Mark Kinver, "The Challenges Facing an Urban World," BBC News, June 15, 2006, http://news.bbc.co.uk/2/hi/science/nature/5054052.stm.

21 Annie Correal, "12,000 Tons a Day, and What to Do with It," *New York Times,* September 18, 2007; John Rather, "A Long, Long Haul from the Curb," *New York Times,* December 4, 2005.

22 See Hawken, Lovins, and Lovins, *Natural Capitalism.*

23 Nicholas Stern, *The Economics of Climate Change: The Stern Review* (Cambridge University Press, 2007), Overall financial impact and benefits of early action; Gordon Brown speech on climate change, WWF, November 19, 2007.

24 CO_2 concentrations are measured in parts per million (ppm), a standard method of measuring the concentrations of atmospheric gases. CO_2 in 2007 was estimated at 380 ppm, versus about 280 ppm in 1850.

25 The scientific convention for measuring CO_2 flows is in equivalent tons of carbon per year. Estimates on how much of present emitted CO_2 is absorbed by the biosphere and oceans range from 2 to over 3 billion tons a year. J. Hansen and M. Sato, PNAS 101,16109, 2004; Greenblatt, Princeton.

26 John Sterman and Linda Booth Sweeney, "Cloudy Skies: Assessing Public Understanding of Global Warming," *Reflections: The SoL Journal* 7, 3 (2007); Linda Booth Sweeney and John Sterman, "Understanding Public Complacency about Climate Change: Adults' Mental Models of Climate Change Violate Conservation of Matter," *Climatic Change Journal,* February 2007, Vol. ,80, No. 3-4, 213-238.

27 Long-term data on CO_2 and temperature fluctuations, basd on ice-core studies, shows cycles in both, such as have produced periodic ice ages, but at no time was CO_2 above 300 ppm (as compared to today's 380 ppm). The Industrial Age came at the end of a long warming period where CO_2 levels had risen to about 280 ppm by 1850.

28 Examples of these "tipping points" are melting ice cover leading to reduced reflectivity of the earth and further warming (the albedo effect); melting artic permafrost releasing stored greenhouse gases, also leading to further warming; and rising temperatures reducing forest cover, leading to less carbon sequestration and still more warming.

29 S. Pacala and R. Socolow, "Stabilization Wedges: Solving the Climate Problem for the Next 50 Years with Current Technologies," *Science* 305 (2004): 969–72.

30 For example, on March 11, 2002, in a speech given at Stanford University, Sir John Browne, then chairman and CEO of British Petroleum, explained why his company broke ranks with other oil corporations in 1997 and decided to face up to climate change. First, it was clear that reputable science could not be ignored. The science wasn't complete—but science is never complete. Still, they knew enough to say that there were long-term risks and that precautionary action was necessary if we were to avoid the greater risk—of delaying until the point where draconian action was unavoidable.

31 For example, the Sustainable Development Commission in Britain (involving many senior business and government executives) is working on setting targets for reductions in emissions from all forms of personal mobility of 30 percent by 2010 and 60 percent by 2020.

32 While a 60 percent reduction relative to present global emissions (8 to 3 gtc/year) might be sufficient, the 80 percent target is needed because of uncertainties regarding whether carbon sinks can continue to absorb this much excess CO_2 and virtual certainties that China and India will be unable to achieve such 60 percent decreases.

Chapter 3: Life Beyond the Bubble

1   Jared Diamond, *The Third Chimpanzee* (New York: HarperCollins, 1992) and Jared Diamond, *Collapse: How Societies Choose to Fail or Succeed* (New York: Viking, 2004).

2   Edward O. Wilson, "The Ecological Footprint," 2000 Kistler Prize Acceptance Speech, Carnegie Foundation, 2001, www.policyinnovations.org/ideas/policy_library/data/01373: "In the real real world governed by both the market and natural economies, all of life together is locked in a Cadmean struggle. Left unabated, the struggle will be lost, first by the biosphere, and then by us."

3   For example, see: Lane, R.E., *The Loss of Happiness in Market Democracies.* Yale University Press, New Haven, 2000; Smil, Vaclav. *Energy at the Crossroads: Global Perspectives and Uncertainties.* Cambridge, MA: The MIT Press, 2003; Kasser, Tim. *The High Price of Materialism.* Cambridge, MA: The MIT Press, 2002; Max-Neff, M. *Development and Human Needs.* In P. Enkins and M.Max-Neff, *Real-life Economics: Understanding Wealth Creation.* London: Routledge, 1992; and Daly, Herman and J. Cobb. *For the Common Good: Redirecting the Economy Toward Community, the Environment and a Sustainable Future.* Boston: The Beacon Press, 1989. *Sustainability by Design: A Subversive Strategy for Transforming Our Consumer Culture* (New Haven, CT: Yale University Press, 2008).

4   In this version of the shifting-the-burden pattern, the side effects of take-make-waste solutions, damage to social and environmental systems, are shown to the right. As shown above, these end up creating still more problems, prompting still more short-term fixes.

5   This is a phrase we learned from Native American friends.

Chapter 4: New Thinking, New Choices

1   Mark Lynas, Carbon Counter, HarperCollins, 2007, quoted in "Big Foot" by Michael Specter, *The New Yorker,* February 25, 2008, pp. 44–52.

2   For example, the Canadian Standards Association, the Forest Stewardship Council, the Programme for the Endorsement of Forest Certification, and the Sustainable Forestry Initiative Program have developed different forest certification schemes.

Chapter 5: Never Doubt What One Person and a Small Group of Co-Conspirators Can Do

1   www.baff.info/english/.

2   www.greenzone.nu/index_e.shtml.

3   Lars Christensen, *Formation for Collective Action: The Development of BioFuel Region,* Visanu (Swedish National Programme for Development of Innovation Systems and Clusters), October 2005, www.biofuelregion.se/english.cfm?open=eng: Case study of Sweden's BioFuel Region.

Chapter 6: Aligning an Industry

1   For more on creating a "container" for dialogue, see Peter Senge et al., *The Fifth Discipline Fieldbook* (New York: Doubleday, 1994), 354ff.

Chapter 7: Unconventional Allies: Coke and WWF Partner for Sustainable Water

1   WWF is the brand image for The World Wildlife Fund. WWF is a global federation co-ordinated by WWF International, based in Switzerland, with major organizations based in the United States, Germany, the Netherlands, and the United Kingdom. By some in-dicators, such as total budget and brand recognition, it could be regarded as the world's largest NGO.

2   Chapagain A. K. and A.Y. Hoekstra, Water Footprints of Nationa, Vols. 1 and 2. Unesco-IHE Value in Water research reports series no. 16. http://www.waterfootprint.org?publications.htm; "Hidden Waters," A Briefing, February 2007, Joanne Zygmunt, http://www.Waterwise.org

3   The seven major regions are the Danube; the Rio Grande and Rio Bravo in the south-western United States and Mexico; southeastern rivers and streams in the United States; rivers and lakes of eastern Africa; the Mekong in Laos, Thailand, and Cambodia; the Yangtze in China; and the Mesoamerican Reef, which stretches along the western shore of Central America.

4   Part of WWF's global plan is to focus on seven major river systems as a laboratory for developing more integrated water management (see note 3 above). Coke is also part of one of these projects in the United States, the southeastern rivers and streams.

5   See www.worldwildlifc.org/climatesavers/

6   Current targets and progress can be found on both Coke and WWF's websites.

Chapter 8: Risks and Opportunities: The Business Rationale for Sustainability

1   Ari Levy, "Google Plans to Develop Cheaper Solar, Wind Power," Bloomberg.com, Novem-ber 27, 2007, www.bloomberg.com/apps/news?pid=20601087&sid=a_yeVlId3yug&refer=home.

2   Brad Stone, "Google's Next Frontier," *New York Times,* November 28, 2007.

3   GlobeScan: Corporate Social Responsibility Monitor, 2007, 12.

4   "Taking the Earth Into Account," *Time,* May 2, 2005.

5   Ibid.

6   Juergen H. Daum, *Intangible Assets and Value Creation*, New York: Wiley, 2002.

7   GlobeScan: Corporate Social Responsibility Monitor, 2007, 33.

8   Mark Borden, Jeff Chu, Charles Fishman, Michael A. Prospero, and Danielle Sacks, "50 Ways to Green Your Business," *Fast Company,* November 2007, www.fastcompany.com/magazine/120/50-ways-to-green-your-business.html

9   Ibid.

10 Ibid.

11 Adapted with permission from Bob Willard, *The Next Sustainability Wave* (Gabriola Island, BC: New Society Publishers, 2005), 28.

12 Cornelia Dean, "Executive on a Mission," *New York Times,* May 22, 2007.

13 Bob Willard, *The Sustainability Advantage,* (Gabriola Island, BC: New Society Publish-ers), 2002 and *The Next Sustainability Wave,* (Gabriola Island, BC: New Society Publish-ers) 2005.

Chapter 9: Positioning for the Future *and* the Present

1   S. Hart and M. Milstein, "Creating Sustainable Value," *Academy of Management Executive* 17, 2 (2003). Also see Stuart Hart, *Capitalism at the Crossroads,* (Philadelphia: Wharton School Publishing, 2007).

2   In 1999, Brian Kelly founded the Sustainable Enterprise Academy (SEA) at York University's Schulich School of Business, with the mission of supporting business leaders in the transformation to corporate sustainability. He brought together a small group of leading thinkers to develop and offer a four-day executive leadership program, focused on the business opportunities inherent in sustainability. He also included, as guest presenters, senior business leaders of companies already moving to integrate sustainability into the core of their business. Stuart Hart contributed the sustainable value matrix to the SEA program, which became an important tool for the business leaders attending to create sustainable value within their organizations.

3   Adapted with permission from S. Hart and M. Milstein, "Creating Sustainable Value," *Academy of Management Executive* 17, 2 (2003). Also see Stuart Hart, *Capitalism at the Crossroads* (Philadelphia: Wharton School Publishing, 2007).

4   Frank J. Lechner and John Boli, *The Globalization Reader* (Oxford: Blackwell, 2000).

5   The Cleantech Group, LLC

6   As quoted in *Vanity Fair,* July 10, 2006.

Chapter 10: Getting People Engaged

1   *The Fifth Discipline Fieldbook* (New York: Doubleday, 1994), a compendium of tools and methods, is one of the most complete resources we can recommend.

Chapter 11: Building Your Case for Change

1   As reported in the *Globe and Mail,* November 15, 2007.

Chapter 12: The Tragedy and Opportunity of the Commons

1   "Climate Change 2007," IPCC Fourth Assessment Report AR4. This synthesis report can be downloaded at http://www.ipcc.ch/press/index.htm. Also see Millennium Ecosystem Assessment, *Ecosystems and Human Well-being: General Synthesis* (Washington, DC: Island Press, 2005), www.millenniumassessment.org/en/Synthesis.aspx.

2   Fish Banks, Ltd., was developed at the University of New Hampshire by Dennis Meadows. The game is available at www.unh.edu/ipssr.index.html. A similar version is available on the Cloud Institute for Sustainability Education website at www.sustainabilityed. org. A simplified version that does not require computers is described in Linda Booth Sweeney and Dennis Meadows, *The Systems Thinking Playbook and Companion DVD* (Waltham, MA: Pegasus Communications, 2001).

3   Attendees were from the many companies from the SoL Sustainability Consortium, organizations committed to utilizing organizational learning tools and principles to address sustainability challenges. See www.solsustainability.org.

4   The company even invented a "circle structure" where three executive circles replace the

traditional functional hierarchy: make product (which includes R&D as well as manu-facturing), sell product (marketing, sales, and service support), and the leadership circle, whose job is to support the others. The intent of the circles is to "force people to have to continually talk with one another across boundaries," says retired CEO Rich Teerlink. For more on this, see Rich Teerlink and L. Ozley, *More than a Motorcycle* (Cambridge, MA: Harvard Business School Press, 2000).

5   To be precise, the stock falls most rapidly when the excess of the outflow over the inflow is greatest; as the fish stock falls, the regeneration rate does also, so the point where the stock is falling most rapidly may actually come some time after the fish catch is at its peak—which means that the longer the fishing companies wait to curtail their fishing, the more the population and the regeneration rate drops, making regeneration still more difficult.

6   Advocates of free markets often claim that rising price signals are sufficient to protect commons, yet it is not prices but how people respond to prices that matters. In most real settings where commons are being depleted, prices usually start to rise as supply falls (or rises more slowly than demand); but customers often respond to rising prices slowly at first (especially if there are not ready substitutes for the product), and rising prices also cause producers to work harder to keep expanding production, as the fishing companies do in Fish Banks. By the time prices have risen so high that demand declines signifi-cantly, it may be much too late to save the fishery.

Chapter 13: Spaceship Earth

1   EPA, 2007, Report to Congress on Server and Data Centre/Energy Efficiency.

2   Energy Information Administration, US DOE, Annual Energy Outlook 2008.

3   Calculation based on: If Internet grows 16.7 percent per year (four-year doubling time), vs. 3.3 percent for electricity use (overall global economic growth rate), internet/total electricity grows at about 14 percent per year. This is a doubling T of about 5 years. If internet is currently 4 percent of electricity use, this would make it 32 percent in three doublings or fifteen years.

4   The Earth Charter, a declaration of principles for building a just, sustainable world, is an outgrowth of the UN Conference on Environment and Development (the Rio Confer-ence), held in 1992, and can be found at www.earthcharter.org/ or http://en.wikipedia.org/wiki/Earth_Charter.

5   For a complete discussion of archetypes, see Peter Senge et al., *The Fifth Discipline,* rev. ed. (New York: Doubleday, 2006), and Peter Senge et al., *The Fifth Discipline Fieldbook* (New York: Doubleday, 1994); also see the publications of Pegasus Communications, at www.pegasuscom.com.

6   The category of SUVs, vans and pickup trucks as a percent of all U.S. vehicles has grown from 28% in 1987 to 50% by 2007. Not surprisingly, engine technology advances have largely gone into increased power to move heavier vehicles rather than higher fuel econ-omy and reduced emissions—average horsepower has almost doubled, while overall fuel economy has decreased by 9%. U.S. EPA, 2007, Light-Duty Automotive Technology and Fuel Economy Trends: 1975 Through 2007.

Chapter 14: Seeing Our Choices

1   Nike's commitment to industry-leading transparency in its social responsibility reporting has led to the company being named the top U.S. company and one of the world's top 10 in the latest Sustainability Global Reporters Program ranking. See www.greenbiz.com/news/news_third.cfm?NewsID=34235.

2   www.indigodev.com/Kal.html.

3   Malcolm Gladwell, *The Tipping Point: How Little Things Can Make a Big Difference* (Boston: Little, Brown, 2000).

4   Peter Marsh, "Solar Energy Demand Soars," *Financial Times,* April 4, 2007.

5   "Wind, Solar Power Gain Users," *Wall Street Journal,* January 18, 2008.

6   *Economist,* February 23, 2008, 84.

7   "Installed U.S. Wind Power Capacity Surged 46% in 2007," news release, American Wind Energy Association, January 17, 2008.

8   "US, China and Spain Lead World Wind Power Market in 2007," news release, Global Wind Energy Council Brussels, February 6, 2008.

9   "The Renewables 2007 Global Status Report," Renewable Energy Network for the 21st Century, in collaboration with the Worldwatch Institute.

10   In principle, to assess the waste by-products of any of these examples you must look at the total life cycle "footprint" of the product, such as whether fossil fuels were used for growing the food or transporting the fibers or producing the hydrogen (and therefore CO_2 was generated in its production or use). See Appendix for resources on conducting such footprint analysis.

11   William McDonough and Michael Braungart, *Cradle to Cradle* (New York: North Point Press, 2002).

Chapter 16: Convening: "Get the System in the Room"

1   See J. Jaworksi, *Synchronicity* (San Francisco: Berrett-Koehler, 1996); Peter Senge, Joseph Jaworski, C. Otto Scharmer, and Betty Sue Flowers, *Presence* (New York: Doubleday, 2005).

2   In the interviews done for *Presence* with diverse scientists and entrepreneurs, Joseph Jaworski and C. Otto Scharmer would often ask, "What is the question that lies at the heart of your work?" See www.dialogonleadership.org.

3   Dialogue, as described by the late quantum physicist David Bohm, is a conversation of shared exploration toward greater understanding and possibility. See David Bohm *On Dialogue* (New York: Routledge, 1996), and William Isaacs, *Dialogue and the Art of Thinking Together,* (New York: Doubleday, 1999).

4   C. Otto Scharmer, *Theory U* (Cambridge, MA: Society for Organizational Learning, 2007), 288.

Chapter 17: Seeing Reality Through Others' Eyes

1   From 1950 to 2000, the average world price for the largest traded agricultural commodities fell: 80% for soy; 90% for corn; 80% for wheat; 90% for cotton; 70% for dry beans; 50% for potatoes. USDA.

2   See the Sustainability Institute website, www.sustainer.org.

3   The initial convening group, and formative strategic microcosm, included André van Heemstra, a member of the management board at Unilever; Barbara Stocking, president of Oxfam GB; Oren Hesterman, director of agriculture programs at the Kellogg Foundation; Joseph Jaworski and Adam Kahane from Generon Consulting; and Hal Hamilton of the Sustainability Institute, founded by Donella Meadows to work on global agriculture systems, which eventually became the coordinator of the lab.

4   The whole process of building systems intelligence, collaboration, and collective creative capacity was organized using Theory U for aligning inner and outer change (described in Peter Senge, Joseph Jaworski, C. Otto Scharmer, and Betty Sue Flowers, *Presence* (New York: Doubleday, 2005), and in C. Otto Scharmer, *Theory U* (Cambridge, MA: Society for Organizational Learning, 2007).

5   Chris Pomfret, speech at IPA Sustainability Conference, May 2002.

6   The Ladder of Inference has its roots in anthropology, where field researchers had to develop rigorous disciplines for making explicit their interpretations of cultures very different from their own, and has become a cornerstone of all organizational learning projects. See Peter Senge et al., *The Fifth Discipline Fieldbook* (New York: Doubleday, 1994), 242–61.

7   See Susan Sweitzer, "Sustainable Food Lab Learning History," www.sustainablefoodlab.org/learning-history. All quotes from Lab Team members come from this source.

8   If a team is too big to travel together throughout a learning journey, they can be split into subteams, maintaining as much of the diversity as possible. This is what was done in the Food Lab's Brazilian learning journeys, which were taken in three groups of about ten to fifteen each, after which all the groups assembled for a ten-day retreat two months later.

Chapter 18: Building Shared Commitment

1   Bill Bowerman, track and field coach at the University of Oregon, trained thirty-one Olympic athletes and co-founded Nike.

2   During this time Flies had worked with Roca, the pioneering youth leadership organization in the Boston area, and learned of their "peacekeeping circles," an approach she started to incorporate into her Guatemala meetings. More info can be found in Kay Pranis, Barry Stuart, and Mark Wedge, *Peacemaking Circles: From Crime to Community* (St. Paul, MN: Living Justice Press, 2003).

Chapter 19: Innovation Inspired by Living Systems

1   The ideas behind Zero-to-Landfill business models have been developed by many people, including Swiss economist Walter Stahel, who originally coined the term "cradle to cradle." See, for example, "product of service" in Paul Hawken, Amory Lovins, and E. Hunter Lovins, *Natural Capitalism* (Boston: Little, Brown, 1999), and the writings of industrial ecologist John Ehrenfeld.

Chapter 20: Unleashing Everday Magic

1   Martin Luther King, Jr., "Letter from Birmingham Jail," April, 16, 1963.
2   The particular way of articulating this principle comes from the work of Robert Fritz, who refers to it as "structural tension." See Fritz, *The Path of Least Resistance* (New York: Ballantine, 1989); and *The Path of Least Resistance for Managers* (San Francisco: Berrett-Koehler, 1999).
3   David Whyte, *The Heart Aroused* (New York: Currency/Doubleday, 1994), p. 231
4   For an excellent summary of these, see Mohandas Gandhi, *"Hind Swaraj," and Other Writings* (Cambridge: Cambridge University Press, 1997).

Chapter 22: From Low-Hanging Fruit to New Strategic Possibilities

1   See Peter Senge et al., *The Fifth Discipline,* rev. ed. (New York: Doubleday, 2006), 259–60.
2   This capital investment plan included the gas business. BP is not the only major oil company with significant investments in alternative energy, but they are one of the largest.
3   Presently, these power stations will produce hydrogen from fossil fuels such as coal, petroleum, and natural gas, with the plan to capture and store underground 90 percent of the CO_2 produced in the process.

Chapter 23: It's Not What the Vision Is, It's What the Vision Does

1   According to OSHA records, DuPont historically has been the safest large company in the United States in the post–World War II era.
2   See http://www.greystonbakery.com
3   Although full life cycle analysis of products is being done more often by companies, it is still far less common than simply tracking waste within the firm's own processes ("waste from manufacturing" in the simple systems framework presented in Chapter 2) because of the time and effort required but also because, unlike the costs associated with your own manufacturing waste or energy use, total life cycle waste is a cost to someone else and requires a broader boundary of management concern.
4   Many mission-based businesses are begun by social entrepreneurs, and organizations such as Ashoka (www.ashoka.org) have formed to support them as they develop solutions to some of the world's most urgent problems.
5   The key findings of this study were not published for almost fifteen years, when they appeared in Arie de Geus, *The Living Company* (Boston: Harvard Business School Press, 1997).

Chapter 24: Redesigning for the Future

1   There is a significant body of guiding ideas, experience, and science to draw on in doing this redesign work. One set is Requisite Organization principles, practices, and tools, which have proven to be a good fit for designing sustainability into the core of a business (developed by Elliott Jaques and his collaborators over the last thirty years). The meaning of the term *requisite* is "required, necessary, or indispensable for a particular purpose

or position, as in the requisite skills of an engineer." Elliott Jaques, *The Requisite Organization*, revised second edition (Arlington, VA: Casson-Hall, 1996).

2 We wish to thank Sue Simington for her contributions to this chapter, based on her experience in redesigning organizations and businesses for sustainability.

Chapter 25: The Future of the Corporation

1 *The Economist*, October 7th, 2006 "A Survey of Talent," p. 4.

2 See Arie de Geus, "Planning as Learning," *Harvard Business Review*, March–April 1988, and Arie de Geus, *The Living Company* (Boston: Harvard Business School Press, 1997).

3 S. Lydenberg, "Long Term Investing: A Proposal for How to Define and Implement Long-Term Investing," in *Paper Series on Corporate Design*, Summit on the Future of the Corporation, available from Tellus Institute, www.tellus.org. Many similar critiques of excessive short-termism in corporate management have been published in recent years (e.g., M. Tonello, "Revisiting Stock-Market Short-Termism," Conference Board, 2006, 42); conversely, several recent studies have lauded the benefits for investors of longer-term more responsible management (e.g., see Goldman-Sachs "GS SUSTAIN" Global Investment Research, July, 2007).

4 Current work groups from the meeting include: common ratings system (à la LEEDS for building the future corporation); mandating longer-term holding periods for stock; implementing more accountable corporate governance practices; rewriting incorporation laws; mandating social and environmental risk assessment; and developing alternatives to GDP that incorporate social and environmental indicators.

5 Handy was part of a ten-year study commissioned by Tony Blair to review company law—though, for the time being, the outcomes have been minimal under the new prime minister Gordon Brown's administration.

6 One of the attendees, a senior executive in one of the country's largest banks, had to leave in order to attend to the unfolding crisis. Later, he commented that the crisis, which cost his CEO his job and eventually tens of thousands of others theirs, came about through "interactions of aggressive strategies and computer-mediated investment decisions that no one will probably ever understand."

Chapter 26: The Future of Enterprise Variety

1 Paul Hawken, *The Ecology of Commerce: A Declaration of Sustainability* (New York: Harper Business, 1994).

2 Paul Hawken, *Blessed Unrest: How the Largest Movement in the World Came into Being and Why No One Saw It Coming* (New York: Viking, 2007), 1.

3 John Keane, *Global Civil Society* (Cambridge: Cambridge University Press, 2003). According to researchers at Johns Hopkins, if civil society organizations (including foundations) were a separate national economy, it would be the eighth largest in the world, with $1.2 trillion in expenditures.

4 Hawken, *Ecology of Commerce*, 3.

5 The World Health Organization estimates that 1.5 million infants die each year because they are more vulnerable to diseases due to being bottle-fed.

6   See www.pioneersofchange.net and also Peter Senge et al., *The Fifth Discipline,* rev. ed. (New York: Doubleday, 2006), 370–76.

7   Hawken, *Ecology of Commerce,* 2.

8   Chang Tsai [Zhang Zai], "The Western Inscription," in Wing-tsit Chan, trans. *A Source Book in Chinese Philosophy* (Princeton: Princeton University Press, 1963) p. 497.

9   T. Berry, *The Dream of the Earth* (San Francisco: Sierra Club, 1988); T. Berry and Brian Swimme, *The Universe Story* (New York: Penguin, 1994). See also *The Great Work,* (New York: Bell Tower, 1999).

10   Eric Jaffe, "Mirror Image: The First Evidence That Elephants Can Recognize Themselves," www.smithsonian.com, November 7, 2006; J. M. Plotnik, F. de Waal, and D. Reiss, "Self-recognition in an Asian Elephant," *Proccedings of the National Academy of Science,* October 2006, www.pnas.org/cgi/content/abstract/0608062103v1.

Chapter 27: The Future of Leadership

1   The program, originally called the Uganda Food and Peace Project, was funded intially by small private contributions raised mostly in Europe and the United States by Hans and Silvanna Veltkamp to pay for field workers such as Mwalimu Musheshe.

2   The school won the prestigious Forum for African Women Educationalists (FAWE) award in 2002, for the promotion of girls' education and innovative achievement in female education.

3   The organization's five founding principles are: "(1) The people of Uganda, like people all over the world, are KEY to their own development—'no one can develop you until you make the choice.' (2) Lasting change is possible when people shift to a creative rather than a reactive orientation. (3) A people with a common vision can transcend traditional prejudices caused by tribal, religious, political, gender and age differences and work together to achieve what is most important to them. (4) People have innate power and wisdom which they can tap to transform the quality of their lives and that of their communities. (5) Training, education, and information sharing are key critical ingredients for rural transformation."

4   Today worldwide CO_2 emissions are about 8.5 gtc/yr. As explained in Chapter 2, stabilizing CO_2 concentration in the atmosphere would require global emissions in the vicinity of 2–3 gtc/yr. China's estimated emissions in 2007 were estimated to be slightly in excess of 2 gtc/yr.

5   India, obviously, is the other industrializing giant that will shape the twenty-first century and how we meet the 80-20 Challenge (today its emissions are roughly half those of China but also growing rapidly), and the two countries are likely to influence each other in many ways, including in energy strategy.

6   Others include the US-China Center for Sustainable development (http://chinauscenter.org/initiatives/default.asp) and Per Carstedt's biofuel project.

7   The losses, typically, might include 70 percent of energy in a power plant that generates electricity 8–10 percent of the energy remaining is then lost in transmission,

another 10 percent in an electrical motor, which drives a pump, which loses another 25 percent, which then sends the hot gas through pipes with a throttle that loses another 33 percent to another string of pipes, where another 20 percent is lost before the gases reach their end use. The net of these losses is that for every 100 units of energy that goes into the power plant, 9.5 units eventually reach the end use.

8   For its accomplishments, the company was recently honored by the Communist Party as the first host of its Annual Learning Organization Conference (previously held in Beijing), where the Party recognizes excellence in organizational learning practice among Chinese businesses.

Chapter 28: The Future of Our Relations

1   Including a MacArthur Fellowship; the Heinz, Lindbergh, World Technology, and Right Livelihood ("Alternative Nobel Prize") awards; and the Blue Planet, Volo, Nissan, Shingo, Mitchell, and Onassis Prizes. *Time* named him one of the "Heroes for the Planet," and *Newsweek* called him "one of the Western world's most influential energy thinkers." Lovins was one of the youngest dons in the history of Oxford University and is a fellow of the American Association for the Advancement of Science.

2   See *Natural Capitalism, Factor 4* (Ernst Ulrich von Weizsäcker, Amory und Hunter Lovins, Earthscan, 1998), and *Winning the Oil End Game* (Amory B. Lovins, E. Kyle Datta, Odd-Even Bustnes, and Jonathan G. Koomey, Rocky Mountain Institute, 2004)

3   See *National Geographic,* March 2008, 57.

4   Ibid.

5   R. Fouts, *Next of Kin: What Chimpanzees Have Taught Me About Who We Are,* (New York: William Morrow, 1997).

6   Ibid, p. 291.

7   The author Daniel Quinn calls this the "law of limited competition"; see his *Ishmael,* (New York: Bantam, 1992).

Chapter 29: The Future of Us

1   The Sant Bani School, www.santbanischool.org.

index

acknowledgments

No project like this ever comes to realization without countless contributions, tangible and intangible.

First, this book would never have been possible without the many people who have been leading by example all these years, both those whose stories are contained in the preceding pages as well as many whose stories, due to the inevitable constraints of space, are not. Their passion, courage, and imagination have been an inspiration to us, and their lessons illuminate the paths we are all seeking toward a regenerative future. Though few think of themselves as examples, and many are their own harshest critics, they have become mentors and friends. Their names can be found throughout the pages of this book.

In turn, the opportunity for so many of us to work together has arisen through the development of overlapping learning communities such as the SoL (Society for Organizational Learning) Sustainability Consortium, the Global Sustainable Food Lab, and the Sustainable Enterprise Academy (SEA). We would especially like to thank Bernie Bulkin of BP and Ray Anderson, Joyce Lavalle, and Jim Hartzfeld of Interface Inc., Sarah Severn and Darcy Winslow of Nike, Tim Savino of Harley Davidson, and Roger Saillant and John Elter of Plug Power for helping to bring the SoL

Sustainability Consortium into existence; Barbara Stocking of Oxfam, Andre van Heemstra of Unilever, and Hal Hamilton and Don Seville of the Sustainability Institute for stewarding the Food Lab since 2002, along with Adam Kahane, its initial designer and facilitator. We appreciate the leadership of Brian Kelly in founding the Sustainable Enterprise Academy in 1999, and bringing together the initial core faculty, including Stuart Hart, John Ehrenfeld, David Bell, David Wheeler, and Arthur Hanson.

Early in the formative stages of this book, longtime colleague Art Kleiner helped to develop the initial project concept and plan, a role he had played in our earlier Fifth Discipline Fieldbook series. Along the way, Paul B. Brown, Mike Bryan, and Glenn Rifkin, along with Art, helped to sharpen arguments, supplement research, and clarify the overall flow of the book. A special thanks to Sarah Rainone, our editor at Doubleday, whose patience and keen criticism were invaluable, and to Roger Scholl and Michael Palgon, whose enthusiasm for the importance of this book sustained us when the task seemed more than formidable than our resources and resolve.

We especially thank our families, without whose understanding and willingness to share the precious commodity of family time, you would not have this book in your hands.

Finally, we would like to thank all our teachers, those who have helped shape us, and the children who will help shape the revolution we are living into.

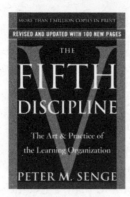

The Fifth Discipline

Trade Paperback, 464 pages
Price: $24.95
ISBN: 978-0-385-51725-6
The completely revised and updated edition of the best-selling classic describes how companies can rid themselves of the "disabilities" that threaten success by becoming a "learning organization"—one in which new and expansive patterns of thinking are nurtured, collective aspiration is set free, and people continually learn how to create the results they truly desire.

The Fifth Discipline Fieldbook

Trade Paperback, 608 pages
Price: $35.00
ISBN: 978-0-385-47256-2
A pragmatic, hands-on guide that shows how to put the theory of organizational learning into practice and create an organization where memories are brought to life, creativity is the lifeblood of every endeavor, and tough questions are fearlessly asked.

Schools That Learn

Trade Paperback, 608 pages
Price: $37.50
ISBN: 978-0-385-49323-9 (0-385-49323-1)
This addition to the Fifth Discipline Fieldbook series offers practical advice, tools, and tips for educators, administrators, and parents on how to strengthen and rebuild our schools.

The Dance of Change

Trade Paperback, 608 pages
Price: $35.00
ISBN: 978-0-385-49322-2 (0-385-49322-3)
Drawing upon new theories about leadership and the long-term success of change initiatives, and based upon 25 years of experience in building learning organizations, *The Dance of Change* fieldbook shows how to accelerate organizational change and avoid the obstacles that can stall momentum.

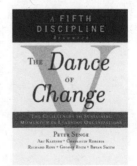